Israel-Palestine

A Mission Study for 2007-2008
by Stephen Goldstein

Study Guide
by Sandra Olewine

Israel-Palestine: A Mission Study for 2007-2008,
copyright © 2007 Women's Division, General Board of
Global Ministries, The United Methodist Church

A publication of the Women's Division, General Board of
Global Ministries, The United Methodist Church

ISBN 978-1-933663-13-5

Library of Congress Control Number 2007924102

Photo Credits

All front cover photos are by Bob May/GBGM.
The two back-cover photos are by Paul Jeffrey/ACT International.
All photos throughout the text are numbered and
credited as follows:

Bob May/GBGM
1-8, 11, 18-19, 21-33, 36-38, 41-43, 45-48, 50-56,
58-65, 67-73, 76-79, 81-82, 85-89, 91-92, 94-112,
115-128, 134, 137, 139, 141-142, 145-240

Beryl Goldberg
9-10, 12-17, 20, 34-35, 39-40, 44, 49, 57, 66,
74-75, 80, 83-84, 90, 93, 113-114

David Wildman/GBGM
131-133, 135-136, 138, 140

Stephen Goldstein/GBGM
129-130, 143-144

Table of Contents

Preface

In the face of long and chronic injustices, many of us in the church are tempted to commit either to indifference or to total resignation. This is especially true in the way many of us relate to the Arab-Israeli conflict, which has been with us for as long as we can remember. It is also true that all the efforts of the warring parties, the United Nations, the United States, the churches, and the international community to resolve the impasse have failed. Nevertheless, for the sake of Israelis and Palestinians who continue to be assassinated, burned alive, injured, incarcerated, tortured, displaced, impoverished, or made to suffer in any way, we must not give up. For the sake of future generations of Israeli and Palestinian children, we must not give up. For the sake of world peace and reconciliation among Jews, Muslims, and Christians in Israel-Palestine and worldwide, we must not give up. For the sake of the survival of the church in the Holy Land and Christian communities throughout the Middle East and North Africa, we must not give up. For the sake of the United States and other countries that are considered Christian nations and their image in the world, we must not give up. For the sake of the Church of Jesus Christ and its witness around the globe, we must not give up.

As long as there is a new sunrise that prevails over the darkness of the night, there is also a sure hope that the darkness of the present time in the Middle East will one day give way to justice, reconciliation, and peace.

The desired peace in the Middle East will come sooner rather than later as more and more people in our churches, towns and cities, schools and universities, and the corridors and offices of our government representatives learn what actually is happening in lands we call holy. Reverend Stephen Goldstein in this book not only provides us with a balanced survey of this long-lasting conflict but also challenges each of us to creatively engage in the art of peacemaking. As *Israel-Palestine* helps the reader to understand the complexities of this conflict, I hope and pray that God's Spirit will also help the reader to soar into the joys and blessings of peacemaking.

Reverend Alex Awad

Introduction

A Just Peace?

It is history that makes Israel-Palestine, a little piece of land no greater in size than New Jersey, so significant. From the August 2005 Israeli unilateral pullout from the Gaza Strip to the anguish of Israeli families being uprooted in the dismantling of the illegal Jewish settlements, from the stunning Palestinian parliamentary elections in January 2006 to the Israeli election of a new Kadima-party-led government in March of that year, we witness the pain and drama of these events on international television. Nothing happens in Israel-Palestine today that doesn't evoke events in the history of Judaism, Christianity, and Islam: the three Abrahamic faiths. This history infuses every event past and present, from biblical times to the wrenching events of the present. The events in Israel-Palestine use more ink in our daily newspapers than any other event in any other place in the world.

An article in *The New York Times* reported on a bilingual Arabic-Hebrew play titled *Six Actors in Search of a Plot,* by Palestinian playwright Mohammed Ahmed Zaher. The cast included both Israeli and Palestinian actors, a somewhat unusual occurrence. During the first five days of rehearsals at Kibbutz Ein Hahoresh near Hadera, Israel, the Palestinian and Jewish actors argued about nearly every line. During rehearsal, both sides said they felt under attack. The Palestinians were "unwilling to give up their attachment to history," Mr. Zaher said. "It's their weapon."[1] It is one wielded by both Palestinians and Israelis.

Anyone who is involved with the struggle in Israel-Palestine understands that the interpretation of both history and memory will necessarily have to be at the heart of any new reality that comes some day to these two peoples. A new reality will also have to take into account an understanding of justice related to two people's histories.

Easy as Pie

The Emperor divides the world
into two parts:
the Good and the Evil.

If you don't accept that,
the Emperor says
You are Evil.
The Emperor declares himself
and his friends: Good.

The Emperor says as soon as
Good has destroyed Evil,
all will be Good.

Simple as one, two, three.
Clear as night and day.
Different as black and white.

Easy as pie.[2]

When Jesus entered Jerusalem to the people's acclaim, the Pharisees rebuked him and demanded that he stop the clamoring of the crowds. Jesus' response was, "I tell you, if these were silent, the stones would shout out" (Luke 19:40). In Israel-Palestine today, the history of the region infuses the stones themselves. Any understanding of what is happening there today demands that we listen for the voices that tell the story of how the past has shaped the present and will continue to shape the future. Because history is so inextricably bound to the reality in Israel-Palestine today, this study book focuses on that history. Participants in the study will find in the study guide information about the peoples who inhabit Israel-Palestine and the cultures through which they express who they are and what they will become.

History infuses every event past and present, from biblical times to the wrenching events of the present.

Abrahamic religion:

any of those religions deriving from a common ancient Semitic tradition and traced by its adherents to Abraham, a patriarch whose life is narrated in the Hebrew Bible/Old Testament. Abraham is designated as a prophet in the Qur'an and is also called a prophet in Genesis 20:7. Abrahamic religions are monotheistic, generally considered to include Judaism, Christianity (Christianity's origins are from Judaism, hence it is also an Abrahamic religion), Islam, and the Bahá'í Faith, and comprise about half of the world's religious adherents.[3]

Throughout history—

a turbulent three-thousand years
when it has been besieged,
burned, sacked, and repeatedly
rebuilt—Jerusalem has been
a beacon of the spirit, yet always
a center of strife. The tension
and the strife remain....
Then walking around the old
walls, I might touch the stones.
Nothing special you might
say, limestone, or what is called
Jerusalem limestone, and
I study the veins of the old stone
as one might read the palms of a
hand and try to decipher what is
written, what is the future....
Always the stones remind me

that the business of Jerusalem
is eternity. Not for this race or this
creed. But at least for these
stones. Tough yet noble, they vary
in shade from a yellowish gray
through pink-gold to russet-gold.
In the old walls, the stones dating
from the Roman days and
Suleiman the Magnificent have
weathered to become yellower
than most, and there are some
hours in the afternoon when
they shine like slabs of gold.
I see the walls, towers, spires, and
pinnacles that represent the
three faiths. Yet, although the Old
City is a holy city to three faiths,

I look upon a scene that
is predominantly Muslim Arab.

Grace Halsell,
Journey to Jerusalem[4]

Anyone involved in the struggle in Israel-Palestine understands that the interpretation of history and memory will have to be at the heart of any new reality that comes to these two peoples.

Chapter 1

History and Memory

Personal History

Before I attempt to review some of the history of Israel-Palestine and the relationships between Israelis and Palestinians, it is appropriate for me to say something about my personal history. What one perceives as reality is grounded in part on who a person is and where he or she comes from. That is certainly the case in terms of my own commitment to a new reality in the Middle East. I don't subscribe to the idea of total objectivity, only degrees of subjectivity.

Although born in the Bronx, I grew up in a Jewish home in the post-World War II New York City suburb of Fort Lee, New Jersey. My parents were both children of Central and Eastern European immigrants, as are most American Jews who came to the United States in the twentieth century. My mother Gertrude's parents came from Hungary. Her father, Stephen, after whom I was named, was Roman Catholic, but her mother, Pauline, was Jewish. They divorced, leaving my grandmother with three young daughters. She worked as a domestic and lacking adequate resources placed my mother and her sister Loretta in a Jewish children's home to ensure their daily maintenance and schooling. The youngest daughter, Mildred, remained with her mother. Pauline's daughters were not estranged from her. They apparently understood their situation was necessary for survival in their circumstances. I never met my maternal grandmother and grandfather, both having died before I was born.

Probably the pogroms that served as the impetus for my father's family's emigration from Russian Poland were those that took place between 1903 and 1906, when two thousand Jews were left dead. News of such atrocities spread within the Jewish communities of the empire, as large numbers of Jewish immigrants to the United States and Canada testified to the trauma they had endured. The Tsar also enacted the harsh

Pogrom (from the Russian, *to wreak havoc, to demolish violently*): (n.) a form of riot, a massive violent attack on a particular ethnic, religious, or other group, primarily characterized by the destruction of its environment (homes, businesses, religious centers). Usually pogroms are accompanied by physical violence against and even murder of the targeted people, in some cases to the degree of massacre. The term has historically been used to denote massive acts of violence, either spontaneous or premeditated, against Jews, but has been applied to similar incidents against other, mostly minority, groups.[5] The Hebrew word for *pogrom* is *praot*.

May Laws of 1882. Thousands of refugees fled the countryside for the greater safety of the cities. Between 1881 and 1914, 2.5 million Jews left the Russian empire and emigrated to America, Britain, the British colonies, and Europe.[6]

The Goldsteins, Herschel and Lena, and their five children came to New York City between 1907 and 1908. My father, Joseph, was born in New York City in 1909, the sixth child. His nickname, an affirmation of their new lives, was "Georgie," after George Washington, the first president of the United States.

My paternal grandparents raised their children in a Jewish-Kosher home. If family lore is reliable, they were not active in their synagogue. It was the practice during the Jewish holidays to charge for a seat in the synagogue, presumably to ensure that inactive folks contributed to the synagogue's upkeep. My grandfather Herschel (changed to Harris by the immigration authorities upon his entering the United States)

was apparently unhappy with the practice, and the family didn't attend services with any regularity, if at all. But that didn't prevent my grandmother Lena from preparing the traditional meal on Friday evening and saying the prayers over the candles to usher in the Sabbath.

My siblings, who were eleven and thirteen years older than I, grew up in a multiethnic Jewish neighborhood in the Bronx. My brother made his Bar Mitzvah, and though it was still an American innovation, my sister made her Bat Mitzvah. Shortly after we moved to New Jersey, when I was five years old, my mother died. My father tried to bring me up religiously. At ten or eleven, I was sent to a nearby Jewish Community Center for Hebrew and religious instruction. My sister was married in the first wedding ceremony performed at the Center.

As I entered adolescence, I became keenly aware that my father was not involved in the life of the Jewish Community

Kosher (from the Hebrew *kasher*, "fit, proper"): (adj.) ritually proper for use according to Jewish law. It is applied especially to the food that Jews are permitted to eat under dietary laws that are derived from passages in the biblical books of Leviticus and Deuteronomy.[7]

The anti-Jewish riots

in Kishinev, Bessarabia (modern Moldova), are worse than the censor will permit to publish. There was a well laid-out plan for the general massacre of Jews on the day following the Orthodox Easter. The mob was led by priests, and the general cry, "Kill the Jews," was taken up all over the city. The Jews were taken wholly unaware and were slaughtered like sheep. The dead number 120 [Note: according to *The Jews in the Modern World* (Hilary L. Rubinstein, Daniel C. Cohn-Sherbok, Abraham J. Edelheit, William D. Rubinstein, Oxford University Press, 2002), the actual number of dead was between 47 and 48.] and the injured about 500. The scenes of horror attending this massacre are beyond description. Babes were literally torn to pieces by the frenzied and bloodthirsty mob. The local police made no attempt to check the reign of terror. At sunset the streets were piled with corpses and wounded. Those who could make their escape fled in terror, and the city is now practically deserted of Jews.[8]

–*The New York Times,* 1903

Center. Unfortunately I felt some negative judgment from the elders in the new congregation about my father's lack of involvement. Coupled with my own rebelliousness and anger as a motherless child, this soured me on the whole experience. I managed to get myself expelled from Hebrew School, and just before turning thirteen I walked away from my Bar Mitzvah instruction. With adolescent honesty, I knew it was hypocritical to undergo a ceremony for which I had no interest and little encouragement. My Bar Mitzvah was to be on a Tuesday rather than celebrated during the Saturday Sabbath service, when a Bar Mitzvah is customarily scheduled with the entire congregation present.

There was little anyone in my family could say with much integrity. I don't recall ever defending my decision. I am sure they worried about me, but as involvement in the Jewish Center was minimal at best on my father's part, it was not a significant matter. When I resisted going to Hebrew School, my father told me that it "wouldn't look nice to the neighbors" if I didn't attend. Since our neighbors were mostly Roman Catholic, I was not persuaded. My father had other matters that surely occupied his attention. He lost his trucking business soon after. Just keeping me clothed, fed, and with a roof over our heads was enough.

What I took away from my religious instruction besides a sense of otherness was an unarticulated awareness of the enormity of the Holocaust for Jewish identity and the centrality of Israel for Jews. I never learned much about God, how the Hebrew of the siddur (prayerbook) translated into English, or why I should follow the religious regulations that they tried to instill in us. But I knew that six million of us had been recently murdered by Hitler (it was only a decade after the War ended) and that we should be committed to this new state in the Middle East, Israel.

I learned about the significance of the Holocaust, but not by talking about it openly. Its horror was still ubiquitous their smokestacks and the miserable emaciated prisoners in striped clothing.

Talk of Israel, however, was a different story. It was the center of much of what was celebrated in that young congregation. There was a display case selling religious gift items imported from Israel in the entrance to the Center. We children were given little blue boxes imprinted with a menorah symbolizing Judaism and the state of Israel. We saved coins to be given to the Jewish Fund for Israel. We were told it was "to plant trees in Israel in the desert which Israelis were turning into a garden." My closest relative, my Aunt Grace, worked for the United Israel Appeal, an organization that raised money for the Jewish Fund. I didn't feel strongly connected to Israel, perhaps because it never came up in conversation at home, but it surely defined part of my sense of what being a Jew meant.

Like most young persons, I had my share of religious concerns and questions. I was a bit more interested than may have in most adult Jewish minds, including my family's. Relatives of my grandparents' generation had been slaughtered (although I didn't know that for some years). But I did know that something very bad was attached to being Jewish. Why else would we not talk about it, and why else would I have internalized a sense of guilt for being Jewish? My brother had left a photographic history of World War II at home after he left for college, the year my mother died. I can still recall the photographs of the death camps and the crematoria with been typical because of negative and unresolved feelings about Judaism and being Jewish. I tried to reject this part of myself. During my high school years, I went out of my way to condemn religious practice of any kind, all the time wanting to know more and to find acceptance. I had plenty of God questions.

I was sent to a private high school, where it was thought I would have more supervision. It entailed a daily two-hour-plus commute by bus, keeping me off the streets on most weekdays. It turned out to be more important for my future growth than could have been anticipated. It was a small coeducational school that afforded significant attention to its students. Some of my professors became significant mentors for me. One of them, the assistant headmaster, an active Christian layman and the son and brother of Methodist pastors, supported me in my search for religious understanding and my thirst for education. He did not try to proselytize me but rather challenged me by nurturing a love for literature and encouraging a search for understanding who I was and what my life was to become. I identified myself as an agnostic, actively denying the little of Judaism that I had experienced, along with any other religion with which I had any contact (for the most part Roman Catholicism). I was attempting to deny being Jewish. If I were an adult, I would have been labeled a self-hating Jew.

Some, however, did try to encourage in me a belief in Christianity. Joel was a close high school friend who was

The significance of God's grace in one's life is always made clear in retrospect. I claim as grace my religious odyssey and my embracing of Christ and Christianity in college. It did not happen in a vacuum but in the midst of the social upheavals of the sixties, including the assassinations of John F. Kennedy, Martin Luther King, Jr., and Bobby Kennedy. I was involved in the Civil Rights movement and the Vietnam anti-war movement. With the encouragement of my high school assistant headmaster and because of a substantial scholarship, I attended the small liberal arts college at Drew University. The college chaplain, a Methodist pastor who stood with us in our search to make sense of the times, became my mentor. The Sunday college chapel services became the context where I sought to make sense of things. His assistant was a seminarian, one of the first female divinity students working toward ordination. She deeply supported and encouraged my journey of faith.

an Italian Protestant—a Baptist. All of the other Italians I knew growing up were Roman Catholic. Joel invited me to attend a Billy Graham crusade with him, an event that almost turned me off to Christianity completely. I found the altar call so intimidating that I was out of my seat before anyone else, only I left the theater. Joel furthered the cause more successfully one year later with a Christmas gift, a Sir Thomas Beecham recording of Handel's Messiah.

The radical Jew of the gospel stories who was martyred by the authorities of his day for nonviolent teaching and advocacy for justice started to impact my life. The support of this Christian community committed to social causes, identified appropriately as Christian concerns, deepened my articulation of religious matters. My experience broadened, but so did my anger, frustration, and concern for what surely was a world gone mad with violence and hate.

One night in powerless despair, I came to see that this Jesus had saved the world and that even with my deepest commitment to do so, I could not and no longer needed to try. In Jesus, God had created a new possibility for life: a way to live a real life in a loving and life-affirming relationship with others that is framed with justice and mystery. In spite of daily violence and hatred, there indeed was a God who had not abandoned us or the world. Our God is at its center, planted on a cross. I came to believe the words of the Eucharistic prayer that I heard at each Sunday worship service in the college chapel: "This is my blood of the covenant, which is poured out for many" (Mark 14:24).

I discovered that I was one of the many, and that the Aramaic translation for many is all. Significant to me was the fact that Jesus lived and died a Jew. My experience, surely a conversion from emptiness and nothingness to a something, felt emotionally and spiritually like a homecoming. It was coming

The year 1968 was a kairos year for me and a momentous year in United States history. Like many others of that time, I can tell you where on campus I was when I received the news that Martin Luther King had been assassinated in Memphis, and later that same year when news came of Bobby Kennedy's death. I also recall hearing news the previous year of the Six-Day War in the Middle East. Although I wouldn't know of its significance until almost twenty years later, I remember feeling some vengeful pride in hearing that the Jews had won a war. "We" had beat somebody else, the "Arabs." Such chauvinism is a telling part of the story.

Upon my graduation and with the arrogance and enthusiasm of a new Christian, along with some encouragement in particular from the assistant chaplain Bonnie Jones (by then a clergy member of the New York Conference), I started seminary. Bonnie and I were married about a year later and had two sons together. I was ordained an elder in the

home to the self I had denied since abandoning and being abandoned by my Jewish roots. I claimed my old self as a Jew and my new self as a follower of Jesus the Jew. I was baptized in Drew College Chapel on the third Sunday of Advent in 1968 by the chaplain and his assistant, Bonnie Jones.

New York Conference, where I now have my membership. In 1980, while we were serving as one of the first clergy couples in the denomination, a friend offered us a free trip to the Holy Land. We immediately accepted the gift with much appreciation.

Holy Land?

It is not possible to publicly discuss Israel-Palestine in the United States critically without inviting judgment, particularly from American Jews. If one is Jewish, such criticism can be divisive in the Jewish community. If one is Christian, criticism can invite charges of anti-Semitism. If one is a Jewish-Christian as I am (though I would be considered a convert or apostate by some Jews), it can be a catalyst for both derision and charges of anti-Semitism. The threat of such derision prevents the story of Israel-Palestine from being told from a perspective that credits both the Israeli narrative and the Palestinian narrative. It prevents fair and impartial coverage in the media and in public forums. It is not unusual for pressure groups to prevent speakers, writers, authors, professors, and others who are perceived to be either pro-Palestinian or who are native Palestinians from making public presentations.

In December 2002 the United Methodist church I attend in White Plains, New York, held two forums, one to which we had invited two Palestinians from Hebron to speak. Zleikha Muhtaseb and Abdel Hadi Hantash are both involved with Human Rights activities in Hebron. They were visiting the United States on a speaking tour sponsored by Americans for Middle East Understanding (AMEU). During the same month, Huwaida Arraf, a Palestinian-American, and her husband, Adam Shapiro, an American Jew, spoke at our church. Along with Ghassam Andoni,[9] they are co-founders of The International Solidarity Movement (ISM).[10] The week before the advertised event, our pastor was alerted by the police to the possibility of violence. In the same week, a representative of the Jewish community in White Plains contacted our pastor and urged him to provide time for a Jewish representative to speak. He acquiesced, and one of the local synagogues

A few years ago, a Presbyterian congregation in Atlanta invited Naim Ateek (a Palestinian Anglican priest, Director of Sabeel Palestinian Liberation Theology Center in Jerusalem) and Marc H. Ellis (an American Jewish theologian and professor currently at Baylor University) to participate in a forum on Israel-Palestine. When the Jewish community in Atlanta applied pressure, the forum was canceled, and the invitations to Ellis and Ateek were rescinded.

flew in from Israel an Israeli spokesperson especially for the event. The climate for such open forums remains the same today.

In a *New York Times* editorial (April 19, 2006), the historian Tony Judt, director of the Remarque Institute at New York University and a British Jew, wrote about an essay titled "The Israel Lobby" from the *London Times Review of Books.* The authors of the essay are two distinguished American academics, Stephen Walt of Harvard

University and John Mearsheimer of the University of Chicago. The article criticizes US foreign policy in the Middle East and blames our foreign policy failures on the uncritical support of Israel, which the authors claim is unduly influenced and distorted by the Israel lobby. The lobby's parent organization is the American Israel Public Affairs Committee (AIPAC). In Judt's words, "…the [Walt-Mearsheimer] essay has run into a firestorm of vituperation and refutation. Critics have charged that the authors' scholarship is shoddy and that their claims are, in the words of the columnist Christopher Hitchens, 'slightly but unmistakably smelly. The smell in question, of course, is that of anti-Semitism.'"

This hypersensitivity to any public conversation about Israel-Palestine is destructive. Professor Judt supports the *Israel Forum,* which "was founded with the goal of providing an open public space where people can come together to discuss the politics of Israel-Palestine. The Forum is comprised of people of all ages, Israelis and Americans, including students from NYU, Columbia University, and other universities in the New York City area."[11] It is important for United Methodists in the United States to become acquainted with both contemporary and historical facts that address the conflict, seek to redress it in a just way, and move toward the establishment of a lasting and just peace.

Judt says that the article has

been criticized in Israel and in the academy on its merits, but has hardly been mentioned in the mainstream US media. Judt reflects on this failure of coverage:

I think there is another element in play: fear. Fear of being thought to legitimize talk of a "Jewish conspiracy"; fear of being thought anti-Israel; and thus, in the end, fear of licensing the expression of anti-Semitism…. The damage that is done by America's fear of anti-Semitism when discussing Israel is threefold. It is bad for Jews: anti-Semitism is real enough (I know something about it, growing up Jewish in 1950s Britain), but for just that reason it should not be confused with political criticisms of Israel or its American supporters. It is bad for Israel: by guaranteeing it unconditional support, Americans encourage Israel to act heedless of consequences…. But above all, self-censorship is bad for the United States itself. Americans are denying themselves participation in a fast-moving international conversation.[12]

Personal History

I have visited the "Holy Land" a number of times in the past twenty-six years, most recently in 2006 immediately prior to the elections mentioned above. I still recall my first visit in 1980.[13] As with most Christian visitors on such tours, the personal religious-spiritual orientation was foremost in my expectations. I sought to visit the biblical sites: a combination of ancient Jewish sites like Masada, Jericho, and Megiddo, as well as the New Testament sites like the Church of the Holy Sepulcher in the Old City of Jerusalem, the Garden Tomb, the Church of the Nativity in Bethlehem, the Sea of Galilee, and the city of Nazareth, Jesus' home.

This commercial tour focused on these destinations and so met my need. The tour guide, licensed by the state of Israel, was attuned to the fact that I was Jewish. The training and licensing of guides is a significant matter and regulated carefully by the Israeli Ministry of Tourism. The guides are

dropped coins in Hebrew School? He certainly knew well the pride and identification an American Jew would experience in seeing that sight.

He was aware that American Jews want to feel at home in the land of Israel. Israel always welcomes American Jews who immigrate to Israel. It is called making aliyah (Hebrew for "going up" or settling in Israel). The Right of Return is an Israeli law. "On the establishment of the state, its founders proclaimed 'the renewal of the Jewish State in the Land of Israel, which would open wide the gates of the homeland to every Jew....'" The Law of Return (1950) grants every Jew, wherever he or she may be, the right to come to Israel as an oleh (a Jew immigrating to Israel) and become an Israeli citizen. For the purposes of this Law, "Jew" means a person who was born of a Jewish mother or has converted to Judaism and is not a member of another religion. Israeli citizenship becomes effective on the day of arrival in the country or of

not only experts regarding the biblical background of the sites but are also accustomed to the Jewish and Christian sensibilities of the tourists (I've been on a tour led by a Palestinian Muslim who honored his professional commitment, whatever his personal sensibilities might have been). As our guide pointed out the hills surrounding the Old City of Jerusalem and the trees growing on them, I'm sure he was quite aware of the special relationship of American Jews to this vista. Did he know about the little box in which I had

receipt of an oleh's certificate, whichever is later.[14] It is Zionist policy to continue encouraging Jewish immigration. Jews may hold dual citizenship in the United States and Israel, and many do.

As we drove past the agriculturally developed areas with modern irrigation techniques in the Jezreel Valley, Israel's breadbasket, we also passed through Samaria and saw small seemingly primitive Arab farms. All one noticed from the tour bus window was the plenitude of rocks and scraggly trees, which I later discovered were olive orchards. The contrasts were quite striking and intentional. "See, the Jews are modern, and the Arabs are not" was the underlying message. When we passed some grazing cattle, the guide noted that they were of a special Israeli breed, part Guernsey and part Holstein; "Goldsteins," he called them. I was even connected through the cattle to Israel!

Most Jewish and Christian religious people who have the opportunity to visit the Holy Land have an expectation similar to mine that they will visit the places mentioned in the Hebrew Bible and/or in the Christian Testament. Both commercial and educational tours are geared to fulfill these expectations. The shorthand for such encounters is "visiting the places where Jesus walked," or making a pilgrimage. But something as seemingly benign as religious tourism is both a political and a theological statement.

In 1992, I again visited Israel-Palestine and Egypt. The trip took place toward the end of the first Intifada (1987-1991), the Palestinian resistance in the West Bank and Gaza strip to the continued Israeli military Occupation.

We had both a licensed tour guide, unusually a Palestinian, and one of our missionaries, Dr. Romeo Del Rosario, who was assigned at the time as the United Methodist liaison to the Middle East Council of Churches. His office was in East Jerusalem, the Palestinian part of Jerusalem. His insights and experiences added a rich depth to our study tour. But this tour was not designed as simply a pilgrimage through traditional Biblical sites, visiting the ancient stones of Bible times, but also as an encounter with the "living stones," Palestinian Christians who live and worship Christ in modern Israel and in the Occupied Territories.

After making our way up to Jerusalem to stay at the East Jerusalem YMCA, an important Palestinian Christian institution,

Intifada: "shaking off," that is, shaking off the military Occupation. It is a focused resistance led by a generation of young Palestinians who had been born and grew up under the Occupation, which was and is a constant presence disrupting and destroying any potential for a normal life for the Palestinians.

The Druze: a Middle Eastern religious sect that originated from the Ismaili sect of Shia Islam in the eleventh century. Religion dominates their habits and customs. Today, the Druze community numbers about one million members who reside mainly in Syria, Lebanon, Israel, and the Israeli-occupied territory of the West Bank (including the Palestinian Authority), and Jordan.[15]

we traveled to Nazareth and stayed at St. Margaret's Guest House attached to Christ Evangelical Episcopal Church. I was standing one afternoon on a balcony admiring the view of the Roman Catholic Church of the Ascension. Arch-Deacon Riah Abu El-Assal,[16] our host, joined me on the balcony. I asked Father Riah if he had been serving St. Margaret's since 1967. "No, longer than that," Father Riah replied. "Since 1948?" "No," he smiled, looking out over Nazareth's snow-covered rooftops, "even longer than that. I have been here 2,000 years! Since A.D. 33 at the first Pentecost. Since Palestinian history began."

Father Riah expanded on this teaching moment when he later addressed our tour group. He introduced himself as a Palestinian Arab Christian citizen of Israel, and an Anglican Priest. In 1991 he had been a priest in Nazareth for about thirty-one years. Father Riah has lived there his entire life, except for a year when he and his family fled to

For Father Riah, this also includes the more than six million Palestinian refugees[19] living in the West Bank, Gaza Strip, and the surrounding Arab nations, and the many who have emigrated beyond. An overriding concern for him has been the large number of Palestinian Christians who have left Palestine. He noted that before 1948 the Christian population of Nazareth was 30 percent, but by 1991 it had dwindled to 1.5 percent.[20] He writes:

> If we do not find a solution quickly, the land where our faith was born and survived for two thousand years will soon be empty of indigenous Christians. The living faith will be represented only by dead stones and their imported custodians. All my effort has been dedicated to preventing this catastrophe.[21]

Ironically the only Christian I had met on my first visit to the Holy Land in 1980 was a Franciscan priest at St. Joseph's

Lebanon. He took Israeli citizenship in 1959 in order to obtain a passport, which is denied Palestinians in Israel, so that he could study abroad. Without a passport, there was no guarantee that he would be able to return to Nazareth.[17] Father Riah has suffered the discrimination all Palestinian citizens of Israel experience, but he has always dedicated his ministry to the vision of peace and justice for all of the residents of the land of the Holy One, whether Jew, Arab, or Druze.[18]

Church in Nazareth, and he was from Fort Lee, New Jersey—my home town!

Chapter 2
Biblical Beginnings to Zionist Zeal

In January 2006 I was with the Reverend Alex Awad while he was addressing a group of African-American Methodist pastors from the Atlanta metropolitan area. Alex often begins his lectures by asking his audience how long the Israel-Palestine conflict has been going on. This time, before he even finished the question, someone interrupted, "Forever." Alex responded as he has in his book, *Through the Eyes of the Victims:*

> In fact, Arabs and Jews lived side by side in relative harmony for hundreds of years. To generalize that they have been fighting for thousands of years or "since Day One" is a false analysis of history.[22]

When it comes to the Holy Land, there is a tendency to bring ancient biblical images and stories to present-day Israel-Palestine without accounting for the long history that has intervened. Another standard perception is to think that the

nor are they found in biblical times. The ascendancy of Islam and the Arab conquests of the Middle East did not occur until the seventh and eighth centuries of the Common Era (C.E.). In the first century C.E., the Romans destroyed the Temple in Jerusalem (First Jewish Revolt 66-70 C.E.) and Emperor Hadrian's armies later (132-135 C.E.) squelched a Palestinian Jewish Messianic rebellion led by Simon Bar Kochba, a Jewish insurrectionist. Rome is cast as the enemy of Israel, not the Arabs. Although it is a simplified interpretation of history, the Jews of Palestine were exiled from their home following this second Jewish Revolt. This exile or dispersion, referred to as the Diaspora, is only a part of the story. The Romans emptied Jerusalem of Jews and prohibited their living there following the destruction of the Temple. But this was by no means the beginning of Jewish dispersion outside of Palestine.

conflict between Arabs and Jews has been going on since biblical times. One might assume that the conflict began with the Abraham-Sarah narrative in Genesis 16-17, in which Hagar is impregnated by Abram and bears a son, Ishmael. Genesis links Ishmael's progeny with what became Edom and the Arabian peninsula;[23] hence the myth of origin for the Arabs.

Exile, Rebellion, Revolt
But the origins of the conflict are not found in the Scriptures;

The first exile of Israel followed the Assyrian conquest of the Northern Kingdom (Samaria) in 722 B.C.E.; these deportees did not generally form a Diaspora community. The Assyrians exchanged the Northern Kingdom population of Israel with those from other subjected areas. It was the deportation of a part of the population of Judah (the Southern Kingdom) by the Babylonians in 597 and later in 587/586 B.C.E. that resulted in the creation of a permanent Jewish community outside of Judea.

The Babylonian exile imposed by Nebuchadnezzar on the Judeans removed the center of Jewish life to Babylon for fifty or sixty years.... The Jews who chose to remain there enjoyed considerable prosperity, as indicated by business documents from nearby Nippur in which individuals identified as Judeans or bearing Jewish names (in Hebrew or Aramaic) engage in various agricultural and commercial activities. The foundations were thus laid for the creative role that Babylonia was to play in the Jewish life of the post-biblical period.[24]

The conflict and mistrust between those Jews living in Jerusalem and those in Samaria originated in part because of the perceived notion that the remaining Samarians had intermarried with "pagans." This mistrust was carried to postexilic returnees and to those residents of Judah who had never gone into exile but had been ruled as a district of "Samaria."[25] The Samarians developed their own religious practices apart from the Jerusalem Temple (II Kings 17) and

than within Palestine.[26] Large Jewish communities thrived in Alexandria in Egypt and in other important urban centers. During the Alexandrian period from the third until near the end of the first century B.C.E., that is, the time of Rome's conquest and the birth of Christianity, Jews had lived outside of Judea and served the various empires, both as peasants in agricultural economies and in trade and commerce. We know of large Jewish communities throughout the Mediterranean world—including in Rome, Antioch, and Damascus—through New Testament writings and histories by Josephus Flavius and others.

It is also significant that the Jews in the New Testament period were not a single unified community. Galilee was not simply the place from where Jesus came. It was a separate territory whose Jewish population was quite distinct from that of Judea. We pick up the historical allusion in Luke, who says that the provinces were ruled separately:

centered their worship on Mount Gerizim in Samaria. The Samaritans acknowledged only their own version of the Pentateuch, the Torah, as authentic Holy Scripture. This discord is reflected by Luke in the parable of the Good Samaritan (Luke 10:25-37), where the cultural and religious distance between Jerusalem and Samaria is clearly ethnic in nature.

At the time of the second Jewish Revolt in the second century C.E. there were more Jews living outside Palestine

In the fifteenth year of the reign of Emperor Tiberius, when Pontius Pilate was governor of Judea and Herod was ruler of Galilee, and his brother Philip ruler of the region of Ituraea [a.k.a. Jordan] and Trachonitis [a.k.a. Syria]..., and Lysanias ruler of Abilene, during the high priesthood of Annas and Caiaphas.... (Luke 3:1-2)

At the time of the Jewish Revolt, the Galileans and Judeans were not a united people and had not been for some time. Since the seventh century B.C.E., the Samaritans, heirs of the Northern Kingdom, and Judeans were most certainly not harmonious in their relations. The regional tension is reflected in the lack of acceptance of Jesus and the disciples, not only because of Jesus' message but because of the regional division in the Jewish community. Echoes of it are heard in Scripture in the Judean slurs against Jesus (John 7:41-44).

The divisions reflected here were symptomatic of later discord. In *Jesus the Jew: A Historian's Reading of the Gospels,* Geza Vermes points out that for the Jews in Jerusalem the residents of Galilee were at best a lesser class and considered peasants, or *'am ha-arez.*

As we move into the more recent history of Zionism and the version of Jewish history used to justify the return to their homeland by European Jews, history has been rewritten to support the politics and projects of the early Zionist settlers and to support the leadership's intentions.

For most of Jewish post-biblical history, the notion of a return home was not a serious expectation for the majority of Jews. Their homes and homelands were well beyond Judea, Samaria, and the Galilee. That is not to say that Diaspora Jews didn't reestablish their Jewish religious identity. But in the course of this long history, a return to Zion was not a significant factor. The establishment of Rabbinic Judaism following the destruction of the Temple in Jerusalem in C.E. 70, which moved the center of Judaism to the Galilee and beyond, brought a substitution for Jewish observance that until then had been centered around the Jerusalem Temple and the cult of sacrifice. Not until the nineteenth century did any concrete idea of a return to Palestine become of significant interest. When analyzed in the context of the historical record, there is little in either the biblical record or the early post-biblical record that can support the proprietary claims of nineteenth and twentieth-century European Jews to Israel-Palestine.

In 2006 it is still part of Israel's self-understanding, at least for some of its citizenry. This will bear further discussion as we follow Zionist history into the early part of the twentieth century. The later ideological use of biblical history to justify and undergird the image of the return to the ancient Jewish homeland was not a one-dimensional reality. It furthered the cause of denying a history to Palestinians.

Islam and the Arab Conquest

The birth of Mohammed in C.E. 570 signals the beginning of a new era, one dominated by a new Abrahamic faith, Islam. Within a century of the appearance of Islam in the Arabian peninsula, the Islamic state extended from the Atlantic Ocean to Central Asia. During this time the Dome of the Rock mosque was built in Jerusalem by Caliph Abd al-Malik ibn Marwan.

From the ninth to the eleventh centuries C.E., Palestine was ruled by the Fatimids, who fell to the invading Seljuks in the late eleventh century. These caliphs elevated religion to a key role in the state. Muslim rulers did not force their religion on the residents of Palestine. It was more than a century before most converted. The remaining Christians and Jews were considered People of the Book and were allowed relative autonomy. They were guaranteed security and freedom of worship, a degree of tolerance that was rare at that time. Subsequently most Palestinians adopted Arabic and Islamic culture.

Palestine was holy to Muslims because the Prophet Mohammed had designated Jerusalem as the first of the directions in which Muslims face when praying. He was believed to have ascended to heaven on a night journey from the Old City of Jerusalem where the Dome of the Rock mosque was later built. For these reasons Jerusalem

of Jerusalem ruled and controlled many holy sites of Islam. Many cities in Palestine, including Jaffa, were captured. But Muslim leader Saladin put an end to the Kingdom in 1187. Successive crusades accomplished little more than the looting and occupation of Constantinople, but the Byzantine Empire was weakened.

In 1453 the centuries-old Byzantine Empire was absorbed by the Ottoman Empire, extending its influence over most of the Islamic world. In 1517 the Ottomans conquered Jerusalem. Largely for practical reasons, the Empire was tolerant toward non-Muslims and did not attempt to convert them. In the sixteenth and seventeenth centuries, the Ottoman Empire was among the world's most powerful states. It steadily declined during the nineteenth century as nationalism swept the world, meeting its demise in the twentieth century after its defeat in World War I along with the other Central Powers.[27]

became the third holiest city in Islam, and remains important to Muslims to this day.

In 1095 Pope Urban II launched the First Crusade and captured Jerusalem, massacring Jews as they passed through European cities. Unlike the first Muslim rulers of Jerusalem, the Crusaders engaged in a campaign to convert the residents, either by gaining their hearts and minds or if necessary by the sword. For a time the Christian Kingdom

Together, the three Abrahamic religions and their adherents have maintained an unbroken presence in the Israel-Palestine region. From the beginning of biblical times, peoples of the region have shared both a history and some common faith roots. All three faiths revere Abraham as a prophet, for example. Over time each faith has gained ascendancy and has wielded its dominance with a greater or a lesser degree of compassion, sometimes living with others peacefully and sometimes with conflict. But from earliest times up through the rule of the Ottoman Empire, Christian and Muslim Arabs and Jews coexisted in a land fraught with meaning for all.

Sweeping Change

Western Europe was in continual turmoil during the latter part of the nineteenth century, dominated by a movement toward the establishment of nation states as defined particularly by shared culture, language, and ethnicity. On January 18, 1871, William I, the Prussian King, was crowned emperor of Germany in the Hall of Mirrors at Versailles, an event that represented the culmination of Bismarck's unremitting efforts for the unification of Germany.[28]

The Dreyfus Case

In France, the fallout from the struggles following the defeat

Alfred Dreyfus, the first Jewish officer to have been assigned to the French general staff, was demoted at a solemn public military ceremony prior to being deported to Devil's Island. Found guilty of handing over secret documents to the Prussian general staff, he was convicted of the crime of high treason.[30]

The charges were completely false. Others in the French military and government were responsible for casting blame on Dreyfus in order to protect themselves. Not until 1906 was he finally exonerated, restored to the service with the rank of major, and decorated with the Legion of Honor. He later served as a lieutenant colonel in World War I (1914-1918).[31]

Present in the courtroom on the day in 1894 when the Dreyfus verdict was read was Theodor Herzl, Paris correspondent for an influential Austrian journal, *Neue Freie Presse*. Although the son of a Hungarian rabbi, Herzl was a liberal assimilated Jew living in Vienna writing drama

in the Franco-Prussian War, the radical attempt of the Paris Commune to establish a socialist government enshrining ideals that affirmed the working man, and the bloody defeat in May of the Paris Commune by government troops[29] all led to turmoil and ferment that exploded in what came to be known as the Dreyfus Case.

Instigated by the French Roman Catholic Church and more conservative civil authorities, anti-Semitism was the backdrop for much of this ferment in France. Captain

criticism. Along with most people, he did not doubt that Dreyfus was guilty. But after Dreyfus was led away, Herzl puzzled over the exaltation of the spectators. Herzl asked time and again, "Granted he is a traitor, how can they find such intense joy in the suffering of a human being?" "You forget," he was told, "that this crowd is elated over the degradation of a Jew."[32]

For months following Dreyfus' conviction, Herzl was in a fever, shaping his response to the revulsion that had so deeply troubled him. A small book emerged from all of these labors: *The Jew's State.* The age-old Messianic longing for Zion was transformed into Zionism—a European conception of a modern national and political movement. In *The Jew's State,* Herzl wrote:

> Anti-Semitism is a highly complex movement, which I think I understand. I approach this movement as a Jew, yet without fear or hatred. I believe that I can see in it the elements of cruel sport, of common commercial rivalry, of inherited prejudice, of religious intolerance—but also of a supposed need for self-defense. I consider the Jewish question neither a social nor a religious one, even though it sometimes takes these and other forms. It is a national question, and to solve it we must first of all establish it as an international political problem to be discussed and settled by the civilized nations of the world in council.[33]

Jewish Nationhood?

Although Herzl is credited as the father of Zionism, he was not the first European Jew to suggest that Jewish nationhood was the solution to European anti-Semitism. Moses Hess, grandson of a German rabbi and an early colleague of Karl Marx, published a small unsuccessful book, *Rome and Jerusalem.* It posits Jewish nationalism and the colonization of Palestine as a solution to anti-Semitism. Hess was a secularist. But he recognized that the more affluent middle-class Jews of Western Europe who were seeking the assimilation of Jews into the majority societies and who were emancipated, at least in public, from parochial Jewish practice, were not about to abandon their newfound place to a barren existence in remote Palestine. He believed that the Jews of Eastern Europe, those who had maintained their traditions and resisted the liberal secularism of the West, were likely to be more willing to accept his vision. Though *Rome and Jerusalem* was addressed primarily to German Jews of the middle class, they were barely tolerant of his ideas. Predictably, they saw themselves first and foremost as Germans, Frenchmen, Englishmen, and Americans, and only secondarily as Jews.[34]

More than five million Jews were living under the Tsar's domination, and they were generally more impoverished than the Jews in Western Europe. They were restricted to the westernmost provinces, living in the towns and cities of Warsaw, Odessa, Vilna, and other smaller urban centers.[35] Only the most prosperous resided in Moscow, St. Petersburg, and Kiev. Few lived on the land.

Other voices who posited Jewish nationalism as a solution to their plight came from this milieu. Leo Pinsker (1821-1891), a respected Odessa physician deeply disturbed by the pogrom of 1881 in Odessa, anonymously published a pamphlet, *Auto-Emancipation: A Warning to His People by a Russian Jew.* His solution was that Jews were to be given a territory of their own—any territory. He neither supported Palestine as the designated place nor rejected it but was inclined toward a Jewish refuge in "the vast open spaces of North America."[36] Though it was addressed in German to the Jews of Western Europe and designed to create compassion for the Jews of the East, response to this pamphlet was no greater than to Hess's.

Other poorly funded groups did attempt settlement in Palestine, but their efforts were mostly in vain. In 1882, Rishon le Zion (First to Zion), a Russian student society, established the first Zionist settlement in Palestine. A small number of others followed but most did not survive the hardships of poverty and disease they encountered. Rishon le Zion, the exception, survived only by turning to the Jewish philanthropist Baron Edmund de Rothschild for charity. His agents took proprietary control with the expectation of developing viticulture as an extension of his French wine

longing was rekindled by fears for their temporal position. As in Herzl, this feeling was the first glow of Jewish solidarity in those who returned to Judaism after having strayed afar.[38]

Herzl was encouraged by this historic piety. He supported this grassroots effort of groups that were caught up in the vision of Jewish settlement in Palestine. At the same time, he lobbied the wealthy and influential in the Jewish community as well as seeking the support of the rulers themselves. His efforts led to the first meeting of the Zionist World Congress in Basel (or Basle), Switzerland, in August 1897. Zionism was born, if not with a unified language or vision, at least with the support of 204 delegates from Europe, the United States, Algiers, and Palestine. Herzl noted in his diary, "In Basle I created the Jewish State."[39]

He was not nearly as successful with the rich and powerful. They were adamantly opposed to any political project, but tepidly in favor of some settlement activity.

business. Eventually it prospered and became well-known for its vineyards, wine cellars, and citrus groves.[37]

Pious Jews were still buried with a little bag of earth from the Holy Land under their heads, so that they might be reunited with their forefathers. This longing for Zion, spiritualized and secularized during the age of emancipation, had yet been kept alive both in Jewish hearts and in the synagogal service. Symbolizing the spiritual unity of Jews in the Diaspora and the hope of Messianic redemption, this

The bride is beautiful but she is married to another man.

Though sympathetic and willing to offer charitable assistance for small settlements, Baron Edmond de Rothschild and other European Jewish philanthropists had a deep aversion to the larger idea of a Jewish state. Yet Herzl persisted. Through family connections, he was able to gain an audience with those close to the German Emperor, William II, who consented to a meeting in the Holy Land (1898) with a Zionist delegation headed by Herzl. Unfortunately, William II discovered the Sultan was adamantly opposed to Jewish emigration into Palestine. After an additional three years of continued lobbying of the Sultan and his court, sanction was given for Jewish colonization anywhere in the Turkish realm except Palestine![40]

Herzl was not deterred. He gained some support from Russian leaders, who were seeking to improve the negative image resulting from the Kishinev pogrom. Then the British under Lord Chamberlain, the Colonial Secretary, offered

came from Russia, where the plight of Jews was most severe. But there was one serious flaw in all of this romantic nationalistic ideology and in the Jewish emigration to the Holy Land that it spawned. Shortly after the Basel Congress, a Zionist delegation of two Viennese rabbis was sent to Palestine on a fact-finding mission. In a cable addressed to the Jewish community in Vienna, the rabbis wrote, "The bride is beautiful but she is married to another man."[42] The Palestinians were already married to the land.

Zionism and Palestinian Arabs in the Land

In 1880 there were approximately 456,000 Arabs living in Palestine, with about 24,000 Jews, that is, 5 percent of the population. Following the 1881 pogroms in Russia, Jews came in what Israel refers to as the first *Aliyah* (return of the Jews).[43] But this was a misnomer. They were not "returning." They were settlers with a nineteenth-century

an autonomous Jewish settlement in Uganda, East Africa.[41] When this was announced at the 1903 Congress, Herzl was severely criticized as a traitor by the Russian delegates. Yet recognition by one of the great powers was extremely heartening. Hurt by the attacks but still pushing until the end, Herzl died in 1904, only 44 years of age.

His vision persisted after him. Jews began to emigrate to Palestine, purchasing land from Arab landowners who would sell to them. Financial support began to develop. Many Jews

colonial ideology emigrating to a land that, until after the First World War and the Treaty of Versailles in 1919, was part of the Ottoman Empire for almost 700 years. During and following the First World War, Jewish emigration from Europe increased. By 1914 the Jewish population had increased to 60,000, about 9 percent of the total population. The idea that these émigrés were settling an uninhabited land (along with the notion that it was a "return") is the central myth of Zionism.

Personal History

On my 1980 tour, Benno Wiseman, the Jewish Israeli tour guide, pointed to our driver, a Sabra *named Jacob. Jacob told me that he was a Palestinian, born there. Another Israeli, Michel Warschawski, explains, "Sabra is the name given to Jews born in Palestine, then in Israel. The word refers to the prickly pear, sharp and thorny on the outside but sweet and sugary inside...."[44] Jacob and Mr. Wiseman were also making the political point that Israelis have as much right to be in the land as Palestinian Arabs. In* On the Border, *Michel Warschawski goes on to point out that the sabra is also the symbol of Palestine in Arabic. It translates as* patience, *a very Palestinian quality, but only remotely Israeli.[45]*

Palestinian Self-Identity

In the literature regarding the early colonization of Palestine, the indigenous population is referred to as *Arab* almost without exception. A myth that was intentionally cultivated during the initial settlement period denies that Palestinian Arabs even existed as an entity residing in Palestine.

In speaking with Palestinian Arab friends and colleagues, I have asked whether they and their forebears thought of themselves as Palestinians. They have always responded in the affirmative. Without exception, all those I have queried affirm that for as long as they can recall, their self-identity has been Palestinian.

Quite self-consciously and intentionally, Jewish Israelis deny the Palestinian Arab claim to the land. This is all the more true with the recent substantial growth of a "native Jewish Israeli" population. By using the ancient biblical narratives as justification, the early Zionists made the same claim. The denial of the validity of the word Palestinian reveals a racism that considers Arabs less than human. Anyone who has experienced the contempt and seen the degradation inflicted

The Zaatara checkpoint, one of more than 180 checkpoints in place (2003)[46] is the main crossing between the northern and central West Bank. Fareed Taamallah, a peace activist and coordinator for the Palestinian Central Election Commission for the district of Salfit, travels daily to his office from his home in Qira.

The distance is about five miles, and it takes him from ninety minutes to two hours to travel through the checkpoint. He has begun reading books in his car while he waits. He relates what occurred on one occasion:

> I looked at the two young soldiers arrogantly manning the checkpoint,

with dozens of people awaiting a sign from them. At last the soldier moved his finger. A taxi edged forward. The driver got out, still far from the soldier, holding the passengers' identity cards. The soldier signaled to the driver to remove his T-shirt. Checking IDs takes ten minutes per car. Palestinians are required to carry Israeli-issued identification cards to present at checkpoints on Palestinian Arabs by Israeli soldiers at checkpoints and border crossings or the abuse and violence inflicted by Jewish settlers in occupied towns like Hebron knows this is not an overstatement. Israelis with whom I have spoken have indicated that, except for soldiers at checkpoints (and settlers), the segregation of Israelis from Palestinians is absolute. It is shocking to note that one can spend days on end in West Jerusalem and not encounter a Palestinian. Yet a couple of miles away, or even less if one enters the Old City, a different world exists.

A Jewish Majority in Palestine

From the outset, the Zionist leadership knew that if the Zionist political and cultural program were to succeed, it would be necessary to create a Jewish majority in Palestine. At best, the Arabs would be offered their civil rights in the Jewish state, which "presupposed that,

in principle, the perspective state would *belong* [my emphasis] to the Jewish people."[47] Or they would have to be relocated, transferred to other Arab lands. Offering civil rights to Arabs was the consensus position of the early Zionist leadership represented by David Ben-Gurion and what became the Labor Party. The later more militant agenda of the early Zionists was represented by Ze'ev Jabotinsky and the Revisionist Zionist Party. However innocent and unaware some early émigrés may have been, their leaders were not naïve, pious, religious Jews. Today's messianic movement has its roots much later, beginning in 1967. At least in the first decades after the First World War, they were realists who were not looking for the Messiah to come and create their state for them. The early leaders were people using every resource available to them to create in Palestine a safe haven exclusively for European Jews.

inside the West Bank. If the soldier keeps the card, the Palestinian cannot travel. I was staring at the soldier as he shouted at a woman holding a crying baby. He ordered her to dump her bag's contents on the ground. Then he forbade her from crossing because she lives in Tulkarm, a city whose inhabitants are currently being collectively punished. A few youths were forced to

sit for hours under the sun just because they are under thirty years old, or for trying to cross the checkpoint on foot. At 9 a.m., it was my turn. The soldier waved me forward with his finger. As I do every day, I stepped out of my car to hand him my ID. On the side of the road, a soldier whose face was partially hidden beneath his helmet pointed an automatic rifle at me,

his finger on the trigger. I opened the trunk and he returned my ID to me without a word. I left the checkpoint wondering whether my generation will witness a day when Palestinians write novels about the old days of suffering under occupation.... What stories will we tell about the checkpoints? Will they be stories of bitterness or steadfastness, pain or hope?[48]

The viewpoint of the early settlers was that of Western European colonialists. Today we would surely judge that outlook as basically racist, and it still is. One of the great failures that still besets Israeli attitudes is that they do not see Palestinians as human beings like themselves. Palestine was there for the Zionist enterprise alone. In the beginning, Zionism was neither a cultural movement nor a religious movement. Zionism at its inception was a movement "that advocated not so much the defense of an ethnic group, as the formation of such a group in Palestine, where those who were thought to fit a certain semi-racial category were to find refuge. It was a lovely dream where all Jews would live happily together and…no one seemed to notice that those who did not pass ethnic muster had no place in the fantasy."[49] That of course means the indigenous Palestinian-Arab population.

Israelis react furiously to charges that Zionism is a racist ideology. Only thirty-one years ago, the United Nations General Assembly passed Resolution 379, which "determined that Zionism is a form of racism and racial discrimination." It further reiterated that "the racist regime in Occupied Palestine and the racist regimes in Zimbabwe and South Africa have a common imperialist origin, forming a whole and having the same racist structure and being organically linked in their policy aimed at repression of the dignity and integrity of the human being...."[50] The resolution caused a major furor and was repealed in 1991.

Today Israeli critics of the latest efforts to derail the Palestinian struggle to establish a viable state equate their government's actions with ethnic cleansing and apartheid. Israeli organizations like The Israeli Committee Against House Demolitions (ICAHD) point out regularly that the equivalent of what their government is doing is what happened

Amos Elon, an Israeli writer,

described the early days from an Israeli perspective:

For the first two or three decades of settlement, the pioneers were hardly aware of the Arabs as the source of a possible conflict. The political imagination, like the imagination of the explorer, often invents its own geography. The settlers did not, of course, consider the country "empty," as did some Zionists abroad. What they saw with their own eyes contradicted the ludicrous dictum attributed to Israel Zangwill, "The land without people—for a people without land," which was current in Zionist circles abroad at least until as late as 1917. Yet even if there were people living in the country, the settlers saw that it was populated only sparsely. They believed they were operating in a political void; and not until the end of World War I were they fully cured of this naïve illusion.[51]

in South Africa. In a statement released on May 27, 2006, *Countdown to Apartheid,* following Prime Minister Ehud Olmert's address to the US Congress, Jeff Halper,[52] ICAHD's coordinator, accused Olmert of Orwellian Newspeak in his address. Jeff suggests that the latest plan (noted above) is not an honest attempt to reach peace with the Palestinians but a continuation of Zionist attempts to control the Occupied Territories.

The Balfour Declaration (1917)

Although Theodor Herzl died before his vision became a reality, his intention of securing a mandate for a Jewish homeland in Palestine from the Great Powers, and the Ottoman Sultan in particular, was taken up by others. But the central figure to further this effort was Chaim Weizmann (1874-1952), a Russian Zionist émigré chemist who had moved to England in 1904 to take up a post at the University of Manchester. When the war began, he moved to London to assist the British government with an improved method for the production of artillery shells. David Lloyd George, soon to become Prime Minister, and Lord Balfour were at the time minister of munitions and first lord of the admiralty, respectively.[53] Weizmann had already begun to lobby for the Zionist project among government contacts that he made through his work. He met Arthur James Balfour, then Foreign Secretary in Lloyd George's Cabinet, who had previously encouraged the Zionists to accept Uganda as a national home. Balfour considered himself a Zionist, and Lloyd George was a biblical romantic sympathetic to the cause. It was in Britain's self-interest to safeguard its colonies and secure control over the Suez Canal. Weizmann suggested that these intentions were sound reasons for support. Furthermore, Britain wished to counter French colonial ambitions and desired to take control over the vast

53   54   55   56

Apartheid: The "A" word was missing from Olmert's speech, but the bottom line of his convergence plan is clear: the establishment of a permanent, institutionalized regime of Israeli domination over Palestinians based on separation between Jews and Arabs. Within six to nine months, according to Olmert's timeline. Olmert may believe that Jews can succeed where Afrikaners failed, but history teaches us that in the end injustice is unsustainable. And convergence/realignment is nothing if not manifest injustice.[54]

Qira is completely separated from Salfit by the "Separation Barrier" (or the *wall*) and the Zaatara checkpoint, which weaves its way deep in Palestinian land around the Ariel Settlement "Bloc." The "Bloc" is home to nearly 40,000 Israelis.[55] If Prime Minister Ehud Olmert's government has its way as outlined in his speech before a joint session of Congress (May 24, 2006), these areas will be entirely separated into what have been likened to the *Bantustans* of apartheid-era South Africa, or more benignly, cantons. Ariel "Bloc" deep in Palestinian Occupied Territory is one of those that will be retained by Israel if the latest convergence plan or a realignment plan comes to fruition.

A shrine was built in the Jewish Settlement of Kiryat Arba adjacent to Hebron, the second largest Palestinian city in the West Bank, honoring Baruch Goldstein, the Israel Defense Forces (IDF)[56] officer and physician who massacred twenty-nine Palestinian Arab civilians during their prayer observance on February 25, 1994, in the Ibrahimi Mosque (Cave of the Patriarchs for Jews). I will never forget the tabernacle and the altar located in a landscaped park-like setting. That such a terrorist act could be celebrated and the perpetrator considered a martyred hero by Jewish settlers only illustrates the contempt with which some Jews regard Palestinian Arabs. Massacres are not daily occurrences. Jewish-Israeli abuse of Palestinian Arabs, whether by settlers or soldiers, is.

oil wealth in the Middle East.[57] Therefore, the government was willing to support the Zionist program.

Other British officials had made overtures to support Arab aspirations following the war. T. E. Lawrence had worked with Husein ibn Ali, the sharif of Mecca, to encourage Arab leaders in their revolt against the Turks. Husein was also promised that his kingdom would be given independence. Sir Henry McMahon, the High Commissioner in Egypt, had indicated this in a letter to the sharif of Mecca in October 1915.[58] The Arabs expected Palestine to be included as part of their independent state, or what would become Transjordan. Britain was surely not in agreement. In 1915 the British approached the French to discuss the post-war alignments in the Middle East. As Britain's involvement in the Middle East had grown, so had its concern with France's interest in Syria. The route between Egypt and India, two of Britain's main colonies, was always a major concern. A French presence might threaten Britain's territories.

Foreign Office

November 2nd, 1917

Dear Lord Rothschild:

I have much pleasure in conveying to you, on behalf of His Majesty's Government, the following declaration of sympathy with Jewish Zionist aspirations which has been submitted to, and approved by, the Cabinet:

His Majesty's Government view with favor the establishment in Palestine of a national home for the Jewish people, and will use their best endeavors to facilitate the achievement of this object, it being clearly understood that nothing shall be done which may prejudice the civil and religious rights of existing non-Jewish communities in Palestine, or the rights and political status enjoyed by Jews in any other country.

I should be grateful if you would bring this declaration to the knowledge of the Zionist Federation.

Yours,
Arthur James Balfour

Sykes-Picot Agreement

A 1916 agreement between Sir Mark Sykes and George-Picot, called the Sykes-Picot Agreement, undercut the promises to support Arab independence. The agreement only addressed creating an independent state for the Arabian Peninsula. Mark Sykes wrote to Lord Curzon:

> My aim is that the Arabs should be our first brown-skinned dominion—not our last colony. Arabs will react against one if one tries to lead them, and they are as stubborn as Jews (sic). But one can lead them anywhere without the use of force if it is theoretically arm in arm.[59]

Clearly the intention of Sykes-Picot was to undermine British commitments made to Husein and other Arab leaders. The Balfour Declaration became another. On the one hand, Britain was counseled by their own officers of the danger of taking sides in the Middle East. Lord Curzon, a member of the War Cabinet who later replaced Balfour, wrote a report that, while not rejecting Jewish aspirations and settlement, argued that the ambiguity allowing for Palestine to be called a national home was a bad idea. Curzon believed the Zionist leadership had the expectation of creating a Jewish state in Palestine. They would be inviting trouble if the Arabs were excluded from the future of Palestine. From the beginning, the Zionists had seen the national home as a sanction to at least start the movement for a Jewish state.

Balfour was more sympathetic to the Jews and understood that as Westerners they were more desirable. He wrote, "Zionism, be it right or wrong, good or bad, is of far profounder import than the desires of and prejudices of the 700,000 Arabs who now inhabit that ancient land."[60] There was also an undercurrent of anti-Semitism in this Christian Zionism that affirmed the declaration for the proposed national home for the Jews in order to encourage or even expel British Jews to Palestine.

The War Cabinet deliberated. It was decided that the President of the United States should be consulted. Woodrow Wilson, who was experiencing his own Zionist lobbying in Washington, reversed his previous opposition. On the afternoon of October 3, 1917, the British cabinet issued the letter to Lord Rothschild, the leader of the British Jewish community. The publication was delayed and not published until November 9. The reactions to the Declaration have always been problematic, and its ambiguity has settled nothing. Arthur Koestler was to write: "One nation solemnly promised a second nation the territory of a third nation."[61] He dismissed the declaration as an impossible notion, an unnatural graft, and called it a "white Negro."[62]

Zionism, be it right or wrong, good or bad, is of far profounder import than the desires of and prejudices of the 700,000 Arabs who now inhabit that ancient land.

The Zionists were elated, even with the Declaration's shortcomings. "Since Cyrus the Great there was never, in all the records of the past, a manifestation inspired by a higher sense of political wisdom, far-sighted statesmanship and national justice towards the Jewish people than this memorable declaration," Weizmann wrote to Balfour.[63] With this occasion Herzl's dream was exhibited for the world to see, and the Israel-Palestine conflict truly began.

Allied forces under British General Allenby advanced into Jerusalem on December 9, 1917, and forced the city's surrender, ending four hundred years of Turkish Rule. The Allied victory was secured in November the following year, and the European powers and the United States began meeting in Paris on January 18, 1919. The Treaty of Versailles, signed June 28, 1919, in the Hall of Mirrors at the Palace of Versailles, included a covenant for the formation of a League of Nations.

One nation solemnly promised a second nation the territory of a third nation.

"Exodus" and *Aliyah*

It is ironic that Prime Minister Ehud Olmert claims that because the elected government of the Palestinian National Authority (PNA) and its Prime Minister, Ismail Haniyeh, refuse to recognize the state of Israel, Israel will not engage in official talks with them. The Hamas-led government has insisted that they will seriously consider recognizing Israel's legitimacy only when Israel is

The League of Nations gave mandates over territories of the former Ottoman Empire to the French and the British with the understanding that these territories would establish statehood in a *short* period of time. Syria and Lebanon were allocated to the French, while Palestine and Iraq went to Britain. Syria achieved independence in 1936, and Lebanon in 1941. Iraq declared its independence in 1931. The story of Israel-Palestine begins here.

prepared to grant the Palestinians their own state in the West Bank within the internationally recognized pre-1967 borders of Israel-Palestine, and when Israel is prepared to end the Occupation. The reality is that Israel has obstructed, fought, demolished, undermined, attacked, and now seeks in this latest chapter the Olmert "convergence/ realignment" plan, to deny the possibility of a viable Palestinian state.

Israel most certainly exists whether the PNA or President Abbas (who has already acknowledged the state of Israel's right to exist in the Oslo Accords of 1993) says so or not. Israel, with the only nuclear capability and the most powerful military in the Middle East, is the region's strongest state. But a Palestinian state cannot exist until Israel is ready to permit it and end the Occupation.

It is often the case that if the powerful say something often enough and for long enough then the perceived notion is taken as reality. But it never becomes the truth. No matter how often Israel makes the claim and the media quote it, each Israeli government since 1948 has tacitly and undeniably refused the establishment of a Palestinian state, just as they had refused to acknowledge the existence of the Palestinian people.

The influential Zionist publicist Moshe Smilansky recalled in 1914 that from the beginning a sense of certainty was created that Palestine was a virgin country. For Smilansky, this myth accounted for the contempt which the Zionist settlers harbored for the indigenous population. But the early propaganda that Palestine was a virgin country was meant mostly for foreign Zionist consumption. Zionists who had already settled in Palestine were keenly aware that it was not a land without a people, and the internal debates of the Zionist movement even at this early date reflected such an awareness.

Who Were the Immigrants?

The 15,000 Jews living in Palestine, primarily in the towns and Jerusalem but seldom on the land, were mostly Ashkenazim and Sephardim. Some Ashkenazim were elderly people who had come from the Russian lands to die and be buried outside the Old City walls of Jerusalem. Others were young students, whose passage had been financed

Sephardic Jews:

Arabic-speaking citizens of the Ottoman Empire who had lived in Palestine for hundreds of years alongside the Palestinian Arabs. Descendants of the Jews expelled from Spain in 1492, they had lived mostly successfully in the Mediterranean basin and the Arab world over those centuries (the Hebrew word *Sefarad* means "Spain").

so that they might concentrate exclusively on the study of Jewish law. All communities lived in extreme poverty, since even those who wanted to earn their own living had few opportunities for doing so. They were largely dependent for support on the annual collections for Palestine made in the synagogues of the Diaspora.

Personal History

My father told me that his grandfather had left Russian Poland in old age in order to die and be buried in the Holy Land. Had I known my great-grandfather's name, I might have investigated to see if he had been buried on the face of the Mount of Olives overlooking the Messiah Gate in the Old City wall where there are many old Jewish graves.

Whatever problems these Ashkenazim may have encountered, they still fared better on the whole in Muslim countries than they had in Christian ones. What both the Ashkenazim and Sephardim shared was an anxiety regarding the new Jewish immigrants, who were for the most part neither religious nor interested in coexistence.

From the First Jewish World Conference in 1897 to the eve of the United Nations Partition Plan in 1947, the immigrant population grew fifteen-fold. In that fifty-year span, the number of Jews grew from about 40,000, representing about 10 percent of the population, to 600,000, more than 39 percent of the population.[64] They came for all of the reasons mentioned previously: because of the belief that it was the Jewish homeland in which they had an historic or divine right to settle, and that life would be better there than in their European homelands, where they encountered persecution and anti-Semitism; and because of the empowerment and enterprise of the early Zionist leadership in the Yishuv who were carving an agricultural

Ashkenazic Jews:

Primarily poor, pious, and less integrated into the Arab culture. The term comes from the Hebrew word *Ashkenaz,* which means "Germany." Ashkenazic Jews had lived in the Rhineland and France until they moved east to Russia and Eastern Europe after the Crusades. Some would eventually move west again during the seventeenth century. Eighty percent of Jews today are Ashkenazic.

and industrial economy out of difficult conditions. Settlements were primarily agricultural in the beginning, with a socialist ideology born out of the Russian Revolution and Marxist thought. When one considers that few of the 25,000 earlier Russian immigrants remained, the initial population increases are perhaps even more impressive.

These earlier immigrants had been far less interested in Zionist and Socialist ideology than in leaving Russia.[65] The lack of cultivatable land and the fact that Palestinians were already cultivating what little there was discouraged almost half of these early self-styled pioneers. The Second Aliyah from 1904-1914 was less successful in retaining numbers than the first. David (Grün) Ben-Gurion, who had emigrated from Russia in 1906, became one of the central Zionist Socialist Labor leaders as well as the first prime minister of the state in 1948. He wrote of the early period:

"Half the immigrants who came to Palestine in those early days took one look and caught the same ship home again."[66]

The second group had a stronger political consciousness and were committed Zionists and Labor Socialists. Even so, perhaps 80 percent returned to Europe or went on to America within weeks or months of their arrival.[67] But those who remained were able to scratch for employment in the farms and support each others' dreams and aspirations.

> It was evident that these were not the usual kind of colonists, not even within the older Zionist tradition of the nineteenth century. Their notion of pioneering was a kind of secularized messianism.[68]

With growing financial support from abroad, the Yishuv increased its land holdings in that same fifty-year span from a little more than 200,000 dunums to 1,802,000 dunums (a dunum is about 1,000 square meters), primarily

Yishuv, literally, "settlement,"
is the term used in the Zionist movement before the State of Israel was established to refer to the Jewish residents in Israel. The residents and new settlers were referred to collectively as the Yishuv.

(*Wikipedia,* the Free Encyclopedia, http://en.wikipedia.org)

Kibbutzim:
Collectively owned agricultural colonies.

Moshavim:
Cooperatively owned agricultural colonies.

Fallahin:
Native Palestinian peasant farmers.

A'yan:
Political and economic notables.

through purchase from absentee landlords who owned large tracts of land.[69] Agricultural colonies, many of which were either collectively owned *kibbutzim* or cooperative *moshavim* increased from 27 to 300. By 1947 half of Jewish cultivated land was accounted for in the collective farms. The other half of the land was held privately.[70] The number of immigrants grew and began to prosper, particularly in relationship to the native *fallahin*, the Palestinian peasant farmers.[71]

Palestinian Economic Development

Because of the growing economic disparity between the Jewish immigrants and the Palestinian *fallahin*, the rising tension between native residents and immigrants was partly economically based. Palestinians had enjoyed significant economic development under the Ottomans before the large influx of Jewish settlers. For the latter part of the

The issue of land ownership is somewhat complicated. In order to justify their growing presence, Zionist ideology has always spoken of the legitimacy of their land acquisition. The Ottoman economy in the latter days of the empire was declining. In the early part of the nineteenth century, the Sultan had passed decrees that improved rights and security for private property. In the 1860s, registration laws were enacted that adversely affected land ownership in Palestine. The regulations' purpose was to raise taxes and identify eligible conscripts for the Turkish army. This facilitated the rise of extensive landed estates privately owned by urban notables from Palestine and Lebanon.

Because peasants were afraid of increased taxation and the conscription of the owner and family members, many registered their land in the names of clan chiefs or urban *a'yan* (political and economic notables). The outcome was that land was expropriated, and the owners lost title to

nineteenth century, Palestine was supplying European, American, and other Middle Eastern markets with commodities such as cotton (during the American Civil War in particular), sesame and olive oil, soap, and oranges grown in the Mediterranean coastal plain. In the last decades of the nineteenth century, oranges were the most profitable. Oranges from Jaffa, a major economic center, were famous for their thick skins that kept them sweet and juicy during transport to Europe and elsewhere.

their lands, forcing them to become sharecroppers, tenant farmers, and rural wage laborers. This fostered a cycle whereby fewer and fewer persons owned more and more of the arable land. The absentee landowners had become the urban *a'yan*, most of them European protégés and European colonists.

Background for the British Mandate

The context for all of this was the British Mandate in Palestine.

As mandatory representatives, the British were charged as follows:

> The mandatory shall be responsible for placing the country under such political, administrative and economic conditions as will secure the establishment of the Jewish national home, as laid down in the preamble, and the development of self-governing institutions, and also for safeguarding the civil and religious rights of all the inhabitants of Palestine, irrespective of race and religion.[72]

The Mandate provisions were met with outright rejection by the Arab delegation, led by Musa Kazim Pasha al-Husseini, President of the Arab Executive. The delegation felt slighted and betrayed by the British, whom they believed had not been forthright in their promises during the war. Pasha al-Husseini had expected that there would be areas within Palestine where Arabs would be autonomous, as well as other benefits for Arabs who

and Arabs could exist in Palestine, and that Britain would not allow an exclusive Jewish claim. But the Arabs were not cooperating. Musa Al-Husseini had sold land to the Jews himself. They acted with the understanding that Palestine could not sustain more inhabitants.[74]

Churchill believed that Arab opposition was rooted in a complex of the feelings that tend to overcome people when newcomers flood in to change their neighborhood. He did not take seriously the depth of the threat to the Palestinian way of life, but was trying to keep a compromise alive and a viable position for Britain.

In June 1922 a non-binding motion was introduced in the House of Lords declaiming the Palestine Mandate as unacceptable. The lords believed that the Zionist effort was too costly to Britain and too problematic because of the Arab hostility. They were also understandably tired of conflict, having just come through the war. The motion

chose to live within the Jewish homeland.[73] Both T. E. Lawrence and Sir Henry McMahon had made such promises to secure Arab military support.

Winston Churchill had become the Colonial Secretary following the war. He was sympathetic to the Jewish enterprise, but in spite of what Balfour and Lloyd George told him about the actual Zionist aspirations for an exclusive Jewish state, Churchill wanted to interpret the Declaration with its ambiguity intact. His position was that both Jews

passed by a two-to-one majority. It was meant to focus the pending debate on the question of Palestine in the House of Commons a few weeks later. In Commons, Churchill gave an impassioned eloquent speech arguing for the importance of having Britain honor its commitments and how during the war it was felt that Jewish support for the war effort was considered a "definite palpable advantage."[75] He also raised the significant cost-saving measures he was enacting as Colonial Secretary.

The speech was a success, and the vote was over-whelmingly in favor of upholding the Mandate. Even though certain compromises reduced the scale of the commitment to Zionism, the Arabs immediately rejected its terms.

Churchill had prepared a White Paper (policy statement) that sought to soften the terms of the Balfour Declaration. One of those compromises had been to emphasize that the Jewish national home was to be founded *in* Palestine. This was to counter Dr. Weizmann's insistence that Palestine would become as Jewish as England is English, and to try to allay the Arab fears concerning the continued support of the Balfour Declaration. The Zionist Organization reluctantly assented to the White Paper, believing their goals could be achieved incrementally. This set in motion an unavoidable collision course among Britain, the Palestinian Arabs, and the Jewish immigrants. Although the establishment of the Jewish national home was not equated with a Jewish state in the minds of all those who identified themselves as Zionists, it is accurate to say that the Zionist project was never anything less than the establishment of a Jewish state. By the time that serious ideas of a nonexclusive Zionism had emerged in the 1920s, its notions of cooperation with the Palestinians had already become unworkable. Too much blood had been shed.[76]

Palestinian National Consciousness

As early as 1911, a Palestinian national consciousness had begun to emerge. Among other things, the Revolt of the Young Turks in 1908 in the Ottoman Empire gave a voice to Palestinians in the Turkish Parliament, as well as freedom of the press. The founding of two Palestinian newspapers solidified the reaction against increasing Jewish immigration sanctioned by the British and land purchase.[77] Although Zionist propaganda later tried to deny that there was any movement for nationalism among the Palestinians, the record indicates something quite different. Even Vladimir Jabotinsky, leader and voice of the radical right Revisionist Zionist party understood:

> [The Palestinians] look at Palestine with the same instinctive love and true fervor that any Aztec looked upon Mexico or any Sioux looked upon his prairie. Palestine will remain for the Palestinians not a borderland, but their birthplace, the center and basis of their own national existence.[78]

It was an unmanageable reality from the very beginning. Britain was to be completely exhausted by their colonial project in Palestine between 1933 and 1947. When they pulled out, they had not accomplished many, if any, of their goals and intentions, noble and ignoble. It was the twilight of the British Empire.

Chapter 3
The British Mandate

Edward W. Said, a naturalized Palestinian-American, was the distinguished Professor of English and Cooperative Literature at Columbia University. Said's now classic work, *Orientalism,* addresses how the narrative of history is framed by the person writing the history and how it looks completely different from the "other's" point of view. In Said's estimation, the whole of Western history uses a lens of imperialism in its interpretation of the Orient.

Personal History

In late 1999, I attended the Third International Sabeel Conference at Bethlehem University. These were the some-what heady and hopeful post-Oslo days when Palestinians were looking to the promise of a state and the end of the Israeli Occupation. The Palestinians were investing both privately and through the Palestinian Authority in the renewal

my understanding of the conflict. Said, who had been a member of the Palestinian National Council from 1977 until 1991, resigned because of the decision by Yasser Arafat and the PLO to support Saddam Hussein in the Gulf War. He considered this a decision disastrous to the interests of Palestinian refugees living in Arab League member states who supported the American-led coalition. Many Palestinians were expelled from their jobs in the Persian Gulf States. Said also became critical of the role of Arafat in the process leading up to the signing of the Oslo Accords in 1993, believing that the Oslo terms were unacceptable. Said's writings were unavailable in the Occupied Territories because of the estrangement between him and the leadership of the Palestinian Authority and President Arafat. I had been reading another of his books during my stay and hoped to have him autograph it if the opportunity arose.

and development of their cities, including Bethlehem. With the millennium year 2000 approaching and the expectation of a major tourist influx, the first traffic light in Bethlehem was being installed near Manger Square.

One evening, Dr. Said was to address the student body of the University, and the Sabeel Conference atten-dees were invited to be present as part of our conference activities. I had read Said's The Question of Palestine *in 1991. It was formative for me and has significantly framed*

Mopsi:

The International and the Soviet Revolutionary Party

Ahdot ha Avodah:

The officially sanctioned Socialist Democratic Party

A Palestinian brother and sister, both in their twenties, were serving as the hotel clerk and concierge in the hotel where I was staying. When I told them that I was going that evening to hear Edward Said, they couldn't hide their enthusiasm or their disappointment. They were not able to get the evening away from the hotel, but the esteem in which they held Dr. Said was palpable. Sorry that they couldn't go to hear him and knowing his books were not readily available, I offered the Palestinian woman my copy of his book. She graciously accepted my gift.

It was particularly unfortunate my young acquaintances weren't able to attend, because Said wonderfully energized and challenged the Palestinian students in his address, raising hope that they would lead their people into a better life, with suggestions about what they could do to accomplish that goal. It had been uncertain whether Said would be able to attend the event because he had recently undergone

Conflicts and Uprisings

If one considers the Arab response to the British Mandate, which was after all an imperialistic military occupation, and add to that what appeared to be bad-faith support of European immigration into Arab lands, it is hardly surprising that there was rebellion.

In May of 1921 a riot broke out in Jaffa, the main port during the twenties and the entry point for Jewish immigration. Just to the north, the new town of Tel Aviv was developing, with the largest population of Jews in Palestine. Among the immigrants from the Soviet Union were Bolshevik Jews committed to the cause of liberation for the working man. They were trying to recruit other working-class Jews and labor groups to the vision of the International and the Soviet Revolutionary Party (Mopsi). Mopsi was a small party and not very successful with its efforts. But on May Day, the revolutionary holiday of the proletariat, Mopsi

treatment for leukemia. Everyone seemed to be aware of his sacrifice to be there. Said was accompanied and attended by Anwar Nussaiba, President of Beir Seit University (a major university near Ramullah), who was introduced as a close colleague and friend. We all could see that Said was somewhat drawn and weakened, but the power and energy of the students and their enthusiastic response clearly enlivened him; he was surely a heroic figure in all our eyes.

decided to break a ban on demonstrating and crossing police lines. Wearing red rosettes, party members marched through the streets of a mixed Jewish-Palestinian quarter in Jaffa, brandishing placards proclaiming the Socialist Revolution.

The Ahdot ha Avodah, the officially sanctioned Socialist Democratic Party, was marching with permission from the authorities. When the two groups encountered one other, they came to blows. Usually such Jewish labor disturbances were treated as little more than curiosities by Palestinians. This time there was a different response.

> Quite suddenly the Arabs seemed to go berserk. Normally law-abiding citizens perpetrated acts of savagery that lasted a week and spread deep into the surrounding countryside.... British-controlled policemen stood between the two groups at opposite ends of a sandy open space.... Neither side would disperse. Somebody began breaking Jewish shop windows.... [A]rmed with sticks, iron bars, knives, and anything that came to hand, they began a general hunt of the Jews.... [T]hey found the Jewish market entirely looted.[79]

Authorities tried to quell the disturbances, but as soon as one was stopped another broke out elsewhere. The police were completely overwhelmed by the situation, so the army was called in. But the riots continued until 200

Jews and 120 Arabs were killed or injured. When it was over, medical authorities were struck by the number and ferocity of wounds on the bodies.[80]

On the second day of rioting, Jews began to seek out Arabs in vengeance. According to the records, they were supported by Jewish police from Tel Aviv. With assistance from the Arab constabulary, a particular target of the Arab mob was the Zionist immigration hostel in the middle of Jaffa. The final casualty toll there was thirteen Jews killed

or mortally wounded and twenty-four more wounded. One Arab was killed and four were wounded."[81]

Although the occurrence was relatively minor weighed against later conflicts, it was not so for the new Jewish immigrants. It was an all-too-familiar reminder of the pogroms in their home countries from which they had recently fled in the hope of leaving anti-Semitic violence behind. That the outbreak was caused by inter-Jewish rivalries, and that the Mopsi came to be despised by the larger immigrant community, did not negate the disturbing reality of the growing hatred and strain between Palestinians and Jews.

The cultural barometers of tolerance and intolerance were also out of any workable balance. Arab-Muslim culture (and no doubt Palestinian-Christian as well) was very conservative and modest in its outward and inward behaviors. The Arabs found these European Jews arrogant and aggressive. From the Arab perspective, the Western mores of these Jews were quite unacceptable and a corrupting influence that was to be neither tolerated nor condoned. To some degree this remains the case today in some Arab countries and cultures.

Shaw Commission Report

The British response to the growing problem of administering the Mandate was essentially as the Arab leadership had feared. Even when the inevitable commissions found that the difficulties of the Arab population needed to be addressed and alleviated (as the Shaw Commission Report concluded in 1929 after riots in Jerusalem), authorities in London remained sympathetic to the Zionist cause. They believed that supporting the Jews would benefit Britain financially and that the Zionist colonization of the country provided justification for the fact that they were there.[82] In spite of strong recommendations from the various commissions, the activism of Jewish and Zionist leadership also stymied the British.

Passfield White Paper and the Black Letter

The findings of the Shaw Commission Report were largely reflected in the Passfield White Paper, a policy paper the British government issued in 1930 in an effort to address the causes of the 1929 disturbances. The Passfield White Paper

proposed that it was time to develop self-rule institutions in Palestine, although the legislative council it proposed was styled after the one in the 1922 Churchill White Paper.[83]

Predictably, Lord Passfield's paper came under vigorous attack from Zionists in Britain and Palestine. Prime Minister Ramsay MacDonald, overwhelmed by the opposition, in effect repudiated and reversed the policy changes of the Passfield White Paper in a letter the Palestinian Arabs dubbed the Black Letter.[84]

The outcome was that the very same social, economic, and institutional injustices that the commission had determined were the cause of the 1929 riots were maintained. In fact, conditions worsened for the Palestinians and led to the Arab Revolt of 1936-1939.

The Arab Revolt (1936-1939)

Just as the early Zionists were internally divided but growing stronger with their disparate political agendas, so the emerging Arab leadership experienced its own divisions and growing pains. The clan and family were the foundation of Arab social structure. The early political efforts and divisions were formed by the wealthy notable extended families of the cities.[85] Throughout the years of the Mandate, the rivalry between the two most prominent Jerusalem families, the al-Husseini and the al-Nashashibi, was a dominant factor. Their self-interests had the al-Husseini

family turning anti-British and hence anti-Zionist while initially the al-Nashashibi family was pro-British and hence willing to accommodate the Zionists, who, early in the 1920s, believed that conciliation was possible. But as time passed and the strength of the Zionists increased in influencing the British, the Arabs became more unified in their efforts for self-determination; this of course was one of the planks of the Mandate as well as the political intention of the United States, or at least that of President

Woodrow Wilson. Self-determination was the cornerstone of his post-war plan, the Fourteen Points.

> XIV. A general association of nations must be formed under specific covenants for the purpose of affording mutual guarantees of political independence and territorial integrity to great and small states alike.[86]

The King-Crane Commission

Although not part of the League of Nations or a signatory to the Versailles treaty, Wilson had deputized in 1919 his own delegation, the King-Crane Commission,[87] which traveled within Palestine and Syria. Its findings were not at all favorable to the Balfour Declaration, but these findings did not come to bear on the situation. The Commission reported, having spoken with British officers, that it was their strong opinion that the inherent injustices in the Zionist program meant that it could only be put forward

The Arab Executive was suing for self-determination. The Jewish Agency had been established with the Mandate, and though the British offered a similar Arab Agency, the Arabs turned it down on two counts. First, they felt any comparison was unjustified because of demographic and historical conditions. Second, the entire Jewish community had elected its representatives to the Agency, yet the British authorities were proposing to appoint the members of the Arab Agency. The British turned down this attempt for Arab self-rule.[89] Resentment continued to grow, and although the Arab Executive had brought the al-Husseini and al-Nashashibi clans together in an organization so that all Palestinians could speak with one voice, the rivalry of the clans undermined the effort to contain the Zionists and the British. Note that the President of the Arab Executive, Pasha al-Husseini, was not the Amin al-Husseini (also transliterated Husayni),

by force of arms. King-Crane wrote: "Decisions requiring armies to carry them out are sometimes necessary, but they are surely not gratuitously to be taken in the interests of a serious injustice. For the initial claim, often submitted by Zionist representatives, that they have a 'right' to Palestine, based on an occupation of two thousand years ago, can hardly be seriously considered."[88] Would that the Allies had listened then and that we would listen now to our own advice.

who became the Grand Mufti of Jerusalem and was the main leader of the Palestinian national movement throughout the years of the Mandate.[90]

With deteriorating economic conditions, continuing immigration, and land settlement, matters could hardly have been expected to improve for Palestinians. The British government had failed to listen to its own commission's findings reflecting the opinions of those on the ground who advised a reversal of pro-Zionist policy. It had refused to honor requests for a Palestinian legislative council providing a modicum of self-rule, and the Black Letter in effect epitomized the failed policy. All of this was a victory for the Zionist cause. Before 1929 the Zionists had to pay attention to the Palestinian claims, since they affected the British reactions. "After 1929" as David Hirst notes, "they [the Zionists] were able to crush the attempt in embryo; for by then they had the strength and self-confidence to do it...."[91]

Zionist Leaders

Who were these Zionist leaders? Chaim Weizmann was the central figure with the British both during the First World War and after his emigration to Palestine. As noted, he was President of the Jewish Agency and became the first president of the state. He was certainly a hard-liner when it came to the goal of establishing a Jewish state.

Sea and down the eastern Mediterranean. Three weeks after leaving his home in Plonsk, he rowed ashore at the rocky port of Jaffa.[92]

Finding Jaffa filthy and depressing, Ben-Gurion made his way the same day to the colony of Petach Tikva, the first Jewish agricultural settlement. It was kept afloat by Baron Edmund de Rothschild's charity. Ben-Gurion hired himself out as a farm laborer. He wrote:

> But who is to complain, to sigh, to despair? In twenty-five years our country will be one of the most blooming, most beautiful and happiest; an old-new nation will flourish in an ancient-new land. Then we shall relate how we fevered and worked, hungered and dreamed.[93]

His vision and determination never left him, and he gave everything he had to create the Jewish state. He was instrumental in the development of various socialist political

But he also was a diplomat who was reluctantly prepared to compromise without abandoning the final goal.

Other potential leaders emerged in Palestine with the growth of immigration. David Ben-Gurion, who arrived in Palestine in 1906 from Russian Poland, became the first Prime Minister of the state in 1948. Of small stature, he was also a man of fierce determination. He left his home at the age of twenty with a small knapsack on his back, traveling as cheaply as possible by train and steamer across the Black

and labor parties as they evolved into Mapai, the Israeli Labor Party. He was an elected leader in the Zionist movement and was elected chairman of the Jewish Agency in 1935. Orthodox in his attitude and in his stand regarding the "Arab question," he revealed at least in his public statements that he saw the conflict between the settler-immigrants and Arabs as resolvable. He did not regard Palestinian Arabs as a separate entity but as part of a larger Arab nation. But underneath his outward political program, he had his own private fears and anxieties. He realized that Arab opposition was grounded in principle and that it amounted to an utter rejection of the entire Zionist enterprise. Ben-Gurion concluded that the inescapable conflict between the Zionists and the Arabs represented a formidable challenge.[94]

He was against the Arab-Jewish integration espoused by one side of Zionist thought, but neither did he advocate with liberal Zionists like Arthur Ruppin, head of the Zionist Organization's Palestine Office. Ruppin believed it was essential to maintain good relations with the Arabs and necessary to redress legitimate Arab grievances, in particular the land purchases that had resulted in the eviction of peasants.[95] Ben-Gurion, a pragmatist whose overriding perspective was always to secure the Jewish state, would do whatever it took to realize this goal without taking strong ideological stands. Everything was understood as a step to his inevitable goal. Throughout his life as one of the formative Israeli leaders, his attitude and dealings with Palestinians were always with the view that they were part of the wider Arab population and culture. Their unique and emerging nationalist aspirations were not of real interest to him, nor did they matter to his Zionist program for a Jewish state.

In contrast, Ben-Gurion's counterpart, Ze'ev Jabotinsky, was a Russian Jew who did indeed take strong ideological stands and represented the radical side of Zionist ideology. He was the spiritual father of the Israeli right. A gifted orator, writer, and polemicist, he applied his considerable faculties to the Zionist cause. During the First World War, he persuaded the British to form Jewish volunteer units within the army. He himself served in Egypt as an officer in the Zion Mule Corps.[96] His new party was the opposition to the majority of Zionist leaders, including Herzl, Weizmann,

Labor and Likud:
Coke and Pepsi

Ben-Gurion, the pacifist A. D. Gordon, and the moralist Berl Katznelson. All these men were humanists, liberals, and social democrats with an instinctive abhorrence of violence.[97] Despite their seeming differences, these Zionist leaders were all single-minded in their support for a Jewish state. The differences between them and Jabotinsky had as much to do with style as substance.

Personal History

I was visiting Israel during the 1996 Parliamentary election when Benjamin Netanyahu was elected Prime Minister, bringing the Likud Party back into power. Yitzhak Rabin, the Labor Prime Minister who had signed the Oslo Accords, had been assassinated in 1995. For a host of reasons, his Labor successor, Shimon Peres, was soundly defeated when elections were called the following year after some serious missteps that alienated the Israeli electorate. Pro-Palestinian American activists and even more liberal Jewish Americans were quite distressed by the return of the Likud, a party that was actively opposed to the Oslo Accords. Arguably, it was Likud's return to power that put the final nail in Oslo's coffin.

I recall, however, the reaction of Palestinian friends. They were clear that there was virtually no difference for them whether Labor or Likud were in power. In fact, some

Jabotinsky's opposition to the Zionist mainstream expressed his radical nationalist perspective. He agreed with Herzl and Weizmann in their belief that it was essential to have the support of a Great Power to succeed, but he also believed in the absolute superiority of Western civilization over that of the Orient. Jabotinsky conceived of Zionism not as a return of the Jews to their spiritual homeland but as an extension or implant of Western civilization in the East. In his view, Zionism was to be permanently allied with European colonialism.[98] He militantly defended the right of the Jews to settle on both sides of the Jordan River[99] (the original border of the Palestinian Mandate), and he believed the Jews had the right to political sovereignty over the entire area.[100]

What was unique about his perspective was that he acknowledged that the Arabs would not be removed from Palestine. In his famous 1923 article, "The Iron Wall," he

Palestinians I spoke with preferred Likud because they were forthright in their anti-Palestinian statehood stance and did not mask their activity in the liberal rhetoric of a benign Occupation. The difference between the Labor and Likud parties was characterized by these Palestinians as similar to the difference between Coke and Pepsi. Likud was the heir, spiritual and otherwise, to the philosophy of Jabotinsky's Revisionist party.

gave the essence of his thought. Although he identified his attitude to Arabs as one of "polite indifference," he posed the question of whether Zionism could achieve its aims peacefully. He believed that was up to the Arabs. He thought his liberal colleagues were mistaken in their belief that accommodation was possible. In his view, a voluntary agreement between Jews and the Arabs of Palestine was inconceivable, either for the present or in the foreseeable future.[101]

Every indigenous people will resist alien settlers as long as they see any hope of ridding themselves of the danger of foreign settlement. This is how the Arabs will behave and go on behaving so long as they possess a gleam of hope that they can prevent "Palestine" from becoming the Land of Israel.

He believed they could not be bought, as it would not alleviate their hostility.

We must either suspend our settlement efforts or continue them without paying any attention to the mood of the natives. Settlement can thus develop under the protection of force that is not dependent on the local population, behind an iron wall which they will be powerless to break down.[102]

Although his philosophy was not officially embraced, I believe that it has become the *realpolitik* of one Israeli government after another. It has only been the rhetoric of

how they maintain their "iron wall" that has differed over the ensuing years since statehood in 1948. In the spiritual heirs of Jabotinsky, Menachim Begin, Yitzhak Shamir, Benjamin Netanyahu, and Ariel Sharon, and now even Prime Minister Ehud Olmert, with his policy of unilateralism, we are seeing the basic Revisionist program in operation. New Historian scholar Avi Shlaim notes that it was not that the Zionists disagreed about the need for an iron wall, but the militarists wanted it constructed with Jewish bayonets, and the more moderate Zionists wanted it built with British bayonets.[103]

Jabotinsky believed that any settlement could ultimately only be achieved when the Arab resistance was defeated by force. He believed in the morality of the Zionist project because it was Western in origin and because it was a positive force, as did all Zionists. In the end, Ben-Gurion and Jabotinsky finally agreed that only the superior Jewish military strength would eventually force the Arabs

It was not that the Zionists disagreed about the need for an iron wall, but the militarists wanted it constructed with

Jewish bayonets, and the more moderate Zionists wanted it built with British bayonets.

to despair of the struggle.[104] "Now, if the cause is just, justice must triumph, without regard to the assent or dissent of anyone else."[105]

The Arabs did dissent. With their legitimate grievances and the compliance of the British government with Zionist aims, the Arab Revolt broke out in April of 1936. One additional factor of major significance that contributed to the boiling over of hostility was the sudden meteoric rise of Jewish immigration in the first half of the 1930s.[106] In spite of the recommendations of one British commission after another to reduce immigration in accordance with the nebulous policy that numbers would bear some relation to the capacity of the economy to absorb immigrants, tens of thousands of Jews poured into Palestine. The rise of Nazism in Germany had pushed them out of Central Europe. Only 4,075 immigrated into Palestine in 1931 and 9,553 in 1932, but the numbers soared to 30,327 in 1933; 42,359

significant. The activism that was growing stronger found an outlet in an underground religious organization led by Sheikh 'Izz ed-Din al-Qassam, who had a concern for social justice and a commitment to direct action. His followers were the rural *fallahin*, the urban poor, and those displaced by the loss of land. With Palestinian violence and Jewish counter-violence intensifying, he and his followers took up arms in the rural areas while outbreaks were transpiring in the cities. The British ambushed and killed al-Qassam and his guerillas in 1935. His martyrdom and activism for Palestinian liberation became a popular model for a new generation of youth who formed guerilla bands they called Ikhwan al-Qassam (Brothers of al-Qassam), launching an armed struggle against both Jewish settlers and the British.

Chaos was descending on Palestine, even as it was breaking out in Europe. The Zionists had formed their own militia, the Haganah, who were organized and retaliating

in 1934; and 61,854 in 1935. The ratio of Jews to Arabs grew from 16 percent in 1931 to 28 percent in 1936.

Rise of Militants

With the death in 1934 of the Palestinian Arab Executive, Pasha al-Husseini, the organization collapsed. A new generation of more militant nationalist parties and organizations emerged with leaders who had a more modern outlook. The Istiqlal (Independence) Party was the most

against the Palestinians. The British declared a state of emergency. On April 19, 1936, the leadership of Istiqlal called a general strike that advanced throughout the county and involved the middle class, professionals, and most of the civil society. To lead the strike, the leadership reorganized and formed the Arab Higher Committee (AHC). It was composed of all the various nationalist groups and parties under the leadership of the Mufti of Jerusalem, al-Haj Amin al-Husayni, who until then had been a conciliatory figure with the British. The AHC announced its goals: the cessation of Jewish immigration, prohibition of land transfer to Jews, and the establishment of a national representative government. The strike lasted for six months, with resistance turning into armed insurrection. Rural families participated fully and organized into guerilla bands. But as the insurrection grew, it became more nationally coordinated, and structures of local governance emerged in the countryside, directly challenging British rule. After a district commissioner was assassinated, the British initiated harsh emergency measures that served only to harden the Palestinian response. Arrests, imprisonment, and deportation of prominent AHC members and other strike and union leaders were carried out. Censorship was imposed, newspapers closed, and strict curfews and other collective forms of punishment were imposed in villages and cities.[107]

spread into major Palestinian cities, including Jerusalem. With the 1938 British attempt to appease Hitler, Britain was able to redirect troops from other theaters to quell the rebellion. British and attendant forces, including six thousand Jewish auxiliaries, outnumbered the estimated two thousand Palestinian rebels by ten to one. But they were nevertheless unable to defeat the Palestinians until 1939, when with their leaders now dispersed and in exile, their struggle was exhausted.[109]

The Woodhead Commission

Attempting to appease the Arab reaction to the Peel findings, another commission, the Woodhead (1938)[110] reevaluated the Peel report and advised, "…the political, administrative, and financial difficulties in the proposal to create independent Arab and Jewish States inside Palestine are so great that this solution of the problem is

The Peel Commission

Typically the British appointed a new commission, the Peel Commission (1937) to investigate. It found, as usual, that Palestinian claims were legitimate, but this time the recommendation was to "end the mandate and to partition Palestine into a Jewish state, an Arab state, and a British Zone around Jerusalem."[108]

The Arabs were outraged at what was a dismemberment of their homeland, and the revolt redoubled and

impracticable."[111] Even so, three partition plans were submitted with this report! They invited representatives of the Palestinian Arabs, of neighboring countries, and the Jewish Agency to confer in London about future policy, including the question of immigration into Palestine.[112] The conference failed, but the government followed up with a new White Paper in 1939 that for the first time reversed its previous policies and responded to Palestine concerns. The paper stated: "His Majesty's Government therefore now declares unequivocally that it is not part of their policy that Palestine should become a Jewish state. They would indeed regard it as contrary to their obligations to the Arabs under the Mandate...that the Arab population of Palestine should be made the subjects of a Jewish state against their will...."[113]

It went on to envision a Jewish national home that would manage immigration for a period of time and establish Arab-Jewish self-governing institutions. Both the Zionists and the Arabs rejected the proposals. The Arab Revolt had failed to achieve its main goal of immediate Palestinian independence.[114] With this failure to foster a workable compromise, Britain was swept up in the war in Europe.

A Grave Setback and Retaliation

The failure of the Arab Revolt marked a grave setback for the emerging Palestinian national consciousness and Palestinian

Houses in villages were demolished and livestock seized as severe collective fines were levied. The economy was in ruins. The British had even authorized one of the Zionist terrorist groups, Irgun Z'vai Leumi to attempt the assassination of the Mufti, al-Hajj Amin al-Husseini, who was in exile in Iraq. It failed.

The Palestinians were politically and militarily defeated, their society psychologically crushed. The forceful spirit of political activism and revolt in the 1930s did not return in full force in the 1940s to resist the ferocious Zionist onslaught of 1947-1948.[117] Perhaps the final image of the collapse of Palestinian resistance as an entity was that when the threat of the German North Africa campaign increased in 1943, seven thousand Palestinians joined the British Army.[118] War creates strange alliances. This ending of the Palestinian-Arab Revolt was punctuated by the issuing of the 1939 White Paper. Though it was too late to

hopes for self-determination. All political parties and activities were banned by the British. Key Palestinian leadership and their fighters in the thousands were disarmed, exiled, or confined in prison or in concentration camps. The overwhelming disproportionality of the British armed retaliation broke the collective will of the struggle.[115] Altogether the British hanged 112 Arabs, in contrast to one Jew. One Palestinian scholar calculated that the dead must have exceeded five thousand and the wounded fourteen thousand.[116]

address real concerns for the Palestinians, it solidified the resistance of the Zionists.

Militias and Forces

The Yishuv continued to expand and strengthen itself both during and after the Arab Revolt. Ben-Gurion used the period of the revolt to develop the Haganah, the armed force of the Jewish Agency. The Haganah received training from the British during the war, and its soldiers grew in numbers, skill, and tactical ability. Underground terrorist groups also became more active. They were not under the supervision and control of Ben-Gurion or the Yishuv leadership.

As the Arab Revolt dissipated, the aforementioned Irgun Z'vai Leumi and the Lohamei, Herut Yisrael (LEHI, a Hebrew acronym for "Fighters for the Freedom of Israel"; or the Stern Gang as the British dubbed it, after Alexander Stern, its founder), became more active against the British authorities. In 1937 the Irgun was created to be the military branch of Jabotinsky's Revisionist party. Although its initial orientation was as an extremist anti-Arab underground militia, it targeted the British with assassination and terrorist bombings after the war. After Jabotinsky's death in 1940, Menachem Begin carried the mantle of the opposition Revisionists until he was elected Prime Minister in 1977, representing Likud, its political heir.

In defiance of the apparent rollback of the Balfour Declaration in the 1939 White Paper, the Zionists took matters into their own hands. The Jewish Agency took on a diplomatic campaign to counter the provisions of the White Paper. With their increasingly active hostility to the British, they turned to the emerging Great Power, the United States, for support.

Biltmore Meeting

A key Zionist international meeting was held in May 1942 at the Biltmore Hotel in New York City. Both Chaim Weizmann and Ben-Gurion had been working to solidify support from the Jewish community and the US government. Through the 1930s and 1940s, the Jewish community had been lukewarm or indifferent toward Zionism. My parents' generation of Jewish immigrants had already found a homeland in the United States. They were intent upon gaining acceptance and assimilating into the great American melting pot. Some

In 1946 the Irgun blew up a wing of the King David Hotel, the British Mandate Headquarters in West Jerusalem, killing ninety-one British, Arab, and Jewish persons. LEHI, considered even more extremist, spun off from Irgun in 1940. To its credit were the assassinations in 1944 of Lord Moyne, a British Minister of State in Cairo, and Count Folke Bernadotte, a Swedish UN peace emissary and mediator in 1948.[119]

As the war in Europe unfolded, sentiment grew in Europe and the United States in favor of the Zionist program.

were actively opposed to the radical notions of Zionism and the creation of a Jewish state. Even if not active in their opposition, they were committed to becoming good citizens of their adopted country. In the climate of wartime and post-war America, anything that could be perceived as partial loyalty to a foreign country was suspect.

At the Biltmore meeting, the Jewish Agency openly put forward its platform for open immigration into Palestine and settlement of unoccupied lands in the country. For the first time, they publicly announced their intention to establish a Jewish Commonwealth in Palestine. The backdrop was the emerging news of the Holocaust. No doubt this influenced some change of heart in the Jewish community, and the conference was a success for the Yishuv. Jewish financial support from the United States grew significantly for the Jewish Agency, and support for the Zionist project deepened as the war continued. The United States Congress passed a resolution in support of the Biltmore program less than two years later in January 1944. With growing American sympathies for the Holocaust survivors, both Roosevelt and Dewey supported the Zionist program, a turnaround. With the passage in 1941 of more stringent immigration regulations, the United States had made it more difficult for Jewish refugees fleeing Europe to enter the country. The same year, the opposition Labor Party in Britain recommended that European Jewish immigration to Palestine be encouraged.

Saudi oil fields were the only ones in the Middle East where an American company held exclusive production rights, and Roosevelt's advisors began to see their potential long-term value.[120] They also had hopes for a military installation apart from British and French control. Looking beyond the combat, Roosevelt nursed the hope that Abdul Aziz, a hero in the Arab world despite his lack of formal education and his country's backwardness, would somehow be helpful in solving a daunting problem that the president knew was coming: the future of Palestine and the resettlement of Europe's surviving Jews.[121]

Despite a fascinating formal meeting with the Saudi on the *USS Quincy,* little except the development of mutual personal admiration had been achieved. Because of the immediate pressure to settle the death-camp survivors, Roosevelt had hoped for some compromise. But upon broaching the matter of the Jewish refugees with the king,

But the United States' interests were not simply altruistic; it had a growing stake in Middle Eastern oil, as had the British. Roosevelt sought to address Arab concerns about Jewish immigration and their aspirations for Palestine. A little-known sidebar of the period was Roosevelt's meeting with Ibn Saud, Abdul Aziz, the Saudi king. The meeting took place aboard the battleship *USS Quincy* upon Roosevelt's return from negotiations with Churchill and Stalin in Yalta on the Crimean coast.

Roosevelt received the following response:

> His majesty replied that in his opinion the Jews should return to live in the lands from which they were driven. The Jews whose homes were completely destroyed and who have no chance of livelihood in their homelands should be given living space in the Axis countries which oppressed them.... Amends should be made by the criminal, not by the innocent bystander. What injury have Arabs done to the Jews of Europe? It is the "Christian" Germans who stole their homes and lives. Let the Germans pay.[122]

Roosevelt's and the King's favorable impression of each other led eventually to significant oil concessions for the United States. It was accomplished under the nose of Churchill and the British, who had been cultivating Ibn Saud's support for Britain and the Allies. The King granted permission for an American training base in Saudi Arabia. Though only a formality, King Abdul Aziz declared war against the Axis Powers, an action that later gained Saudi Arabia membership in the United Nations. Roosevelt had hoped to avert the coming conflict in Palestine, but he died months later. His successor, President Truman, was in a different situation.

Harry Truman met with the US ministers to Egypt, Lebanon and Syria, Saudi Arabia, and the consul-general to mandated Palestine. Informed of his predecessor's agreement with the Saudi king on the question of Palestine, Truman reportedly said: "I'm sorry, gentlemen, but I have to answer to hundreds of thousands who are anxious for the success of Zionism; I do not have hundreds of thousands of Arabs among my constituents."[123]

The Turning Tide

In Palestine the tide was turning toward the Zionists and their intentions. With the war drawing to a close, the Zionists shifted their energies to a terrorist campaign against the British. Truman was in the awkward position of trying to encourage both the Arabs and the Jews. He was trying to change American immigration laws to permit more Jewish immigration to the United States. But the Zionist organization in the United States wanted immigration of displaced persons to Palestine.

Truman pressured the British to accept 100,000 Jewish displaced persons—Jewish refugees living in camps in Europe—into Palestine, but the British in turn had promised the Palestinians to curtail immigration. They understood that the refugee problem was much greater than Zionist political intentions. The United States was not ready to assist the British with military support to impose the immigration on the Palestinians.[124]

By 1946 the British were frustrated and exhausted by the war. They were under increased attack from the still-illegal Haganah, now working in concert with the terrorist groups Irgun and the Stern Gang, which were receiving large shipments of illegal arms with the approval of the Jewish Agency.[125] They refused Truman's request and instituted harsh martial law that legalized military courts and curfews, making Palestine a virtual police state. The British also began to retaliate with terrorist actions of their own.

The Jewish terrorists stepped up their activities. Both the Irgun and Stern Gang had been to Europe looking in the displaced persons camps for possible recruits.[126] Their numbers had increased with the scope of their activity, and the Irgun had doubled in size by 1946. Along with blowing up a wing of the King David Hotel, where the Mandate headquarters were housed, they dynamited bridges and a British radar installation. They targeted sections of the railroad system, the Acre Military prison (freeing Jewish terrorists who were incarcerated there), and police stations. They also assassinated Lord Moynes, mistakenly thought to be an anti-Zionist, and kidnapped British officers for prisoner exchanges. By the end of 1946, Jewish terrorists had killed a total of 373 people. Of that number, 300 were civilians.[127]

It is worth reflecting that because the Jewish cause was increasingly perceived as righteous, it is not generally labeled as terrorism, at least in American history. In their own eyes, Jewish activists certainly were guided by humanitarian concern for Jews. The Nazis' brutality to their victims had the effect of ensuring latitude to the Jewish terrorists for their brutality, if not by the British, then in growing public

opinion. The establishment of a Jewish state (as well as extensive propaganda) made them the victors and bestowed a moral legitimacy on their cause in the public perception, which erases in large part the means by which they attained their state. We should ask whether those accused of terrorism in the Israel-Palestine conflict today should not be judged by the same standards as those whom we are writing about here in the immediate prelude to the Jewish Declaration of Statehood in 1948.

Morrison-Grady Plan

Britain made one final effort to mediate things diplomatically. In April 1946 a joint commission, the Anglo-American Committee of Inquiry, was authorized. They proposed that 100,000 Jewish refugees be admitted to Palestine to satisfy Harry Truman's political needs; that Jewish land-purchase restrictions be eased; that Palestine become a United Nations trusteeship that would become "(1) *a unitary state* for Arabs and Jews together, (2) a binational *federation of two states* with British or UN oversight, or (3) two *independent sovereign states.*"[128]

After discussions by both the United States and Britain, this evolved into the Morrison-Grady Plan, which settled for recommendation on "the immigration of 100,000 Jews to Palestine, the federalization of Jewish and Arab *provinces* under some time-limited British trusteeship— two semi-autonomous provinces (like American states) exercising control over their own intra-community affairs."[129] The British would maintain rule over Jerusalem and the Negev Desert and govern the federation in matters of foreign relations customs and defense. Howard Sacher, the historian, quotes one British official summarizing the Morrison-Grady Plan: "It is a beautiful scheme. It treats the Arabs and the Jews on a footing of complete equality in that it gives nothing to either party, while it leaves us a free run over the whole of Palestine."[130]

A conference was called in London for September 10, which the Zionist Executive declined to attend, insisting that only partition was acceptable. They also recommended that densely populated Palestinian areas be incorporated into Transjordan, and that others be incorporated into the Jewish state.

The Palestinians refused to attend because the Mufti, Amin al-Husseini, was still not permitted by the British to represent them. He was in Cairo in urgent meetings with the recently established Arab Higher Committee and directing affairs from there, including a boycott of all Jewish products. There were also plans to prevent the sale of land to the Zionist entity, as well as support for Arab paramilitary groups. The Arabs submitted a plan that gave an interim role to Britain until a provisional government could be established over a unitary state, with guarantees for freedom of access and religion in Jerusalem. It provided for three Jewish representatives in the new legislature of ten, and Hebrew as the official language in areas where Jews were an absolute majority. Naturalization would be granted to citizens with ten years of residency in Palestine, which excluded any of the Jewish displaced persons from the camps.[131]

Meanwhile, the Americans had threatened to pull out of the London discussions. Truman had grown resentful and negative toward a Jewish campaign he considered to be counter to the interests of both the United States and the Arabs. He was ready to let the Zionists and the British sort things out by themselves.[132] Truman remarked, "Well, you can't satisfy these people.... The Jews aren't going to write the history of the United States or my history."[133]

Public opinion was strained toward the Jews after Begin's terrorist bombing of the King David Hotel. David Niles, Truman's pro-Zionist advisor, warned the leadership of the

It is a beautiful scheme. It treats the Arabs and the Jews on a footing of complete equality in that it gives nothing to either party, while it leaves us a free run over the whole of Palestine.

Jewish Agency to come up with a reasonable plan. Meeting in Paris, the Jewish Agency considered their options. They naturally preferred the Biltmore plan, knowing it would not be acceptable. They were willing to settle for partition without the United Nations or Britain involved, but doubted that the US would accept this. They finally accepted the Morrison-Grady Plan with the provision that the Negev would go to the Jews.[134]

On October 4 immediately before the congressional elections, Truman agreed to the partition for two states and the immigration of the 100,000 displaced persons, but excluded the British altogether because of American Zionist pressure. The British were furious. Perhaps the final blow came when in December of 1946 David Ben-Gurion was elected to succeed Chaim Weizmann as the president of the Jewish Agency. Ben-Gurion was an extremist and activist, while Weizmann had always been understood

issue that provoked the maximalist Zionist demands for Jewish statehood, that ignited the terrorism, launched the illegal refugee traffic to Palestine, undermined Britain's economy, eroded its international reputation, and finally doomed the Palestine mandate itself.[136]

Peter Davies, a missionary with the General Board of Global Ministries who recently served in Israel-Palestine, also served in the British Army in Mandate Palestine in its last days. Davies comments:

> When the UN's partition resolution was adopted, the population of Palestine was close to one million. Sixty-nine percent were Arabs who owned more than ninety percent of Palestine's 10,500 square miles (about the size of Maryland). Thirty-one percent of the population were Jews who owned five percent of the land. Yet despite these verifiable facts compiled by the British, the partition resolution assigned fifty-two percent of the land to [what

by the British as relatively moderate.[135] The issue for the pragmatist Ben-Gurion had always been immigration. Sacher reflects:

> More than any other factor, it was London's preoccupation with Arab goodwill and, correspondingly, Bevin's (British Foreign Secretary in Clement Atlee's Labor Government following the war) agonized intransigence on the immigration

was soon to become] the new state of Israel and forty-eight percent to the Palestinian Arabs.[137]

Now under Ben-Gurion's leadership, the Jewish Agency accepted the United Nations partition plan with reservations and intentions yet to unfold. Obviously it was immediately advantageous to their cause. But it was clearly not in Palestinian interests, and they rejected it.

Chapter 4
From War to War to War: 1948-1973

Personal History

On a visit to Palestine-Israel in 1999, Peter Davies and I traveled with a small group to the Galilee. With us were two young Palestinian women who worked in the gift shop at St. Andrew's Presbyterian Church in Jerusalem. They had never been to the north. Although they lived in Jerusalem, their travel had always been restricted. We stopped briefly at the Horns of Hattin where on July 4, 1187, Salah al-Din (Saladin), the Commander of the Syrian armies, defeated the Crusaders, who were led by two ruthless Europeans, King Guy de Lusignan and Reynald de Chatillon.

Looking down at the plains below where the battle began, you are not far from some celebrated traditional biblical and archaeological sites. To the southwest is the Jezreel Valley and Mount Tabor, the traditional site identified with Jesus' Transfiguration (Mark 9; Matthew 17; Luke 9). A little further

Jewish-Israeli young people visit further down the valley at the biblical tel at Megiddo, the ancient stables which archaeologists now attribute to Jeroboam, who founded the northern kingdom of Israel. It is also where Christian fundamentalists and Christian Zionists visit to meditate on the final confrontation between good and evil when Christ will come in final victory. According to John's Apocalypse, it is to occur "at the place that in Hebrew is called Harmagedon" (Revelation 16:16).

The Palestinian women were excited to be there for the first time, but we didn't linger. We were on our way to visit the site of a more recent war, one that caused the exodus of 750,000 Palestinians from their land; they fled or were forced to flee their homes and farms and villages. This number includes both refugees and the Palestinians who were expelled from their villages—located in what became Israel—and internally displaced.[138] The village we went to visit,

you come to Megiddo, where tradition says Solomon built a palace, and where many biblical battles occurred. According to II Kings 23, King Josiah of Judah was killed by the Egyptian Pharaoh Neco near Megiddo.

As we were looking over the Muslim site, a group of Palestinian young people was visiting. They were reliving their historical narrative as Muslims, when Muslim power was at its apex. On the hillside is a monument commemorating Salah al-Din's victory over the Christian Crusaders. No doubt

destroyed in 1948 by Israeli forces, had no marker except for the remains of stone walls from the buildings. The walls were there for anyone to see, if you searched a little, which we did. This land is now part of an Israeli National Park or Preserve. It is near the junction of a major road where there was a kosher McDonald's restaurant. The two young Palestinian women with us knew of the village because it was where their parents had been born and from which they had fled to become refugees. The women had never visited there before.

It was one of 531 towns and villages that Palestinians left in what they refer to as Al Nakba, the Disaster. Jewish-Israelis call it the War of Independence.

The Jewish Narrative of the War
On November 29, 1947, the United Nations passed "United Nations Resolution 181: The Future Government of Palestine." The Resolution and the partition followed by the war were catastrophic for the Palestinians. By the conclusion of hostilities and the various armistices that were negotiated by the Israelis, Palestine and Palestinians ceased functionally to exist as political entities. What remains are two disparate narratives of what occurred in the 1948 war. The one that has come to be accepted, especially in the United States, is the Israeli narrative. It has entered into the realm of our own national mythology and propaganda. The conventional Zionist version goes something like this:

Palestinians were ordered by their Arab leadership to flee their homes, having been promised they would return in short order after an Arab victory was achieved.

Referring to the standard Israeli narrative, Avi Shlaim in his book *The Iron Wall: Israel in the Arab World* noted:

This popular-heroic-moralistic version of the 1948 war has been used extensively in Israeli propaganda and is still taught in Israeli schools. It is a prime example of the use of a nationalistic version of history in the process of nation building. In a very real sense, history is the propaganda of the victors, and the history of the 1948 war is no exception.[139]

This Israeli version of the story, accepted by many of us at face value, was reinforced at every turn. Consider the 1960 Otto Preminger film *Exodus* and the Leon Uris novel on which it was based. The book mixes historical characters with fictional ones and historical events with invented embellishments.

- Desiring peace with the Arabs, Israel accepted the United Nations Partition Plan. The Arabs did not.

- Tiny Israel was attacked by the giant Arab adversary, seven well-equipped and supplied armies that invaded Palestine at the expiration of the mandate intending to strangle the Jewish state as soon as it emerged.

- An overwhelmingly uneven struggle between a heroic Jewish David and the Arab Goliath ensued in which the

For example, the fabrication that the Palestinians fled at the behest of their leaders is presented as fact. This is but one example of how we in the United States have only been exposed to one side of the Israel-Palestine story.

Films and documentaries that present an alternate perspective that may be damaging to Israel are often prevented from reaching public television affiliates when pro-Zionist groups threaten to withhold support or funding. *People and the Land,* a documentary by Tom Hayes with significant footage showing the brutality of Israeli defense forces in refugee camps during the first Intifada, was prevented from being shown because of what Tom Hayes calls "the information blockade." Out of 283 PBS affiliates, the documentary was screened on only fifteen stations. Abraham Foxman, Anti-Defamation League (ADL) National Director, issued a press release condemning *People and the Land* and expressing outrage at the Corporation for Public Broadcasting for allowing it to be funded at all.[140]

The Revisionists

The events of the 1948 war have been reexamined in the work of a number of Israeli historians and sociologists. They have gained access to documents and records that only became available in Israel thirty years after the war, a standard policy of many governments. Corporately this

judge what is true and what is false in order to provide an accurate and reliable picture of the past.[141]

The new historians have concentrated their scholarly scrutiny in three ways. The first examines the origin of Zionist ideology and practice in the late nineteenth century; the second is an attempt to write the history of the 1948 war using newly available archival documentation; and the third analyzes the state's attitude toward the Palestinian minority and Jewish immigrants from Arab countries.[142]

Pappé says that the other experience that informed this Revisionist perspective was exposure to local Palestinians in the Occupied Territories and their support for the Palestinian Liberation Organization. For the first time, Israeli academicians (and activists) were hearing the Palestinian narrative of 1948, their Nakba. This exposure led a number of Israeli scholars to legitimize some of the major claims that Palestinians had posited throughout the years:

group of historians is known as the Israeli "Revisionists." All of these works had a major impact in exploring beyond the accepted Israeli version of the origins of the state and the 1948 war. Ilan Pappé, one of those historians, wrote regarding this new evaluation of events:

> I cannot overemphasize the fact that it is professional Israeli historians, recognized as such in their own society, who are offering an alternative way of looking at the history of Israel and Zionism. They are accepted as qualified to

In a very real sense, history is the propaganda of the victors, and the history of the 1948 war is no exception.

The major claim accepted by the new scholars is that Israel and the Zionist movement are directly responsible for the Palestinian Catastrophe. Acceptance of this claim alone has far-reaching implications for the present peace process, especially when negotiations address the issue of Palestinian refugees. These scholars may differ with their Palestinian counterparts about the reasons Israel and Zionism were so destructive to the Palestinians, but they agree on the end result. Not less important is the acceptance of the Palestinian claim that the international community was pro-Zionist to the degree that Palestinians had little chance to realize their national aspirations.[143]

In his book, *The Palestinian Catastrophe: the 1948 Expulsion of a People from Their Homeland* (1987), Michael Palumbo calls on sources beyond Israeli government records, including the archives of the United Nations and the British and United States governments. Palumbo observes that the Revisionists tended to accept files that

restitution the 750,000 Palestinian refugees and their descendants will receive, if they are not permitted to return to their homes (some of which still stand and are occupied by Israelis) or to repossess their land. The Israelis have continued to refuse any suggestion that the Palestinian refugees can return to Israel proper, as it would shift the demographic reality to a Palestinian majority, and the Jewish state would cease to exist as such. The second watershed was the 1967 war when Palestinians living in the Jordanian-occupied West Bank again became refugees. The policies and attitudes of current and past leadership are very much informed by how this history is interpreted, presented, and understood.

Who Started the War?

The initial motivation for war was the Zionist realization that a state could not be formed without removing large numbers of Arabs. The Arab population was increasing faster than

had been carefully screened by the Israeli government, without supplementing their work with files available from reliable non-Israeli sources.[144]

The narrative of the actual events of the 1948 war determines much of the contemporary political and public rhetoric dealing with peace between Israelis and Palestinians. It is based on the facts on the ground in 1948. One contentious outstanding issue, which has colored all of the negotiations since Oslo, has been the question of what compensation or

the rate of Jewish immigration.[145] The war was in the Zionists' interest and offered an opportunity to further their goals of expansion beyond the United Nations partition recommendation. The Palestinians had been disarmed even while the Zionists were equipping their forces. The records indicate that the Zionist forces that had numbered around 15,000 in early 1948 increased to over 60,000 by May 1948.[146] The Zionists were also recruiting professional military volunteers.[147]

As early as 1937 Ben-Gurion had said to a gathering of Zionists, "I favor partition of the country because when we become a strong power after the establishment of the state, we will abolish partition and spread throughout Palestine." In a letter to his son a year before, he had written that if the Palestinians could not be removed from the country by negotiations, then "we will expel the Arabs and take their place."[148] During the years immediately prior to World War II and during the war, the Zionists were expanding their military capability. Shortly after war began, the forces of Haganah and the two terrorist groups, the Irgun and LEHI (Stern Gang), were functionally combined. By the second phase of the war they were working together strategically.

When the Arab League and the Mufti Amin al-Husseini finally responded to the need to defend their interests against partition, they assembled a volunteer force of 1,600 irregulars. As local village defenses were organized and the youth groups

organized into eight battalions in central Palestine. But the Arab forces were outnumbered, outarmed, and outclassed by the armed Jewish regulars and their allied international volunteers. The Palestinians were unprepared to defend the integrity and unity of their country.[150]

In reality, the Arab Goliath was ineffectual. Except for the early resistance by the Palestinians in defense of their own villages, the Israelis dominated the war in short order. "Archival documents expose a fragmented Arab world wrought by dismay and confusion and a Palestinian community that possessed no military ability with which to threaten the Jews. The Arab world went about announcing its commitment to the Palestinians in strident, war-like rhetoric, but it did little on the ground to save Palestine."[151]

Throughout this period, the United Nations had been trying to avoid conflict, as well as attempting to broker a truce. Immediately following the British decision to turn over

activated and added to the total, by early 1948 the force may have totaled around 7,000 fighters.[149]

Alarmed by Jewish attacks and because of public pressure from their own people, the Arab League, now consisting of leaders from the recently formed Arab nations, organized and supported a volunteer Arab force, Jayash al-Inqath (Army of Salvation), under the command of Fawzi al-Qawuqji. Nearly four thousand Arab men, including between five hundred and a thousand Palestinians, were

the Mandate to the United Nations, the United Nations Special Committee on Palestine (UNSCOP) had been set up to try to find solutions. The partition plan was its recommendation. A minority report had also been presented recommending two autonomous states in federation with one nationality and citizenship. Arab leadership rejected both the majority and minority reports. They held to their long-standing position that Palestine was an integral part of the Arab world and that from the beginning its indigenous inhabitants had opposed the creation of a Jewish national home in their country. They insisted that the United Nations, a body created and controlled by the United States and Europe, had no right to hand over to the Zionists any part of their territory.[152] They understood that this initiative was a way for the West to salve their conscience for the atrocities of the war and the Holocaust.

Arab violence broke out immediately following the declaration of partition in November and continued until May 1948 when the international phase of the war began with Israel's declaration of statehood. The first attacks were launched by Palestinians against Jews when two Jewish buses were attacked near Lydda airport. On December 2 in Jerusalem, Arab youths ransacked the Jewish market and shopping center. That same day, Arabs all over Palestine went on strike for three days.[153] Into December sporadic Palestinian attacks continued against Jewish settlements in

the north, along the Mediterranean coast and on the routes connecting the main cities. Then the Irgun and the Stern Gang attacked three times between December 23 and January 7. Jewish extremists threw bombs into Arab crowds near the Damascus and Jaffa gates in the Old City.[154] The British Colonial Office saw the Palestinian violence as spontaneous demonstrations against the partition resolution. But the Jews declared to the world that a war of annihilation had begun.[155]

Plan D

The Zionists fought defensively, holding on to the land allocated to them by the partition plan. In April the combined Israeli forces, Haganah, Irgun, and LEHI, launched a violent offensive.[156] The Haganah offensive was orchestrated through what is known as Plan Dalet or "Plan D." The intent of Plan D was the expulsion of as many Palestinians as possible from the heavily populated Palestinian areas in the portions granted to the Zionists—but not simply to expel. The Zionist forces terrorized those they intended to remove from their homes, pillaging, raping women, massacring the old and young, and committing major atrocities. The massacre of the Palestinians at the village of Deir Yassin five miles west of Jerusalem has become emblematic of the brutality that the Jewish forces wreaked on the ill-defended Palestinians. The Palestinians of Deir Yassin had agreed to a non-aggression pact with the Haganah and with Jewish

neighbors in surrounding villages. But on April 9, a combined force of Irgun, Stern Gang, and Haganah, called Operation Unity (because the goal was to demonstrate cooperation among the three Zionist forces) attacked Deir Yassin.[157] Palestinian sentries were posted around the village. They were armed with old Mausers (World War I vintage rifles) and Turkish rifles that had been fired only to hunt rabbits. When one of the sentries spotted the terrorists, he fired his rifle and screamed, "The Jews are coming."

At first the Zionists made little progress. Though barefoot and half naked, scores of residents of Deir Yassin were able to reach neighboring villages. Those who were unable to flee put up a valiant defense. Meir Pa'il,[158] an eyewitness, noted the ineffectiveness of the terrorists. "They just managed to occupy the eastern half of the village, they couldn't occupy the higher western half. About ten or twelve Arabs shot at them using only rifles, no automatic weapons, and pinned them down on the eastern side."[159]

The Palmach, Jewish commando units, reluctantly came to the assistance of the Irgun and Stern Gang, who were not yet under a unified command. These additional forces allowed them to complete the occupation of the village. Had it stopped there, it would have been the same as hundreds of other Israeli operations. According to Pa'il, however, the terrorists were out for revenge against the Palestinians for their attempted resistance and because of their own need for

Following the massacre, Menachem Begin sent an order of the day to the attackers of Deir Yassin: "Accept congratulations on this splendid act of conquest…. Tell the soldiers you have made history in Israel."[161] The Irgun and Stern Gang held a joint press conference in order to publicize their victory at Deir Yassin. An Irgun representative told the newsmen: "We intend to conquer and keep until we have the whole of Palestine and Transjordan in a Greater Jewish state. This attack is the first step."[162]

Menachem Begin later recalled in a memoir:

Arabs throughout the country, induced to believe wild tales of "Irgun butchery," were seized with limitless panic and started to flee for their lives. This mass flight soon developed into a maddened, uncontrollable stampede. The political and economic significance of this development can hardly be overestimated.[163]

Haganah back-up assistance. One of the Deir Yassin residents, Mohammad Aref Sammour, recounted the savage slaughter that followed not far from his own house:

There were twenty-five people, twenty-four were killed and only one could escape through a window. They used grenades and after they stormed the house they used machine guns. In another house they captured a boy who was holding the knee of his mother. They slaughtered him in front of her.[160]

In all, 254 men, women, and children were killed. Survivors were paraded from the backs of trucks for the purpose of terrorizing the surrounding villages and inciting Palestinians to flee their homes out of fear. No doubt Arab fighters carried out atrocities as well. But aside from being an instance of savage atrocity, both the severity of Deir Yassin and the story spread by Arabs and Zionists alike created vast Arab panic. This terror and flight affected the demographics of the UN-designated territories along with the outcome of the war.[164]

There have been disagreements and controversy around whether the Deir Yassin massacre was premeditated, as described in "Plan D," or a more randomly-driven occurrence. Benny Morris, another Revisionist historian, claims it was not part of a plan but a less intentional strategy. In weighing the evidence, Pappé notes the mass expulsion of more than half of the Palestinian population, sometimes accompanied by massacres, rape, and pillage. Regardless, he concludes that the mere reference to what the Israelis had done to put Palestinians to flight stands in stark contrast to the mainstream Zionist version of the war's history. The official version is that the Palestinian leadership called upon its population to leave so that they would not get in the way of the invading Arab armies. No recognition of atrocities beyond Deir Yassin is given in this version, and even this atrocity is attributed to renegade right-wing terrorists, not to the Haganah, the main military

of which evidence does not exist. After reading many narratives and analyses, I cannot see any other explanation except a willful policy of expulsion and transfer on the part of the Zionists.

Establishment of the Jewish State

By April 1948 the Zionist forces were in charge of the war, and the ill-fated Palestinian resistance was spent. On May 14 the last of the British forces departed from Haifa. That same day, David Ben-Gurion declared to an audience of Jewish Yishuv leadership and over the radio to the world the "establishment of the Jewish State in Palestine, to be called *Medinath Yisrael* (the State of Israel)":

> The State of Israel will be open to the immigration of Jews from all countries of their dispersion; will promote the development of the country for the benefit of all its inhabitants; will be based on the principles of liberty,

force. The New Historians, on the other hand, attribute other massacres to the Haganah, and some have even discovered a link between the Haganah and the Deir Yassin massacre.[165]

The Israeli historian Meir Pa'il gave this estimate of the overall Palestinian exodus: around one-third fled out of fear; one-third were forcibly evacuated by the Israelis; about one-third were encouraged by the Israelis to flee.[166] Meir Pa'il still attributes the exodus to a prior Arab conspiracy,

justice, and peace as conceived by the Prophets of Israel; will uphold the full social and political equality of all its citizens, without distinction of religion, race, or sex; will guarantee freedom of religion, conscience, education, and culture; will safeguard the Holy Places of all religions; and will loyally uphold the principles of the United Nations Charter.... With trust in the Rock of Israel, we set our hand to this Declaration, at the session of the Provisional State Council, on the soil of the Homeland, in the city of Tel Aviv....[167]

The first country to acknowledge Israel was the United States, which it did the same day. With Cold War politics in the offing, the Russians followed suit immediately. The international phase of the war began at once. With King Abdullah Hussein at its head, the Arab Legion crossed the Jordan River at the Allenby Bridge. Therein is a significant story that also testifies to the actual imbalance of the conflict in contrast to the official Israeli narrative. Avi Shlaim writes in his book, *The Iron Wall: Israel and the Arab World* (2000):

> As far as the military balance is concerned, it was always assumed that the Arabs enjoyed overwhelming numerical superiority. The war was persistently portrayed as a struggle of the few against the many.... But in mid-May 1948 the total number of Arab troops, both regular and irregular, operating in the Palestinian theater was under 25,000, whereas the IDF (Israeli Defense Forces, formerly the Haganah, and the terrorist organizations) was over

35,000. By mid-July the IDF mobilized 65,000 men under arms, and by December its numbers had reached a peak of 96,441. The Arab states also reinforced their armies, but they could not match this rate of increase. Thus, at each stage of the war, the IDF significantly outnumbered all the Arab forces arrayed against it, and by the final stage of the war, its superiority ratio was nearly two to one. The final outcome of the war was therefore not a miracle but a reflection of the underlying Arab-Israeli military imbalance. In this war, as in most wars, the stronger side ultimately prevailed.[168]

Other significant factors contributed to the Israeli success. The most effective of the Arab forces was King Abdullah's Arab Legion from Transjordan, whose commanding officer was a British General, John Glubb. Glubb served with the Arab Legion in Transjordan through World War II and the Mandate until 1956. But the Arab Legion was fighting with one hand tied behind its back. Abdullah had been secretly negotiating with the Zionists, who through diplomacy had sought support for their plans from the leaders of the surrounding Arab lands. With King Abdullah, the diplomatic efforts were fruitful. On November 17, 1947, well before the war broke out, Golda Meir, Ben-Gurion's agent, had reached a secret agreement with King Abdullah:

> [Abdullah's] many critics suggested that he was prepared to compromise the Arab claim to the whole of Palestine as long as he could acquire part of Palestine for himself. "The internecine struggles of the Arabs," reported Glubb, "are more in the minds of Arab politicians than the struggle against the Jews. Azzam Pasha, the *mufti* and the Syrian government would sooner see the Jews get the whole of Palestine than that King Abdullah should benefit.[169]

As a son of the Sharif of Mecca, Abdullah's ambition was a driving force. Beyond his status as a British client, he had designs on creating a more significant kingdom that he had hoped would include all of historic Palestine (once called Greater Syria). Abdullah was not forthright in his support of the Palestinian cause in his dealings with the other Arab leaders in the Arab League.

The substance of the agreement was that when Palestine was divided, part would go to the Jewish Agency and part to Transjordan. In exchange for the West Bank, the Arab Legion under the King's authority would not interfere with Israel. With the armistice, the West Bank was incorporated into Transjordan, and Israel gained significant territory beyond that proposed in the partition plan: 78 percent of historic Palestine, well beyond the 44 percent of the UN plan. Palestinian territory was reduced to only 22 percent. Gaza came under the military control of Egypt. Hundreds of thousands of Palestinians became refugees in the parts of Palestine under Arab control and in neighboring Arab countries, and Palestine ceased to exist.[170] It is not an overstatement to say Abdullah's was a major betrayal; as Shlaim notes, "The losers were the Palestinians, who have been without a homeland ever since."[171]

Armistice, But No Peace

It has been a perennial part of the public face of Zionism, and now of Israel, to claim that they have persistently sued for peace with the Arabs and have always been rebuffed, threatened, or attacked. They have seldom taken responsibility, at least publicly, for their belligerence and their intentional undermining of attempts at resolutions to the conflict. Israel has chosen to create the perception that they are perennial victims, even in the face of their military superiority and the large numbers of dead Palestinians. Israel's internal political dialogue has also created intentional ambiguity in its professed policies so as to confound potential agreements with Arab states and to manipulate its international supporters.

It is likewise true that Arab nations and their leadership have been unable to maintain a unified strategy regarding Israel or the question of Palestine. Arab intransigence in the face of Israeli and world-power diplomacy, and their own intractable intra-Arab rivalries and conflicts have correspondingly contributed to the failure of a lasting peace.

The Bernadotte Assassination

Israeli bellicosity as observed in the massacre in Deir Yassin and the expulsion of Palestinians from their homes during the 1948 war reveals the depth of the error in the perception of Israel as victim. Another incident casts in bright contrast how misleading is the rhetoric offered by Israeli leadership for the world's consumption with regard to the pursuit of peace. The United Nations appointed Count Folke Bernadotte, a highly regarded veteran diplomat, to try to reach a settlement between the Israelis and the Arabs.

Bernadotte, formerly vice president of the Swedish Red Cross, had negotiated in 1945 for the Allies with Heinrich

Himmler for the complete surrender of Germany. He successfully delivered the surrender to President Roosevelt and Prime Minister Churchill. He seemed a highly competent, credible choice. Bernadotte had also been deeply involved with the rescue of Europeans from the Nazi concentration camps. After the first peace plan had been rejected by both Arabs and Israelis, Bernadotte proposed a second settlement plan for a resolution to the war that included a portion of Palestine being merged with Transjordan, an international administration for Jerusalem, and significantly, a provision to ensure the right of the Palestinian refugees to return to their homes. On September 17, 1948, Bernadotte was assassinated by a gang of LEHI terrorists led by Yitzhak Shamir (Prime Minister of Israel from 1983 to 1984 and again from 1986 to 1992). The day before the assassination, Israeli Foreign Minister Moshe Sharett

remaining members of the gang were given amnesty eight months later. No one was ever put on trial for the killing.[173] Historian Howard Sachar notes that Yehoshua Cohen, Ben-Gurion's friend, was believed to be the trigger man.[174]

This incident is indicative of Israel's lack of commitment to finding peaceful solutions after the 1948 war and reveals an extremist streak in the heart of the Zionist program. Zionist policy has been to initiate terrorist actions while claiming impotence or self-defense or of being innocent victims of provocation, all the while pursuing territorial expansion, a bottom line of Zionist policy.

In her 1994 book about the assassination, *A Death in Jerusalem,* Kati Marton likens Bernadotte's assassination by the extremist Stern Gang to Baruch Goldstein's assassination of Prime Minister Yitzhak Rabin in February 1994.[175] This is not to say that Israelis are a nation of extremists and terrorists, but that the foundational record

publicly accused Bernadotte of being biased against Israel and in favor of the Arab states.[172]

The outside world was horrified by this act of Zionist brutality. Immediately following Bernadotte's assassination, the Israeli government granted visas to thirty members of the Stern Gang to travel to Prague in Eastern Europe. They left Palestine within weeks. The Israeli government later revealed that most of the Stern Gang members who had been rounded up had been released within two weeks. The

exposes something more than the popular images set before us of a beleaguered minority in the Arab world. The Israelis have more frequently been the aggressors in the Middle East. This has been the case even up to the present, with the unwavering support of the United States since the 1967 war. We have consistently allowed Israel to have its way even when, in the eyes of the rest of the world, Israel's actions have been unjust and detrimental to any lasting program of peace in the Middle East.

Armistices, Truces and Stand-Offs

The period following the 1948 war saw not peace but a series of bilateral armistices, truces, and stand-offs between Israel and the principal Arab players: Egypt, Syria, Transjordan, and Lebanon. Of more importance later were relationships with Iraq, Saudi Arabia, Turkey, Afghanistan, and Iran (the latter two not being Arab nations.) The cessation of declared war was merely a prelude to ongoing violent confrontations and cross-border incursions. The good offices of Count Bernadotte's successor, Ralph Johnson Bunche, brokered the various armistices between Israel and the Arab states from January to July 1949.[176] These armistice lines defined Israel's boundaries until the 1967 war. It was a terribly frustrating endeavor. None of the humiliated Arab countries wanted to acknowledge officially that they had been defeated, and Israel had no need to make peace.[177]

quotes Ben-Gurion in the *Herald Tribune* in July 1949 as remarking: "I am prepared to get up in the middle of the night in order to sign a peace agreement—but I am not in a hurry and I can wait ten years. We are under no pressure whatsoever."[179] With regret, the Conciliation Commission decided to terminate the conference on November 21. Neither party was willing to substantially back down from its rigid position to seek a solution through mediation.[180] It took another thirty years for Israel to sign a peace treaty with Egypt (1979) and it was Ben-Gurion's nemesis, Menachem Begin, who reluctantly signed it.

Dominating all of the maneuvering and machinations in the Middle East during this period was the expanding Cold War. Both the United States and the Soviet Union, the principal powers seeking to dominate the world for their own interests, used the Middle East as one of the theaters to vie for power and control over the economic, political,

Bunche won the 1950 Nobel Prize for Peace for his successful negotiation of these Arab-Israeli truces in Palestine after the war.

But peace agreements and treaties were another matter. The United Nations-sponsored Palestinian Conciliation Commission (PCC) meeting in Lausanne tried to move beyond the initial armistice agreements. The positions of Israel and the Arabs were so far apart and so inflexible as to make the gap between them unbridgeable.[178] Avi Shlaim

and (if one were to believe some of the Cold War rhetoric), moral assets of the region.

A number of simultaneous tracks in the Middle East contributed to the main narratives of the Israelis and the Palestinians. The first was the continued post-war imperial ambitions of the French and British. Another was the emergence of the Arab states from the colonial era as independent entities, each striving for autonomy, stability, and improved lives for their citizens. Their internal struggles were in some cases monumental. A contributing factor was the need for the Arabs after their defeat in the 1948 war to define their national aspirations against the fact of the Jewish state with its territorial ambitions. The Arab states' internecine struggles for dominance in the Arab world were born out of the colonial period, World War I, and the Mandate period that followed. The other main event was the reemergence of the struggle for Palestinian self-determination and the emergence of the Palestinian Liberation Organization as the embodiment of Palestinian aspirations.

The individual political events and incidents that populate these tracks are more numerous than can be faithfully contained here. But some few contribute to the larger picture in significant ways. First is the emergence of Egypt under Gamal Abdel Nasser and the Suez Crises of 1956.

authority in the region. These culminated in 1955 in a regional alliance, the Baghdad Pact among Iraq, Turkey, Iran, and Pakistan. The United States supported Britain but did not join until later.[181]

A series of coups d'etat in the Arab countries heightened tensions throughout the region. In 1949 Colonel Husni Zaim staged a military takeover in Syria. In July 1951 King Abdullah Hussein was assassinated. Palestinians were angry over his clandestine negotiations with Israel to expand Transjordan and to absorb part of the West Bank, understood by them as a betrayal and a barrier to establishing a national home. In July 1952 a group of Free Officers—young nationalist officers of the Egyptian army, led by Gamal Abdul Nasser, a hero of the 1948 war—overthrew King Farouk and the Egyptian monarchy.[182] The officers' motivation was to liberate Egypt from its British colonial legacy and the corrupt monarchy. Nasser emerged as the leader of the movement

Egypt and Nasser

Following the loss of much of their empire, the British wanted to continue their dominance as much as possible. Keeping control of the Suez Canal as access to the Indian Ocean through the Red Sea was of great economic importance, as was reliance on Middle Eastern oil imports. At the same time, European powers feared that the Arab nations would align themselves with the Soviets against Western interests. Britain engineered a number of initiatives to retain its

and was President of Egypt from 1954 until his sudden death in 1970 following the Black September revolution in Jordan.

The driving force for the Arab states was not fear of the Soviet Union but the more palpable threat of Israel. Nasser's vision of Arab unity, Pan-Arabism, became the dominant force in the Middle Eastern Arab nations. This included the nascent leadership of the Palestinians, later to emerge in the Palestinian Liberation Organization, and its related movements, Fatah, the Popular Front for the Liberation of Palestine (PFLP), and others.

> It also gave the Palestinian refugees, who were poorly treated in many Arab countries, a larger sense of identity, which gave the promise of protecting them from such pressures. Thus, for a time, 'Abd al-Nasser's picture was on the walls of many homes in the Palestinian refugee camps; and in Israel, in Jordan, in the Gaza Strip, as well as in all of the countries of the Palestinian diaspora....[183]

Nasser wanted the Arab states to be free of any post-colonial Western or Eastern European dominance. He was therefore opposed to the Baghdad Pact. He was shrewd in his dealings with the Cold War adversaries, sometimes gaining support from one or the other, as he furthered Egyptian interests, especially in opposition to Israel. Because of Nasser's non-aligned stand, the US Secretary of State, John Foster Dulles, refused his request for arms. Nasser then turned to the Soviet

Reparations and Water Rights

The United States' interests were defined by containing the Soviet Union's expanding influence. Its identification with Israel as a client to counter Soviet influence was not as yet established, and Eisenhower's administration, although sympathetic to Israel, also saw the need to maintain ties to the Arab states. Eisenhower was prepared to maintain financial support for Israel because of Western sympathy for the sufferings of the Jews throughout twenty-five hundred years of history. And also because of the Holocaust.

> At the same time, [Eisenhower] did not want to impair Arab relations by creating a unique US-Israeli defense treaty or supply of weapons. In fact, he judged that the existing balance of military power favored Israel and he knew that Israel was receiving arms from France.[184]

Union and brokered an arms deal through Czechoslovakia in 1955 for armaments, including tanks and aircraft.

Initially, Nasser was open to peace with Israel. His primary goal was the social and economic development of his people, not a perpetual state of defense against Israel. He was also keenly aware of Egypt's military weakness. But Nasser's diplomatic program to garner support and arms from the Soviet Union for Egypt's interests soured cooperation with the United States.

Israel was increasingly perceived by Dulles and Eisenhower as the aggressor. Eisenhower was neither the first nor the last US president to think agreements ought to have been possible in the conflict. During the early 1950s Israel continued to carry out raids across border areas into Syria, Jordan, Egypt, and Gaza, claiming that they were preventing Palestinian infiltration. The Palestinians were generally refugees attempting to return to their own lost homes. In 1952 when West Germany settled on reparations to be paid to Israel and restitutions to Jewish refugees and their families, Israel still refused to repatriate or compensate Palestinian refugees for their lost land. In 1953 when Dulles called for Israel to pay parallel restitution to Palestinian refugees, Israel refused.[185]

Another stir came over water rights and alleged violations of the armistice agreement with Syria:

> These violations, Syria charged, consisted mainly of the following: (1) draining of the Huleh marshes and the straightening and deepening of the bed of the Jordan River between Lake Huleh and Lake Tiberias; (2) military occupation of the demilitarized zone; (3) firing on Syrian military outposts; (4) forcible evacuation of indigenous Arab inhabitants of the demilitarized zone and the demolishing of their villages; and (5) bombing of El Hamma and Syrian military outposts.[186]

whom it had signed armistices. Military incursions on the Syrian border increased into the 1960s. Although the Arab states were hardly innocent of hostility, the burden was surely on Israel as the aggressor. Eisenhower and Dulles thought so as well.

Israel's militants, especially Moshe Dayan, Ben-Gurion's military chief of staff, had advocated a more belligerent policy of reprisals that changed Israel's strategy from one of basic security to one of serious deterrence. It was in line with Ben-Gurion's attitudes as it presumed force rather than diplomacy as the instrument of foreign policy. In a speech to army officers in 1955, Dayan gave the rationale for the new policy of reprisal.

> We could not guard every water pipeline from being blown up and every tree from being uprooted. We could not prevent every murder of a worker in an orchard or a family in their beds. But it was in our power to set a high

Israel claimed that it was justified in its actions and that Syria had violated the armistice agreement with armed incursions to stop the drainage project. Syrians had attacked an Israeli police patrol, killing seven and wounding three others. The United Nations Security Council mediated and passed a resolution that resolved nothing. The underlying issues of the Palestinian refugees and setting of permanent borders between Syria and Israel had not been addressed, as was typical of the disputes between Israel and those with

price on our blood, a price too high for the Arab community, the Arab army, or the Arab governments to think it worth paying....[187]

In his younger years Dayan, with a patch over one eye lost presumably in combat, was something of a warrior icon. It is revealing that historian Avi Shlaim describes him as a sensitive man who understood the injustice perpetrated on the Palestinians. He is also representative of a generation of Israelis whose basic assumption was that Israel would be in perpetual conflict with its neighbors because of its original sin. Israel's survival was always at stake. Shlaim likens Dayan to the early settlers in the United States who prided themselves on being Indian fighters. Dayan and his generation saw themselves as Arab fighters, typical of second-generation settlers in a country where newcomers must fight the native population.[188] Dayan believed without reservation in military force against civilians. Shlaim quotes Dayan as having told a meeting of government officials of his party: "Harassing the village, including women, children, and elderly people…is the only method that proved itself effective, not justified or moral, but effective, when Arabs lay mines on our side."[189] It is also the policy that contributed to the Suez crises.

The Suez Crisis

Having returned to the government, Ben-Gurion was intent on provoking Egypt and Nasser rather than furthering peace.

the shipping passage through the Straights of Tiran with access to the Red Sea. Egypt had barred Israel from use of the Suez in 1948.

The stage was set. The Israeli, French, and British interests in removing Nasser from power converged. In 1956 the United States was preoccupied with a presidential election, and the Soviet Union was occupied with the uprising in Hungary.

The plan was to have the three nations invade Egypt: Israel would land paratroopers at the canal, where they would be joined by land forces coming across the Sinai. Upon reaching the Suez Canal, France and Britain would issue an ultimatum for Israel and Egypt to withdraw their respective forces to ten miles from the canal. They knew that Nasser would never agree. At this point, the joint British and French forces would appear at the canal to separate the Israeli and Egyptian armies.

For all of the reasons mentioned, and because of the personal make-up of Israeli leadership (perhaps excluding Moshe Sharret, who continued to respond to peace feelers and indirect conversation from Egypt through mediators), Nasser and Egypt were to be treated as a threat. The Gaza raid finally shut the door. Israel wanted to go to war with Egypt before their procurement of weaponry could be made effective, but also because of Israel's continued interest in territorial expansion in the Sinai, and to ensure access to

Israeli commander Ariel Sharon arrived at the Suez Canal. Egypt engaged Israeli troops and the ultimatum was proffered and rejected. The Europeans bombed Egyptian airfields and landed at Port Said. The United Nations almost immediately passed a unanimous resolution calling for a ceasefire. With Russia and the United States strenuously condemning the action, the British and French consented to the resolution. Israel did not and went on to capture the entire Sinai Peninsula.

Britain's prestige nose-dived in world affairs. Years later (January 16, 1977) *The New York Times* wrote: "[Sir Anthony] Eden was the last prime minister to believe Britain was a great power and the first to confront a crisis which proved beyond doubt that she was not."[190]

Even with the defeat, Nasser emerged as a hero representing Arab Nationalism and anti-Imperialism. Although forced by the United Nations and the United States to withdraw from the Sinai and Gaza and now perceived to be an agent of Western imperialism and militarism, Israel was also viewed as a formidable military force in the Middle East. The United Nations placed UN Emergency Forces (UNEF) in Gaza and in the southern end of the Sinai to prevent clashes between Egypt and Israel. Egypt retained the right to dismiss them.

The Eisenhower Doctrine
On the international level, the Suez crisis and war marked the

happening around the world in the aftermath of colonialism: the rise of indigenous nationalism. The rivalries and conflicts between the Arab states were of far greater moment than any concern about communism. Avi Shlaim captures the basic reality: "[B]y identifying the radical Arab regimes with international communism, the Eisenhower Doctrine instead pushed them into the arms of the Soviet Union."[191] Conversely, countries like Israel and the conservative Arab oil kingdoms, threatened by radical Arab regimes, sought to become clients of the United States in the struggle against communism. That card continues to be played today, only now it is called the "war against terrorism," with the Bush doctrine replacing that of President Eisenhower.

From 1958 until 1967 there was a period of relative calm in the Middle East. But there were continuing border incidents across the armistice lines and significant internal political activity in Israel and in the Arab states. Then on

end of an era and the beginning of another. Fearing the continuing influence of the Soviet Union, the United States initiated what was called the Eisenhower Doctrine, an ill-timed and misconceived reaction to the events in Suez. Simply put, it offered military and economic aid to any Middle Eastern nation threatened by communism. Washington was locked into a Cold War mentality in which containing communism was viewed as the only game in town. But what was happening in the Middle East was also what was

November 13, 1966, Israel abruptly departed from its pattern of small acts of retaliation against Jordan. It launched a devastating attack on the village of Samu, south of Hebron on the West Bank.[192] The reason given was that mines had been planted on the Israeli side of the border. Jordan was still in control of the West Bank. Staged in broad daylight by a large force with tanks, the attack resulted in the death of dozens of Jordanian soldiers and the destruction of forty-one houses.[193]

Both the United Nations and the United States condemned the attack. It underlined the weakness of King Hussein (Abdullah's grandson), who perceived the attack as a betrayal of Israel's previously expressed commitment to Jordan's stability and safety.[194] It was also an embarrassment to Nasser (the scion of Arab unity), who took no action. Before his death, Hussein noted in an interview with Avi Shlaim that it "created a devastating effect in Jordan itself because… [it] was not something that Jordan condoned or sponsored or supported in any form or way."[195] Even Yitzhak Rabin was shocked by the consequences of the raid. Up to this point, Israel had only been taking reprisals against Palestinian civilians, not against Hussein's Arab Legions who were generally keeping the peace.[196] As Jordan is the only Arab nation to have granted Palestinians citizenship and issued passports to them, 60 percent of Jordan's population is Palestinian.

But though the period was relatively calm, it was nevertheless characterized by the continuing search and cultivation of Cold War benefactors for increased armaments. Ben-Gurion was succeeded by Levi Eshkol, who was not a strong ideologue. Eshkol's attitude toward the Arabs was one of live and let live. Yet regardless of his personal proclivities, his government followed a policy of solidifying the country's security by acquiring the latest military hardware.[197] Beginning with the Kennedy administration, the United States drew ever closer to Israel, supporting in particular her military interests.

Israel and the Nuclear Problem
During Eisenhower's administration, Israel had obtained assistance in developing nuclear power for the development of energy. To that purpose, they built a uranium reactor north of Tel Aviv. But in secret Ben-Gurion began construction

By identifying the radical Arab regimes with international communism, the Eisenhower Doctrine instead pushed them into the arms of the Soviet Union.

of a reactor that would enable Israel to build nuclear weapons. He did not bring the matter to the Knesset or any of its committees for discussion. The government ministers were internally divided about it, both because of its crippling costs and the perception that it would take resources away from the development of conventional weaponry and the economy. Aside from Ben-Gurion, its advocates included Shimon Peres (who has been called the father of nuclear energy in Israel) and eventually Moshe Dayan.

The United States discovered the project through surveillance with U-2 spy planes in 1960. Kennedy, who had adopted a policy of global nonproliferation, distrusted Israel's long-term intentions. He was also wary of starting an arms race in the Middle East. Further, he was reluctant to offer Israel significant armaments, including the long-range missiles that Israel coveted. Early in his administration in 1961, during a meeting with Ben-Gurion, Kennedy intended

to extract a pledge from Israel that it would not develop nuclear weapons and would accept compliance by permitting international inspections. Backed by two distinguished Jewish-American physicists who had visited Dimona and had reported on its intended peaceful use, Ben-Gurion was able to deflect Kennedy and to reiterate Israel's security needs.

By 1962, Kennedy had reversed his decision against the sale of surface-to-air missiles to Israel. He hoped that this would discourage Israel from seeking to develop a nuclear option. Further, he wanted to signal to the Arabs more clearly than in the past that the United States was committed to the defense of Israel.[198] Kennedy gave a nod to seeking a resolution for the refugee problem, but it was ineffective. He continued to press Ben-Gurion about international inspection at Dimona until 1963 when on June 16, Ben-Gurion resigned from the government. Inspections never occurred, Israel developed nuclear weapons, and after

If the Arab population of Palestine had not been sure of their identity before 1948, defeat, dispossession, and exile guaranteed that they knew their identity soon afterwards: they were Palestinians.

Kennedy's assassination, the Johnson administration was far less reluctant than Kennedy to support Israel's security concerns and its arms requests.

Rivalries and Conflicts in the Arab World

In the Arab arena, Nasser continued his bid for Arab leadership. He was in a rivalry with the different regimes in Syria, where the Baath Socialist party eventually won out over Syrian communists. From 1958 through 1961, the Baathists formed a union with Egypt, the United Arab Republic (UAR), which Nasser sought to dominate. In 1961 Nasser imposed nationalization on the Syrian economy as he had done previously in Egypt. Even with Syrian Baathist socialism, Syria was essentially a traditional private economy. Most Syrians supported their country's withdrawal from the United Arab Republic and the formation of a new government from which the Baath party was excluded.[199] Syria was a theater

a growing population of Shia Muslims. Lebanon's years of fragile stability were near an end. The other Arab states lined up on one side or the other. The decade was characterized by these rivalries, internal debates, and conflicts in the Arab nations.

The Refugee Problem

The Palestinians were forgotten by the United States and by the Soviet Union. They had been treated not as a people but as the "refugee problem," a footnote that continued to undermine Israel's search for security and served as a bludgeon for the Arab nations to use against relations with Israel. But they emerged with a number of political entities and revolutionary movements both inside the host Arab nations and in the West Bank and Gaza Strip.

In his book *Palestinian Identity,* Rashid Khalidi notes rather sardonically:

in which the Soviet Union and United States could ply their Cold War tactics of military support and coup d'état, with the CIA in the thick of it. The Eisenhower Doctrine was proclaimed, and the United States signed onto the Baghdad pact. Lebanon accepted the Eisenhower Doctrine, with its fragile coalition government apportioned among Maronite Christians, Druze and Sunni Muslims, but with a growing population of Palestinian refugees. The refugees were mostly Sunni Muslims, though there was

If the Arab population of Palestine had not been sure of their identity before 1948, the experience of defeat, dispossession, and exile guaranteed that they knew what their identity was very soon afterwards: they were Palestinians.[200]

Birth of the PLO

The Palestinian Liberation Organization was born out of an Arab League summit meeting in January of 1964 in Cairo, Egypt. The summit had been called to address the serious problem for the Arab nations of Israel's water diversion project from the Sea of Galilee (Lake Kinneret) in the north to irrigate land in the Negev in the south. The project was completed in 1964. Syria had retaliated by diverting water from the sources of the Jordan and by allowing Palestinian attacks on Israel, but in a series of violent confrontations Israel had gained the upper hand. Things were seriously heating up.

The Arab statement from the summit was inflammatory. Its preamble:

> The establishment of Israel is the basic threat that the Arab nation in its entirety has agreed to forestall. And since the existence of Israel is a danger that threatens the Arab nation, the diversion of the Jordan waters by it multiplies the dangers to Arab existence. Accordingly the Arab states have to prepare the plans necessary for dealing with the political, economic, and social aspects, so that if the necessary results are not achieved, collective Arab military preparations, when they are completed, will constitute the ultimate practical means for the final liquidation of Israel.[201]

Army (PLA), with branches in various Arab countries. The Arab leaders had chosen Ahmad al-Shuqayri as its head. He was a veteran of the 1948 war and had served as Saudi Arabia's United Nations representative. He was also Nasser's choice, by whom Nasser hoped to keep the PLO powerless and confined to a symbolic representation. But even symbolically it was perceived as a problem to Jordan, with their majority Palestinian population. Hussein barred all PLO activity in Jordan, including recruitment. The Syrians, however, were more sympathetic to the cause for their own purposes: they planned to use the Palestinians to conduct cross-border raids.

The nascent nationalist identity of Palestinians was beginning to emerge from the decade of invisibility and defeat. "In the refugee camps, the workplaces, the schools, and the universities where Palestinians congregated in the years after 1948, we find the beginnings, the prehistory as it was

It was the first collective public Arab statement calling for the destruction of the Jewish state.

The preamble was followed by individual decisions: one was to establish the Palestinian Liberation Organization (PLO), and another was to establish a unified Arab military command under an Egyptian General. The PLO was under the jurisdiction of the Arab League and Egypt, and it was Nasser's desire to keep control of it. But the PLO had already spawned military arms, the Palestinian Liberation

of a new generation of Palestinian nationalist groups and movements which started clandestinely in the 1950s...."[202] One group of these young leaders had fled to Gaza following the 1948 war in which they had fought, were educated at Cairo University in the 1950s, and after the Suez War left for Kuwait, where they found better-paying jobs than in Egypt. Among the early leaders was Salah Khalaf, Khalil al-Wazir, and, as Rashid Khalidi notes, "a young clean-shaven engineering student...later to become known as

Yasser Arafat." These leaders founded Fatah, a party that later became dominant in the PLO. Influenced by Frantz Fanon, the theoretician of the armed revolt and struggle in Algeria, they believed that Arab unity would not be possible without the liberation of Palestine.

The Israelis took quite seriously the statements coming out of the Arab summits. In addressing a party forum, Golda Meir, an Israeli Cabinet member, stated that "even though some Arab states went along rather reluctantly with the summit decisions, Israel had to assume that the United Arab Command would not be a mere paper organization." General Yitzhak Rabin saw it as the turning point in the history of the Arab-Israeli conflict. He believed that the origins of the Six-Day War could be traced to the Cairo summit conference.[203]

A second Arab summit in September of the same year approved the plans of the first, including the diversion of the headwaters of the Jordan River and the unified military command. The summit welcomed the establishment of the PLO and issued a proclamation calling for the liberation of Palestine. Israel's representative at the United Nations accused the Arab states of violating the UN Charter by calling for the liquidation of another member state. More significantly, Israel claimed that it had been attacked by the Syrians. Knowing it would constitute a significant act of escalation, Prime Minister Levi Eshkol gave permission to Rabin to use the Israeli Air Force (IAF) to destroy the machinery the Syrians had started to assemble near the border to divert the waters of the Jordan.[204]

The Slide Toward War
With the increasing military activity of Fatah and the PFLP from 1964 to 1967, Palestinian influence on events continued to grow. As 1967 began, Fatah stepped up its infiltrations

In the refugee camps, the workplaces, the schools, and the universities where Palestinians congregated in the years after 1948, we find the beginnings... of a new generation of Palestinian nationalist... movements which started clandestinely....

and left explosives designed to kill civilians and create terror in Israel. This presumably would instigate the hoped-for crises that would unite the Arab governments against Israel and lead to war. Syria was pushing Palestinian militancy even as Egypt and Jordan sought to contain the Palestinian Liberation Organization. All of these events and reactions continued the slide toward war. According to Shlaim, it was a war that none of the adversaries really wanted. "The war resulted from a crisis slide that neither Israel nor her enemies were able to control. Israel inadvertently unleashed this avalanche by issuing a series of threats to act against the Syrian regime unless it stopped its support for Palestinian guerillas...."[205] In May, Chief of Staff Yitzhak Rabin announced he would occupy Damascus and overthrow the Syrian government. Israel misjudged Russia's support for the Baath regime. The Soviets intervened and sent a report to Nasser indicating

in 1966, his primacy had been continually challenged, especially by Hussein and the Jordanians. He had a defense pact with Syria. Most commentators agree that Nasser neither wanted nor planned to go to war with Israel. He embarked on an exercise in brinkmanship that carried him over the brink.[206]

Nasser took three actions. First he sent a large number of Egyptian troops into the Sinai. Then he asked the United Nations to remove the UN Emergency Force (UNEF) from the Sinai, part of his right in the Suez. Secretary General U Thant granted his request, and the Egyptians took over the UN posts on the frontier. When U Thant asked Israel if it would accept UNEF as a buffer, Israel refused. Finally Nasser closed the Straights of Tiran to Israeli shipping, an act that Israel could not but perceive as a cause for war.[207]

Israel paused for two weeks before taking action. It was a traumatic period for the Israelis. Shlaim reports: "During

that Israeli forces were building up on the Syrian border and preparing to invade. Israel's belligerent language played into the perception.

Nasser knew the report was untrue, but he was trapped. He had continued to vie for dominance in the leadership of the Arab states. All through this period his army had been bogged down in a war in Yemen. He was quite aware of Israel's military superiority, but to maintain his credibility in the Arab world he had to do something. Since the Samu raid

the period the entire nation succumbed to a collective psychosis. The memory of the Holocaust was a powerful psychological force that deepened the feelings of isolation and accentuated the perception of threat."[208] Even though they had military superiority, the Israelis experienced these events as an existential crisis for survival. Eshkol and Rabin, who had done so much to prepare the IDF for war, were unequal to the task of leading the nation in a crisis where there was a high risk of war actually occurring.[209] Their indecisiveness contributed to the trauma, so much so that Rabin had a temporary breakdown.

Out of their failure and a series of internal gyrations, a unity government was formed. Against the wishes of Eshkol and Golda Meir, Moshe Dayan was named the Minister of Defense. Menachem Begin became a minister without a portfolio. Dayan severely undermined Rabin's authority by activating the IDF reserves. When Rabin consulted with the now retired Ben-Gurion, the old man brutally dressed Rabin down for mobilizing the reserves:

> I very much doubt whether Nasser wanted to go to war, and now we are in serious trouble. You have led the state into a grave situation. We must not go to war. We are isolated. You bear the responsibility.[210]

Rabin was incapacitated at home for a day, received medical attention, and returned to full activity the following day.

Egypt, who had defense pacts with both Jordan and Syria, decided for one more attempt at accommodation. When a car filled with explosives exploded at a Jordanian border post, Hussein broke off relations with Syria.[212] Nasser's allies were now enemies. It did not preclude a unified success. Though he was planning to send his vice-president to the United States to seek a way around the confrontation in the Straits of Tiran, it was too late. On June 5, Dayan attacked the Egyptians and nearly obliterated the Egyptian air fields. In the space of three hours, Israel had already dealt a death blow to Egypt's greatest threat. The rest was cleanup.[213] On June 8 Egypt accepted a ceasefire, and by the next day Israel had reached the Suez Canal, occupied Sharm al-Shayak on the Straits of Tiran, and occupied Gaza.

Israel offered Hussein a ceasefire on the first day, but Hussein had entered the pact with Egypt weeks before

Israeli Foreign Minister Abba Eban was in Washington seeking support to have the United States (or France or Britain) force the Egyptians to open the straits of Tiran. He failed. Meeting with President Lyndon Johnson, he was told that "it was the unanimous view of his military experts that there was no sign that the Egyptians were planning to attack Israel and that if they did attack, the Israelis would 'whip the hell out of them.'"[211] They did.

in May. With the largest number of Palestinian refugees, Hussein had little choice but to begin shelling Israel.[214] The IDF responded with full force. Within two days Hussein sought a ceasefire. But by then Israel had moved into the West Bank toward the Jordan River.

On June 9 Syria, which had contributed so much to the crises and little to the fighting, asked for a ceasefire as well. There had as yet not been a serious engagement with them. Israel had destroyed the Syrian Air Force at the same time as the Egyptian. Without informing either Eshkol or Rabin, Dayan ordered an all-out assault.[215] Though angered by Dayan's actions, Eshkol wanted him to proceed as far as possible into Syria to capture the headwaters of the Jordan River. Israel agreed to a ceasefire on June 7, but continued their offensive into Syria, occupying the key town of Qunaitra on June 10 after it had been abandoned by the retreating Syrians.[216] The war was over.

The *U.S.S. Liberty*

Even though the United States had been supportive of (or at least did not seek to stop) the Israeli aggression, on June 8 Israel attacked an intelligence-gathering naval vessel, the *U.S.S. Liberty.* Thirty-four Americans were killed and more than seventy were wounded. The incident was covered up for thirty years, and only then was the complete story told and the survivors honored.

pilots reporting back to base that the ship was American and that he could see the flag.[217]

Israel claimed it was accidental, and the Johnson administration backed them up. Despite the anger of many top-level government officials privy to what had happened, they fumed in private. No investigation was authorized that might endanger Israel's account of the incident. Johnson ordered Clark Clifford to prepare a report without benefit of independent inquiry. The Clifford Report accepted the Israeli explanation and was classified Top Secret.[218]

In a grim way, this little-known incident also illustrates US support for Israel, even when it is against US interests and cost the lives of innocent Americans. The full story is published by Americans for Middle East Understanding (AMEU) on their website (as listed in the bibliography, in the online resource at http://resources.gbgm-umc.org/israelpalestine).

The *Liberty* was positioned in international waters off Gaza and assigned to monitor communications of the Israeli and Arab armies. Starting at 0600 hours on June 8, the fourth day of the war, Israeli planes began a series of eight reconnaissance flights to observe the ship. James Ennes, Jr., saw seven of the eight overflights from his position on the bridge. At 1000, two Mirage III fighter-bombers flew close enough that he could see the pilots through binoculars. "If I could see the pilots in their cockpits, the pilots could certainly see our flag and no doubt the ship's name and number." *Liberty* radio operators overheard one of the

The June 1967 War, or the Six-Day War as Israel calls it, was Israel's most spectacular military victory. Because of the completeness and speed of the victory, Israel has been accused of deliberately provoking the war in order to fulfill their long-standing territorial ambitions. Avi Shlaim, an Israeli historian unafraid of criticizing Israel, categorically denies this. "The Six-Day War was a defensive war. It was launched by Israel to safeguard its security, not to expand its territory. The main enemy was Egypt."[219]

Implications of the War

The victory changed the whole complexion of things in the Middle East for Israel, for Palestinians and the struggle for statehood, and for United States foreign policy. It completely obliterated the Arab nations' self-image and standing. The Arab world was reeling from the defeat and suffering from a sense of doom, especially in the defeated countries.[220] Nasser resigned in humiliation but was restored to his presidency with the acclamation of his public. The victory also radically changed the perception of Israel for the Jewish community in the United States and elsewhere. The war and its aftermath still haunt the continuing Israel-Palestine conflict of today. With the acquisition of Gaza and the West Bank, Israel controlled 1.1 million Palestinians: 600,000 in the West Bank, 70,000 in East Jerusalem, and 350,000 in Gaza (200,000 West Bank Palestinians had become refugees and had fled or were expelled into Jordan).[221] In occupying the Old City of Jerusalem, Israel immediately bulldozed 135 homes and evicted 650 people to create a plaza at the base of the Haram al-Sharif, called by the Jews the Temple Mount, and the Western Wall. Within days of the war's end, Israel took over some twenty-five miles of the West Bank beyond the 2.3 square miles that had been Jordanian Jerusalem. Israel annexed this territory to the municipal boundaries of Israeli Jerusalem, or, as it became known, West Jerusalem.[222]

Resolution 242

The area that Israel claims as East Jerusalem was not part of the city but part of the West Bank. Neither the international community nor the Palestinians recognized the annexation of the territory and its incorporation into Israel by the Israeli Knesset. The international community through the United Nations Security Council passed Resolution 242 to counter Israeli actions following the 1967 war. The resolution remains at the heart of any possibility for a just peace in Israel-Palestine (see UN Resolutions, found at http://resources.gbgm-umc.org/israelpalestine, for the text of the resolution).

In every peace proposal from 1967 to the present, the starting point is this resolution (SC 242), which insists that the Palestinian state be situated on the land that Israel conquered in the 1967 war, and that Israeli armed forces withdraw from territories occupied in the conflict, including East Jerusalem. There were arduous negotiations surrounding the passage of the resolution. The Israelis insisted on changing one of the sentences which originally read, "from *the* territories occupied or all the territories occupied" to "from territories occupied," in order to protect their own understanding of what their borders would be, and from their perspective to ensure Israeli security. The Arab nations expected a return to the status quo before the war, a complete Israeli withdrawal from all Occupied Territories, much as they had after the Suez War.

The Allon Plan

Levi Eshkol, the prime minister after the victory, informed the Israeli public that, "there should be no illusion that Israel is prepared to return to the conditions that existed a week ago.... We have fought alone for our existence and security and are therefore justified in deciding for ourselves what are the genuine and indispensable interests of our state...."[223] The Israeli Cabinet deliberated, considering their options after their unexpected victory, and settled on a plan that addressed security needs. The plan is referred to as the Allon Plan, named after Yigal Allon, the Deputy Prime Minister. It called for incorporating certain occupied territory into Israel, including:

> ...a strip of land ten to fifteen kilometers wide along the Jordan River; most of the Judean desert along the Dead Sea; and a substantial area around Greater Jerusalem including the Latrum salient.[224]

Israel was coming to grips with the new reality for their state as they considered territory three times larger than existed following the 1948 war. It was also pursuing bilateral peace agreements with the Arab nations as they had in the 1948 armistice process. Israel initially was prepared to turn back parts of the captured territories for peace.

The Three No's

In August, however, the Arab nations held a summit meeting in Khartoum (without Syria, which boycotted the meeting). The summit concluded with a resolution containing what are called the Three No's: "namely, no peace with Israel, no recognition of Israel, no negotiations with it, and insistence on the rights of the Palestinian people in their own country."[225] It was not meant, however, to be as strident as the No's made it seem. The preamble of the statement indicated that international negotiations

The plan would have incorporated the fewest Palestinians possible. Israel would have allowed for the rest of the West Bank to be an autonomous region linked economically to Israel. The Allon Plan was neither accepted nor rejected. Other discussions included establishing army bases and sending Jewish settlers into the West Bank. This was initiated almost immediately in the Golan Heights and was Moshe Dayan's preferred course of defense.

were an option and could proceed in order to obtain Israeli withdrawal; however, the No's seemed to negate the preamble. Israel's immediate response was to seal itself off from any serious peace settlement or negotiation. What was not known at the time was that the Arab resolution was partly a face-saving device. It was also a compromise for Nasser, who was attacked by his former Arab allies and blamed for losing the war. By opening the door to international and diplomatic initiatives,

Nasser was trying to find a political settlement. The No's were intended to placate Syrian intransigence and Palestinian fears.

In a conversation that King Hussein reported to Avi Shlaim, Nasser had urged King Hussein to "go and speak of a comprehensive solution to the problem and a comprehensive peace and go do anything you can short of signing a separate peace."[226] But it was not to be. The outcome was the Arabs would not consider peace without Israeli withdrawal and Israel would not consider withdrawal without direct negotiations that would lead to a peace agreement that incorporated secure and recognized boundaries.[227]

SC 242 is another ambiguous document in the list of politically equivocal papers and resolutions that have punctuated the Arab-Israeli conflict from the days of the Mandate. There is one explicit, unambiguous declaration that has had lasting impact: the inadmissibility of the acquisition of territory

The War of Attrition

The period from the 1967 war until the Yom Kippur war in 1973 was characterized by failure and hostility. The Soviets and the United States appropriated arms for their respective Cold War clients and engaged in diplomatic and political posturing. From 1968-1970 there was a period dubbed the War of Attrition. It was during those years that Richard Nixon, William Rogers, and Henry Kissinger managed American foreign policy and sided ever more closely with Israel. The War of Attrition was costly to both Israel and Egypt and barely brought a hiatus to hostilities, let alone peace. Although Egypt got by far the worst of the conflict, both sides exaggerated the punishment in arms and life inflicted on the other. A reasonable estimate is that about 10,000 Egyptian civilians and military were killed, compared to fewer than 400 Israelis who died on the Egyptian front.[230] The conflict ended in a ceasefire that the Israelis claimed

by war. But SC 242 reduced the Palestinians to the "refugee problem." They are mentioned only indirectly in a hope for a just settlement of the refugee problem.[228] Still controlled by Egypt, the Palestinian Liberation Organization rejected the resolution because it ignored the right of the refugees to return to their homes.[229] The Palestinian hope for self-determination was dimmed, but by 1967 they were preparing to take their future into their own hands.

as victory because of the perseverance of the Israel Air Force (IAF) and its retention of forces on the eastern shore of the Suez Canal. But in fact the casualties were proportionally higher for Israel, and the grind of the war depleted Israel's self-image of military superiority.

The Egyptians in turn considered the war a success, since Egypt had held its own militarily, punishing the Israeli lines, albeit with the significant support of the Soviet Union. During this time, Egypt gained a self-confidence that seemed to have been irreparably damaged in the previous defeats of 1948, 1956, and 1967.[231] Indeed, during the last stages of the war, it seemed that Egyptian aircraft defenses had found a way to contain the IAF. Egyptian General Gamsay recorded that although the War of Attrition had been "a tremendous burden on both Egypt and Israel…in the final analysis it was beneficial to Egypt and proved harmful to Israel."[232]

In 1971 Egypt under Nasser's successor, Anwar al-Sadat, tried to sue for peace, offering to sign a treaty and open the Suez Canal to Israeli shipping if Israel would remove its forces a few miles from the canal. Still under Golda Meir's premiership, Israel would not consider it, largely ignoring the overtures from Sadat. So did Nixon and Kissinger. But Sadat persisted.

The United Nations dispatched special envoy Gunner Jarring to negotiate an even more comprehensive agreement that would include Israel's withdrawal to the pre-1967

of the US State Department, Joseph Sisco, who stated: "Israel will be considered responsible for the rejection of the best opportunity to achieve peace since the establishment of the state."[233]

The 1973 war was in large part a response to Sadat's frustrated attempts to reach a settlement. Under Ariel Sharon, commander of Israel's southern command, brutalities increased in the Sinai, as well as in the refugee camps in Gaza and against Palestinian civilians and feda'iyyin guerillas in Lebanon, now aligned with the Fateh leadership in the Palestinian Liberation Organization. In February 1972 Sharon's operations drove around 10,000 farmers and Bedouins from northeast Sinai. Sharon's forces destroyed crops and wells so that Jewish settlements and a resort could be built.[234] This foreshadowed Israeli policy for the next three decades. Mirroring earlier patterns when a Palestinian raid from southern Lebanon

borders. In exchange, Egypt would agree to respect Israel's independence, its right to live within secure borders, and its right of passage through the Suez Canal and the Strait of Tiran. Subject to further deliberation, Sadat agreed to discuss the more significant proposal. But Golda Meir again refused, reiterating that there would be no return to the pre-1967 borders. Another major opportunity for peace with at least one Arab neighbor failed. The general international consensus was reflected by a senior official

killed three Israelis, the IDF went into Lebanon, killing sixty persons and wounding 100. In September 1972, when two Israeli soldiers were killed in the Golan Heights, Israel again went into Lebanon, killing twenty-three Lebanese civilians, eighteen Lebanese soldiers, and thirty Palestinian guerrillas.[235]

The hostilities continued to escalate, and once again war appeared to be in the offing. In 1972 between 700 and 1,000 Arabs were killed, as well as thirty-six

Israelis,[236] including the Munich athletes at the Olympic Village in Munich, Germany. In 1973 Israel attacked Syrian aircraft, razed the Syrian village of Dail, and shot down a Cairo-bound Libyan airliner that had strayed into Israeli airspace over the Sinai. The United Nations General Assembly, over the objections of the United States, passed three resolutions condemning Israeli destruction of almost 16,000 homes in Gaza, reiterating the right of return of the 1967 refugees, and a declaration of the Palestinian right to self-determination.[237]

Fearing another war in the Middle East and reacting to the failure to mediate any significant agreements during Secretary of State William Rogers' various initiatives, the United States sent Henry Kissinger to a summit meeting in Moscow. Kissinger successfully convinced Leonid Brezhnev, the Soviet Premier, to accede to a status quo policy in the Middle East in exchange for US trade credits

Sadat then finally acted after a summit in Washington when Golda Meir refused US mediation to withdraw from the Sinai. Sadat had received funding from Saudi Arabia to purchase Soviet armaments. Saudi King Faisal had mistrusted Nasser and distanced himself from him because of the leftist leanings of Pan-Arabism and its Third-World liberation rhetoric that he believed to be communism. Faisal, a conservative, understood both communism and Zionism as threats to his monarchy and to the Middle East, in that order.

Sadat gained more credibility with the King and with that, financial support. Anwar al-Sadat and Hafaz al-Assad saw the Israeli occupation of the Sinai and other Arab lands as an intolerable situation. Coupled with growing dissent on the part of his Egyptian subjects, this led Sadat to a military agreement with Syria to force Israel into a two-front war in the hope of restoring a positive Arab self-image after the debacle of 1967.

and technology. Both Sadat and President Hafez al-Assad of Syria came to realize that Arab humiliation and the occupation of Arab lands by the Israelis was of no real interest to the Soviets. With the Soviets' refusal of additional armaments for Egypt, Sadat expelled thousands of Soviet advisors from Egypt, surprising both the Russians and Americans. Kissinger thought it was a victory for his diplomacy. Instead, fearing a complete loss of influence, the Soviets armed President Assad.

The Yom Kippur War

Kissinger's hope for the status quo to continue came to an end on October 6, 1973, as Syria attacked Israeli forces in the Golan Heights, and Egyptian forces attacked the IDF in the Sinai. It came to be known as the Yom Kippur War in Israel and the West, as it was launched on the Day of Atonement, the holiest day in the calendar for religious Jews. Because it was also the anniversary of Muhammad's first military victory at Badr in 624 C.E., it was called

Operation Badr by Syria and Egypt. Regardless of the name, there was nothing religious about the war.

The war came as a significant setback for Israel. Although Israel ultimately prevailed, the Syrians and Egyptians fought with significant effect. Among other weaponry, the Syrians were armed with Russian-made missiles (SAM: surface-to-air missiles used to counter aircraft) and two armored divisions with tanks. At the outset, on the Syrian front, the Israelis were outnumbered by more than five-to-one in armored vehicles and twenty-to-one in guns. During the next four days, the biggest tank battle since World War II was fought.[238] Israel finally overcame the Syrians and pushed them back into Syria. But reinforced by Iraqi and Jordanian forces, the Syrians were not broken and still presented a tenacious opponent.[239]

In the south, the Egyptians were more soundly defeated. But they won two six-mile strips of territory in Israeli-occupied

Council Resolution 338 (see UN Resolutions, found in the online resource at http://resources.gbgm-umc.org/israelpalestine, for the text of the resolution).

Israel came out the victor, but it was a major blow for its leaders. Although the vaunted Israeli Intelligence agency knew that Syria and Egypt were prepared to go to war, they had not informed Golda Meir and Moshe Dayan until midnight the night before the attacks[241] that war was imminent. They decided against a preemptive attack. The Agranat Commission was set up after the war to determine why Israel was not better prepared. It determined that it was not a failure in intelligence but a failure to read the information correctly. Avi Shlaim, however, sees the failure as one of Israeli policy that was overconfident in its "power to deter the Arab attack."[242]

The political fallout created the most significant change in Israeli politics since the 1948 war. Although reelected in

Sinai and held onto them. The Egyptians also won back their self-respect. Fearing it would serve as a provocation to the Russians, the United States reluctantly airlifted supplies to Israel, including a $2.2 billion aid package. King Faisal countered by imposing an oil embargo against the Americans and any European nations rendering aid to Israel and the United States.[240] On October 22, with Moscow's initiative, a ceasefire was negotiated with Kissinger. The United Nations responded with Security

December 1973, Golda Meir and Dayan were both severely attacked for failing to anticipate the war and for their conduct of foreign policy. The dissatisfaction with the old guard of the Labor party led to demonstrations calling for their resignations. On April 10, Golda Meir, feeling her seventy-five years and wracked by guilt, resigned. Yitzhak Rabin and Shimon Peres succeeded her. The real failure was Israel's failure to come to grips with the Arab world. Golda Meir and Ben-Gurion before her saw the world as black and white, a world in which Israel could do no wrong and the Arabs no right.[243] Shlaim sums up Israel's and Golda Meir's inability to change their iron-wall approach to the Arab nations.

> More than most Israeli leaders, she exhibited the siege mentality, the notion that Israel had to barricade itself behind an iron wall, the fatalistic belief that Israel was doomed forever to live by the sword.... In her five years as prime minister she made two monumental mistakes. First, she turned down Jarring's suggestion that Israel should trade Sinai for peace with Egypt, the very terms on which the Egyptian-Israeli peace treaty was to be based eight years later. Second, she turned down Sadat's proposal for an interim settlement, thus leaving him no option except to go to war in order to subvert an intolerable status quo. Few leaders talked more about peace and did less to give it a chance to develop.[244]

Chapter 5

The Aftermath

There are three significant matters related to the 1967 war that are of particular significance for contemporary events. First is the rise of religious Zionism and Jewish fundamentalism in Israel and Islamic fundamentalism or the Islamist movements in the Arab nations and in the Occupied Territories. Second is the ascendance of Fateh and the feda'iyyin guerilla groups within the larger framework of the Palestinian Liberation Organization. Third, because of the nature of the change it represented, is the cultural, religious-emotional, and nationalistic adoption by American Jewry of the Jewish state, when previously the majority of American Jews were at best lukewarm toward Israel.

Rise of Fundamentalism

On May 14 immediately preceding the June 1967 war, Israel celebrated its nineteenth Independence Day. At the Merkaz

All this land is ours, absolutely belonging to all of us, non-transferable to others even in part. It is clear that there are no "Arab territories" or "Arab lands" here but only the lands of Israel, the eternal heritage of our forefathers to which others have come, upon which they have built without our permission and in our absence.[245]

The address on this day was different. Rabbi Kook recalled his sorrow on that first Independence Day when the United Nations presented the partition plan that divided the land. He lamented: "Yes, where is our Hebron—have we forgotten it? And where is our Schechem and our Jericho, where—will we forget them? And all of Transjordan—it is all ours, every single clod of earth, each little bit, every part of the land is part of the land of God—is it in our own power to surrender even one millimeter of it?!"[246] His devoted disciples (called Gahelet, or embers) asked whether they should attend the military parade the

HaRav Talmudic Academy in Jerusalem the guests were gathered to hear Rabbi Tzvi Yehuda Kook give his annual address marking the occasion. Israel was on the verge of a major conflict and in a severe economic depression. As noted above, the country was experiencing high anxiety. Rabbi Kook was a proponent of a Jewish messianic theology that looked forward to the restoration of the biblical Eretz Israel, the whole land of Israel. That included the West Bank, then still under Jordan's rule. Rabbi Kook wrote:

next day. He urged them to do so, as the army was there to liberate Eretz Yisrael.

When Israel's lightning conquest of not only the West Bank but the Sinai and Golan Heights occurred just weeks later, Rabbi Kook appeared divinely inspired. Some of his graduates were part of an elite paratrooper unit. One student recalled Rabbi Kook saying after the war that God had done his part, and it was now up to them. What was their part? "Our part was of course settlement," the student recalled. Rabbi Kook's followers, particularly the Gahelet, became leaders of Gush Emunim (the Block of the Faithful), an extremist movement that would play a key role in the colonization of the West Bank with settlements, following the 1973 war.[247]

The New Messianism

Up until the 1967 war, Orthodox Jews were not Zionists. Most Orthodox sects were clear that the establishment of a new Israel was to be the work of the Messiah when he came. To force religion onto politics was vehemently opposed. But a new messianism was born out of the unexpected victory. Rabbi Tzvi Yehuda Hacohen Kook (1890-1982) was the son of Rabbi Avraham Yitzhak Hacohen Kook the elder (1865-1935), who was the Chief Rabbi of Palestine from 1920 to 1935. It was Kook the elder whose thought and teaching were the origin of the

marriage between Jewish messianism and political action. It is not unlike Islamic and Christian apocalyptic messianism. Rabbi Kook's ideology assumes the immanent coming of the Messiah and asserts that the Jews:

> aided by God, will triumph over the non-Jews and rule over them forever (presumably good for the non-Jews.) All current political developments will either help bring this about sooner or will delay it. Jewish sins, in particular a lack of faith, can postpone the coming of the Messiah, but not for long. Even the worst sins of the Jews cannot alter the course of redemption. The calamitous events of modern history are examples of punishment. The elder Rabbi Kook did not pretend to hide his joy over the loss of lives in World War I; he explained that this was necessary in order to begin to break Satan's Power.[248]

Rabbi Kook the younger capitalized on the urgency and imminence of the religious ideology following the 1967 war,

It is clear that there are no "Arab territories" or "Arab lands" here but only the lands of Israel.

and his followers expanded the political project. He was the leader of the settler movement, Gush Emunim. Both the elder and the younger Kooks taught that secular Zionists, through their conquests of the Land of Israel (Eretz Yisrael), had unwittingly brought about the beginning of the messianic age. Gush Emunim supporters believe that the coming of the Messiah can be hastened through Jewish settlement on land that they understand God has allotted to the Jewish people as outlined in the Hebrew Bible.

This and the growth of other branches of Jewish fundamentalism, the Haredim and their political projects, have combined to alter the face of Israeli politics. These movements, aligned often with one or the other of Israel's political parties, have continued to undermine any settlement with the Palestinians, who as non-Jews are not part of the religious parties' aims or objectives for Eretz Israel. These political parties have exercised major influence in the Knesset and over both the Labor and Likud governments that have been in power in Israel since the 1970s and especially with the election of Menachem Begin (1977) and his successors, Benjamin Netanyahu and Ariel Sharon (recall that Begin was a follower of Lev Jabotinsky, the founder of the Revisionist Zionist Party). The National Religious Party (NRP) includes a number of these associations, realignments, and coalitions of different groups.

Return have become citizens of Israel. Others hold joint US-Israeli citizenship and are permitted to vote in elections in the United States. Often, prior to US presidential elections, subsidized flights return these Israelis to the United States in order to exercise their franchise. This is further evidence of the special relationship between the United States and Israel. (In a conversation with an American-Israeli, Jeff Halper, coordinator of the Israeli Committee Against House Demolitions {ICAHD}, I mentioned my opposition to this Israeli-American joint citizenship. He laughed and said that if the religious settlers had to choose loyalties and either one citizenship or the other, the settlements would empty and the settlers would return to Brooklyn!)

In his book, *On the Border,* Michel Warschawski, an observant Orthodox Jew and a major activist for Palestinian rights, reflects on the strong impact of these movements on Israeli life:

These parties are proponents of a religious racism which some scholars insist is inherent in some of the traditional writings and interpretations of Rabbinic Judaism regarding the non-Jew. They have also spawned the religious settler movements that have terrorized the Palestinian populations of the West Bank and Gaza since Gush Emunim was founded in 1974.

Significant numbers of religious settlers are American Jews who have moved to Israel and because of the Law of

Fifty years after the birth of the Jewish State, the divide that fractures Israeli society is likely to leave very little room for those who defend a vision of a society based on democracy and solidarity, who are secular but respectful of cultural diversities, who are open to the Arab world but enriched with the democratic traditions of the French and American Revolutions.... We must engage simultaneously in a struggle against those who want to make Israel the advance post of the new neoliberal crusade against the nations of the Middle East and those who want to imprison it within an armed ghetto, led by the rabbis of a new messianism, in which fundamentalism and nationalism reinforce each other.[249]

Fateh and Feda'iyyin Guerillas in the PLO

The Palestinian Liberation Organization became the central voice and identity for Palestinian aspirations and self-determination following the 1967 war. After the defeat of the Arab armies in 1967, the Palestinian feda'iyyin was the only group able to counter the Israeli occupation through guerilla raids into the Occupied Territories. Hoping to mobilize Palestinians in the West Bank against the Israelis, they began to organize cells in the West Bank.

It seemed that the classical pattern of Revolutionary War from within could now be applied, and that Fateh's great hour had come. People and weapons were hastily smuggled to the West Bank. Yasser Arafat himself came to lead

1971-1972, it was perhaps in failure that Fateh grew in its importance. In 1968 Israel launched a punitive "invasion" across the Jordan to the town of Al-Karameh, where there was a Palestinian refugee camp and a base for the feda'iyyin and Fateh guerillas.[251] They held their ground against the much greater Israeli forces and fought a heroic battle. By so doing, they inspired the regular Jordanian forces who were deployed in the hills. Together, the Jordanians and the feda'iyyin forced the Israelis to retreat behind their ceasefire lines in the Occupied West Bank.[252]

The Palestinians lost the battle, but it was important in the formation of Palestinian identity for ideological reasons. The Arabic word *al-karameh* means "dignity," and the battle was understood as the beginning of restoring Arab dignity.[253] It gave credence to the Palestinian revolutionary ideology and aspirations for liberation from the Occupation. Al-Karameh became a symbol used by Palestinian nationalist groups both

the organization of his network. Some groups began to be active. However, almost all their cells were detected by the Israeli authorities and their members were put in prison. In a matter of weeks the whole network collapsed.[250]

The Fateh members retreated across the Jordan River and established bases there from which to launch the insurgency. It will be recalled that Jordan had a majority population of Palestinian refugees since 1948. Although organizing resistance was more successful in Gaza until

to expand their ranks with fresh recruits and to pressure Arab regimes to allow them greater freedom of action. It helped to make the PLO a force to reckon with in Arab politics. The battle of al-Karameh was a case of a failure against overwhelming odds being recast as heroic myth.[254]

Through this growing narrative of resistance, the Palestinian Liberation Organization constantly struggled for survival. The PLO kept the Palestinian dream alive in the face of brutal setbacks like Black September (1970), when

King Hussein, increasingly threatened by guerilla activity and politically seeking accommodation with Israel and support from the United States, launched an assault on the feda'iyyin bases in the refugee camps around Amman. It was a costly defeat for the guerillas.[255] With the blessing of the United States, Israel was prepared to enter the conflict if the Syrians had entered in support of the feda'iyyin. But Nasser actively intervened to end the fighting in Jordan.

The defeat of the feda'iyyin and Nasser's death later that year were the tacit end of the revolutionary movement in the Arab world. The feda'iyyin moved to Lebanon where they became victims of the Civil War. In 1975 three Palestinian refugee camps near Beirut were overrun by militias backed indirectly by both Israel and Syria. The inhabitants were either killed or expelled from the camps.[256] The PLO continued to be in the middle of the turmoil in Lebanon, capped by an Israeli incursion into the south

assistance well beyond the scope of the militant cadres of earlier years. The PLO was exiled to Tunisia, Libya, Yemen, the Sudan, Iraq, and Syria. It was a terrible setback, recalling the exodus of 1948 and again from Jordan. One of the hardest things for the Palestinians to accept was that in Lebanon they had lost the support of a local population that had been sympathetic to their cause, due mostly to their own political mistakes.[258]

What followed in the 1980s was serious soul searching by the leadership and much dissension from factions as well as among the Palestinian Refugee leadership from the diaspora. It became clear that unless they could operate within the Occupied Territories, they were becoming obsolete as the voice of Palestinians, of whom another generation was experiencing the oppression of the Israeli Occupation. One could easily argue that the reliance on armed struggle and terrorist actions like the kidnapping and murder of the

of Lebanon in 1978. An invasion by Israel followed, with a nine-week siege of the PLO in Beirut in the summer of 1982. The PLO, the Palestinians, and the Lebanese suffered heavy casualties, an estimated 19,000 killed and 30,000 wounded.[257]

The United States brokered the PLO expulsion from Lebanon where they had built their organization in significant ways. For ten years they had provided support for the Palestinian refugees through social and commercial

Israeli Olympic athletes in 1972 was counter-productive to their goal. Yet they were able to maintain their identity as Palestinians through all of these catastrophes. The Intifada, a spontaneous grassroots uprising in 1987 in which the PLO was initially uninvolved, rejuvenated the nationalist movement. Palestine itself was also reestablished as the center of gravity of Palestinian politics, rather than in the Palestinian diaspora, where it had been located for so many years.[259] It was the Intifada (1987-1991) that eventually led to the world's recognition of the injustice and brutality of the Israeli Occupation, culminating in the failed Madrid conference, the Oslo Declaration of 1993, and the installation of the Palestinian Authority in Jericho and Gaza.

American Jewry and the Jewish State
Personal History: Holocaust Ideology

If my father's stories were representative of his parents' attitude, neither Lena nor Hershel were nostalgic for the old country. When my father was a little boy and a relative or acquaintance from the old days came to visit the Goldsteins on Lenox Avenue in Harlem, there was an aversion to recalling the difficulties of their European past. Once, when a certain cousin was visiting, he referred to one of the pogroms in Poland from their previous lives. My grandmother was intent on shushing him. The past was past. However their former days were remembered, it was a life from which they were

I was vulnerable to verbal abuse and racial epithets from some Gentile schoolmates. I'm sure I didn't think being called names qualified as anti-Semitism, nor did I view the young perpetrators as anti-Semites. Though I had not had any dramatic encounters to solidify such feelings, I was aware of being "different." The one occasion when I was beat up in a fight, however, I doubt my antagonist could have been considered anything but a bully.

The other element that made it problematic for American Jews of my father's generation was the sense of shame they felt toward the victims and survivors. "Had they left Europe as we did, this never would have happened" or "If they hadn't remained in their isolated and parochial communities in the shtetls[260] of Russian Poland and tried instead to be like everyone else, this might not have happened." In our home, Orthodox Jews were not thought of fondly. The eighteenth-century garb of Eastern European Jews was looked upon with

thankful to have been delivered. They clung to their new one in the United States.

Perhaps for even more significant reasons, this ambiguous mindset regarding the slaughter of Jews by the Nazis was carried to my father's generation. Words were inadequate to express the profound pain, fear, and shock elicited by the disclosure of the enormity of the death camps and the world's having turned its back on the Jews of Europe. The lesson I learned was that being Jewish carried some kind of liability.

Intifada:

a spontaneous grassroots uprising.

disapproval, and Hasidic Jews were viewed with disdain. They represented the culture and lifestyle my forebears had fled for a new life here.

In my family circle, overt demonstrations of religious piety or practice were greeted with either embarrassment or antipathy. Along with the abandonment of the old country for the new came a perspective that insisted we were now Americans and shouldn't demonstrate any of the outward signs that defined being Jewish. We wanted to fit in, to be invisible in this post-war America. I even felt mildly uncomfortable wearing a yarmulke when I went to the synagogue.

In the nineteenth and early twentieth centuries, the Jews of Germany and in Austria were intentional in abandoning their distinctive public Jewish behaviors, their religious and cultural norms, in order to find acceptance in the German culture which they had come to love and with which they identified. Austrian and German Jews who were visible in

a desultory way. Since he was a native-born American whose family had come in the early 1900s, I expect he was protecting his own identity by distancing himself from identification with recent European Jewish immigrants. These newcomers had accents and spoke English as a second or third language. Whatever the source of his feelings, I heard his lack of charity for some of his Jewish colleagues who had arrived as recent immigrants, mainly from Germany. But his feelings revealed his ambivalence in responding to the horror of what was then all too recent history.

In a photograph collection I inherited from my aunt some years ago, there was an old heavy cardboard-stock photo of a very fashionably and formally dressed couple from the early years of the twentieth century. On the back in either German or Yiddish was a note to my grandparents, the gist of which was: "Look at us prospering here visiting the famous mineral spring and resort Carlsbad [now in the

upper-class cultural and political circles embraced modern enlightenment thought and believed that whatever anti-Semitism still existed could be overcome by education, the liberalization of society, and Jewish self-improvement. The reward for this assimilation would be acceptance and citizenship. Ultimately, they were mistaken.

I was aware of a mild disdain my father felt for Jews who had fled Hitler's Europe and came to the United States in the 1930s and early 1940s. He referred to them as "refugees" in

Czech Republic]. Aren't you sorry at having fled to the United States?" The couple were probably friends or cousins of Lena or Herschel's, perhaps eventual victims of the Holocaust if they had remained in Europe. Such things were simply not discussed.

More than sixty years have passed since the events of World War II and the nearly successful elimination of European Jewry. It remains a defining element of the Jewish psyche and a significant part of the self-understanding of Israelis. It is not an exaggeration to say that the substance, memory, and presentation of the Holocaust have been a prime factor in the birth and development of the state of Israel; the Holocaust continues to influence the actions and identity of its citizens. The depth of these scars and their impact on the Israeli or any Jewish psyche cannot be underestimated. The pain, the self-imposed sense of failure, and the attendant rage has infected Israeli society in terribly corrupting and unhealthy ways.

The early Zionists had intended Israel to be a safe haven for persecuted Jews, yet ironically Israel had come into existence without being able to save the dead millions. To this day there is a latent hysteria in Israeli life that springs directly from this source. It explains the paranoiac sense of isolation that has been a main characteristic of the Israeli temper since 1948. Generations of Israelis

have been brought up on this grim tenet: Jews were singled out to die not because of their religion or their politics or because of what they did; but simply because they were there, they existed. The message has been instilled in them for years and with far-reaching political, cultural, and religious consequences.[261]

And it has been the single most significant factor in Israel's unwillingness to trust their Arab neighbors or the Palestinians, whose land they have colonized, and who are being victimized on a daily basis.

Since 1948, the Holocaust and the fear of anti-Semitism have also created a consciousness that has contributed significantly to preventing Israel from making peace with its Arab neighbors. This Holocaust consciousness has detracted from and undermined the ongoing search for peace in the Middle East. It is critical that we understand the dynamic that is perpetuating suffering for the Palestinians, a people who

The substance, memory, and presentation of the Holocaust have been a prime factor in the birth and development of the state of Israel; the Holocaust continues to influence the actions and identity of its citizens.

have no substantive connection to the events of the Holocaust. Neither Palestinians nor any other Arab residents of the Middle East were protagonists in the actions of Nazi Germany. The obsession with the Holocaust and anti-Semitism that pervades so much of current Jewish and Israeli discourse and political motivation and action is lethal for the Palestinians living under Occupation, but it is self-destructive for Israelis as well. The burden of this Holocaust consciousness also prevents progressive US Christians from making the necessary connections that would lead to actively raising concern about the Israeli Occupation of what is left of *Palestinian* Palestine.

It is a troubling reality to acknowledge Christian complicity in the destruction of European Jewry. The Nazis in large part were European Christians. The Lutheran and Roman Catholic Churches of Germany and Austria, though also victimized, were generally passive in their opposition to the murder of the six million Jews and of the hundreds of thousands of other innocent victims of genocide in the death camps. We are constantly reminded of the Holocaust through the arts and in the media, as well as in our schools, museums, civic commemorations, and religious institutions. Coupled with these reminders are the political rhetoric and the unexamined blanket support for Israel by our government and in large part by our churches. This has paralyzed our ability to have the serious discourse that might help us examine what it would mean to live in a post-Holocaust day of healing.

This conflict has turned history's most celebrated victims, the Jews (and in this case Israelis), into victimizers of the Palestinians. As Christians, we must find our voice and work responsibly to say that the Holocaust does not afford Israel or its supporters the right to perpetuate an illegal and immoral occupation. Thanks in part to the

Standing behind each Arab

or Palestinian, Israelis tend to see SS men determined to push them once again into gas chambers and crematoria.[262]

United States, Israel is the most powerful country in the Middle East. They were arguably never and certainly have not been for the last forty years at the mercy of anyone in the Arab world, in spite of the torrential propaganda that floods our media.

One strong voice in Israel belongs to Amira Hass, the *only* Israeli journalist who lives and reports from the Occupied Territories. She lived for a time in the Gaza Strip and currently resides in Ramallah, the largest Palestinian city in the Occupied Territories. The daughter of death-camp survivors, she has used her parents' experience and the subsequent witness of their lives to move beyond the horrors of that former time. Her parents had stories to explain their own commitment to justice.

> These narratives were my parents' legacy—a history of resisting injustice, speaking out and fighting back. But of all of their memories that had become my own, one stood out beyond the others. One summer day in 1944, my mother was herded from a cattle car along with the rest of its human cargo, which had been transported from Belgrade [then Yugoslavia, now the capital of Serbia and Montenegro] to the concentration camp at Bergen-Belsen. She saw a group of German women, some on foot, some on bicycles, slow down as the strange procession went by and watch with indifferent curiosity on their faces. For me, these women became a loathsome symbol of watching from the sidelines, and at an early age I decided that my place was not with the bystanders.[263]

our exposed nerve. I needed to know the people whose lives had been forever altered by my society and my history, whose parents and grandparents, refugees, were forced from their villages in 1948.[264]

I believe that you and I have a responsibility not to be bystanders to this Occupation and to these injustices. It is frightening that the same indifference that in part allowed the Nazi Holocaust to occur is again paralyzing us from acting. Is it too simplistic to insist that as Christians we are called to witness to something deeper and wider than death, more powerful than the symbol of all of humanity's inhumanity? Are we not called to witness to the cross of Jesus Christ and to the possibility of life beyond such manifest oppression? Are we not called to testify when oppressors use their identity as the oppressed with stories of sixty years ago but through some failure of perception cannot see what transpires now in the shadow of the Holocaust? Is our response one of

Ms. Hass writes that her reason for moving from the security of Israel proper to Gaza was that she could not bear to be a bystander:

> ...from my need to understand, down to the last detail, a world that is, to the best of my political and historical comprehension, a profoundly Israeli creation. To me, Gaza embodies the entire saga of the Israeli-Palestinian conflict; it represents the central contradiction of the State of Israel—democracy for some, dispossession for others; it is

despair or indifference that witnesses to the "death of God" rather than the Resurrected Christ?

Marc Ellis, in his book *Ending Auschwitz: The Future of Jewish and Christian Life,* provides a theological understanding that can address this Holocaust mentality. Dr. Ellis asks whether Jewish piety as expressed by those lost in the ovens, was a witness not to the silence of God (to quote Eliezer Berkovits, an Orthodox Jewish theologian) but rather the possibility of taking "cognizance of the tragedy and promise of existence and whether one may hold on to the promise in spite of the tragedy."[265]

Ellis asks his questions within a radical critique of Jewish power and struggles with the full integrity of his thought and his identity as a modern Jew, and also within the context of listening to what Christian thinkers have said about the same concerns. Ellis sees, I believe, a glimmer of the cross and of resurrection as constructs in his search for meaning in our post-Holocaust world. While not embracing Christianity, he is willing to cross the barrier between the two faiths to find a just answer to both Auschwitz and the Occupation. In his struggle, he concludes with this reflection, honoring those like Rubenstein and Greenberg but wanting something more for the future:

> I, along with others of my generation, would soon be on our own; for the generation forged at Auschwitz is giving way to a new generation, one that champions and dissents....

Would we one day...find ourselves in the unexpected role as guardians of a tradition we challenged and thereby helped to create? The creation is, of course, not nearly as easy as the critique; nor is living at the end when others are celebrating a rebirth. But what could one hope for after Auschwitz and 1492 [a reference to the expulsion of the Jews from Spain in that year], except to end those events, thus holding out the promise of a new and unpredictable beginning.[266]

For me, this points to a theology of resurrection, offering a hope beyond spiritual captivity to a world "shrouded in darkness," where the Jewish experience of Holocaust "is a paradigm for the future of other peoples...."[267]

A response had to be found to the apparent meaninglessness of religion and its rituals or of a belief in an omniscient and moral God in the face of the terrible images, narratives, and memories that the Holocaust created. Given the absolute impossibility of finding an easy solution or answer, existential

US Aid to Israel

- Total grants and loans to Israel from the United States in 1997: over $5.5 billion.

- Total US aid to Israel from 1949 to 1996 was the same as US aid to all of sub-Sahara Africa, Latin America, and the Caribbean combined.

- From 1948 to 2003, direct US aid to Israel totaled $89.9 billion, not including loan guarantees and cancelled debts.

- Since 1975, Israel has been the largest recipient of US aid on an annual basis (Egypt, with a population twelve times that of Israel, is second).

- Aid to Israel from the United States has some unique features, such as waiving the repayment of loans. Israel receives all of its US aid in the first thirty days of the fiscal year

(other countries receive aid in three or four installments).

Sources: "The Washington Report on Middle East Affairs," quoting the Congressional Research Service (The Library of Congress) Fact Sheets on Israel-Palestine (http://www.pcusa.org/worldwide/israelpalestine/resources.htm. See the website for sources for the fact sheets.)

or spiritual (as if one could be had in some simple creedal equation or religious proscription or doctrine), a living possibility was substituted. Israel, with its unexpected and perhaps inexplicable victory, resonated with a contradiction to the narrative of powerlessness and defeat. It was also the time of the Vietnam War in the American consciousness, a time for many of doubt, despair, and anger. Was there not anything good to be found anywhere at all? Although I demonstrated against the wars in Southeast Asia, I recall finding something laudable in Israel's victory over the Arab Goliath, but I knew next to nothing about the actual history, let alone the narrative of the Palestinian people. The Palestinians were to me merely an enemy that Israel rose from the ashes to defeat in order to survive. It was a practical response to begin venerating Israel and perhaps also a way to avoid the darker questions that the Holocaust raised, even for those not claiming theological sophistication or

distant from our awareness. Visiting Israel, we are presented with a narrative that feeds the empty space in our beings and gives us something palpable to embrace.

I think that Ellis underlines my sense in his analysis of Elie Wiesel's role as the spokesperson for the unspeakable nature of the Holocaust.

> In Wiesel's written works and public presentations there is no mention of biblical claims to the land of Judea and Samaria—or even the land that comprises the 1967 borders of Israel—nor is there discussion of settlements and settlers or religious shrines and attachments. Jerusalem is spoken about in an abstract, mystical way, as is the 1967 war, where for Wiesel the Israeli soldiers carried Jewish history and innocence into battle that was forced upon them by the Arab world…. Jews are innocent in suffering *and* empowerment.[268]

The process has come to its fruition in the teachings of

commitment to an articulated faith. It became an object of the faith that was rehearsed in the biblical stories of the Hebrew Scriptures. Never mind the ensuing millennia and all the narratives of the Arab and Muslim nations so

contemporary Jewish theologians and rabbis. Israel has become a major tenant at the heart of any expression of Jewish faith. In the American Jewish community, I believe this is a direct result of the events of the 1967 war.

Chapter 6
Reframing the Questions

This final chapter will provide a survey of events in the history of Israel-Palestine for the last twenty-seven years, concluding with the failure of the Oslo Peace Accords and the negotiations at Camp David in 2000 in the final days of the Clinton administration. Oslo and Camp David cast a shadow over much of the recent experience in Israel-Palestine and provide a tragic commentary. What is occurring in the news is strongly connected to the history and policies of Israel and the United States and their relationships, or lack thereof, with the Arab nations of the Middle East since the First World War and the years of the British Mandate. Although some would suggest that the past is something to be gotten past, I take the view that the original sin against the Palestinians directly connects to contemporary events. Justice has not been done, and until a just resolution is determined, the words of the prophet Micah will continue to ring in our ears:

conflict can assist us in discovering the connections that make things comprehensible and will assist us in making a just evaluation of events as they unfold.

A recent example illustrates the problem. Accepting at face value the assertion that the capture of Israeli soldiers across the "blue line" between Lebanon and Israel by Hezbollah militia is the sole or even the main reason for the recent conflict (July-August 2006) is a failure to go beneath the surface. A deeper analysis of events must take into account at the very least the Lebanese Civil War of 1975-1976, Israel's incursions in the late 1970s, its invasion in 1982, and its occupation of Southern Lebanon until 2000, when Israel withdrew its troops. Any evaluation of this situation must take into account Israel's part in the rise of Hezbollah because of its occupation and the large numbers of Lebanese being imprisoned by Israel. To explain the conflict as merely resulting from the July capture of the IDF

He has told you, O mortal, what is good; and what does the Lord require of you but to do justice, and to love kindness, and to walk humbly with your God?

Micah 6:8

Much too often, the media report things as if in a vacuum, ignoring essential historical background that bears closely on what is occurring in the present. The oft-repeated dictum that the situation in the Middle East is too complicated to comprehend is really not accurate. Seeing the roots of the

soldiers is too tidy an equation. Israel and the United States have framed the message of self-defense with the myth of Israel's dominant victim narrative. As we have seen, it is a misrepresentation of the actual story. It surely does not reveal the motivations for what Israel's aggression has unleashed. The current ceasefire "agreement" (August 14, 2006) and attendant UN Security Council Resolutions 1559 and 1701 are the culmination of years of ongoing aggression against Lebanon.

It is my hope that with the information in this study, the reader will be able to reframe the facts as they are presented, particularly by the mainstream media. Then it will be possible to assess public statements by the major participants and move beyond the accepted propaganda to a more accurate portrayal of the actual meaning of events.

At present, the United States and Israel are trying to interpret everything in the conflict through the lens and rhetoric of the war on terror. The latest chapter in this sad history is part of Israel's intention to destroy Arab resistance and continue its hegemony by force of arms. In this most recent conflict, the media portrayed Israel as acting in its own self-defense. Meanwhile, Israel has killed more than fifteen hundred Lebanese civilians, with many thousands of innocent persons displaced from their homes and the infrastructure of a sovereign nation blown to bits.

Robert Fisk, senior correspondent on the Middle East for the British newspaper *The Independent,* reflected in his column on the irony of Israel's insistence that United Nations Security Council Resolutions be scrupulously observed:

> One cannot but wish the Israelis always paid such attention to UN resolutions. If only they would be so keen to adhere to UN Security Council Resolution 242, for example, as they are anxious to ensure Hezbollah and the Lebanese army abide by 1559 and 1701. Few readers will need to be reminded that [SCR] 242 calls for the withdrawal of Israeli troops from territory occupied in the 1967 war in return for the security of all states (including Israel) in the area.[269]

The present conflict is not an isolated occurrence brought on by a recent border crossing. Nor is it what Israeli and United States propaganda claim.

Reframing the conflict would start with evaluating what has actually occurred and examining the question of the disproportionate use of military force. One needs to ask what Israel was trying to accomplish and why, and how it fits with what has been the ongoing narrative of Israeli policy. One cannot answer these questions without asking what the interests of the United States are and what bearing they have in the presentation of events. One then needs to ask the same questions of Lebanon and the other players in the Middle East.

The Bush administration operates with the notion that, when confronted by military might, the "forces of terror" will collapse or see the light and come over to join the "forces of freedom." That may be how it happens in apocalyptic fantasies, but it's not how it happens in history. That is not what has happened in Iraq, and it is not what is happening in southern Lebanon.[270]

This conflict is about the continued occupation of the West Bank and the occupation of Lebanon that began twenty years ago, not the capture and murder of some Israeli soldiers, however terrible, provocative, and unjustified that may be. Israel chose once more to try to destroy a country instead of addressing the prior injustices. Rather than resorting to military might, they could start by withdrawing from the Golan Heights, territory illegally occupied since 1967.

The Quest for Resolution

Following the Yom Kippur War, there was once again an attempt to find a more lasting resolution to the Middle East conflict. Henry Kissinger with his acclaimed shuttle diplomacy worked out two accords, Sinai I (1974) and Sinai II (1975) or the Egypt-Israel Disengagement of Forces Agreements, in which Israel withdrew from portions of the Golan and the Sinai in exchange for statements of non-belligerency from Syria and Egypt. As was already noted, following the war both Golda Meir and her defense Minister Moshe Dayan

Catholics, Shia Muslims, and the Druze. The PLO represented a threat as well with its leftist factions, who were responsible for continuing cross-border attacks on Israel, inviting retaliation. The Lebanese Muslims were sympathetic, and as a result of the 1969 Cairo Accords, the PLO controlled the refugee camps in the poor neighborhoods south of Beirut. This created a situation much like that of Hezbollah in 2006, with a mini-state within Lebanon.[272] Suffice it to say that between the Civil War and the expulsion of the PLO from Lebanon, the PLO altered its political direction.

At the June 1974 Palestinian National Council Meeting, PLO leaders relinquished the vision of a secular democratic state in all of Palestine and adopted the goal of an independent Palestinian state in any part of Palestine liberated from Occupation. Implicit in this change was the recognition of Israel, as required by Resolution 242.[273] This was confirmed

resigned, and Yitzhak Rabin became the Prime Minister of Israel. It will be recalled that US President Richard M. Nixon resigned in August of 1974, and Kissinger was for all practical purposes unilaterally controlling US foreign policy. All of his efforts brought only limited agreements. He blamed his failure on Israel's intransigence.[271]

The year 1975 saw the outbreak of the Lebanese Civil War with its roots in the increasingly dysfunctional and fragile ethnic-religious coalition between Maronite

by the Arab Summit later that year in Rabat, Morocco. The Arab leaders gave recognition to the Palestinian Liberation Organization as "the sole legitimate representative of the Palestinian people" and further affirmed "the right of the Palestinian people to establish an independent national authority under the command of the Palestinian Liberation Organization...."[274] This gave a boost to Arafat, who addressed the United Nations in New York (November 1974), where the General Assembly passed Resolution

3236, reaffirming "the Palestinian people's right to self-determination...national independence and sovereignty... and the inalienable right of the Palestinian people to return to their homes and property...." The General Assembly also invited the PLO to participate in the work of the General Assembly as an observer.[275]

Unfortunately, the context was Israel's increased resistance under Prime Minister Rabin to any notion of Palestinian identity and nationhood. This was further exacerbated by the parliamentary elections in Israel in 1977 that brought the Likud to power, with Menachem Begin as Prime Minister. Israeli motives in both the Lebanese Civil War and the invasion of 1982 were to prevent Palestinian statehood. This resulted in the massacre of tens of thousands of Palestinians, mostly civilians residing in the refugee camps.[276] Edward W. Said wrote, "Over 20,000 Palestinians and Lebanese Muslims were killed by Israeli troops in the summer of 1982

Likud, the number of settlers doubled in the West Bank, from under 5,000 to 12,500; the number of settlements doubled by 1980. There was also significant growth in the Golan Heights, the Sinai (later dismantled), and in Gaza. In the 1980s, expansion of settlements continued to increase. Mark Tessler comments: "Settlements were often designed to abut Arab communities and often took over their lands, constituting a visible threat designed from Ariel Sharon's point of view to intimidate Arabs and encourage them to leave."[278]

Personal History

I can still recall, prior to the major Likud settlement expansion, being shown what appeared to be new apartment complexes on the hilltops and being impressed by the vast changes and improvements the Israelis were making, transforming the ancient landscape of my personal Bible land imagery into a modern Western country. Was I proud of the Jews for their

alone." He further noted that the ratio of Palestinians to Israeli deaths was one hundred to one.[277]

In the United States, the Carter administration was in power. President Carter was quite sympathetic to the Palestinians and wanted to find a resolution to the conflict. Although the colonizing of the West Bank and Gaza had continued unabated during the labor governments following the 1967 war, it was during Begin's administration that colonization exploded. Over the first few years under the

accomplishments? Was I dismissive of the Palestinian "Arab" villages at the foothills? I expect I was. Riding through Maale Adumim, one of what are now characterized as settlements, I was quite aware of how these very modern townhouses, apartments, and swimming pools could have been gated communities in the southwestern part of the United States, near Phoenix or Las Vegas. Had I been on a commercial tour, I might not have driven through East Jerusalem just outside the Old City walls and seen the settlers building and pushing the

Palestinians off their land; or through Abu Dis, the Palestinian community that Israel is swallowing with its settlement plans. I would not have been aware of what was happening. I might have been dismissive of these poor slum areas and experienced them as eyesores or quaint old neighborhoods in need of gentrification. It is a matter of how what you see with your own eyes can be framed by your understanding.

One of the most troublesome of all the settlements is in Hebron. It was established in 1968 when members of Gush Emunim, led by Rabbi Moshe and Miriam Levinger, occupied a hotel in downtown Hebron, claiming that they wanted to celebrate the Passover near the tombs of the Patriarchs and Matriarchs. They refused to leave, establishing themselves as squatters there. In 1970 the government reached a settlement with the Levingers and gave them some homes and land outside the city of Qiryat Arba. Not satisfied, they conspired with some other settlers to occupy a building known as Beit

largest city in the West Bank, has a population of more than 500,000 Palestinians.

In the ensuing years, the presence of this settlement has closed down normal life for the Arab population. I was told that a garrison of 5,000 Israeli troops was assigned there to guard the small enclave of extremists. I witnessed the abuse of local resident Palestinians by the settlers. In the expansion of the settlements, Palestinian property has been confiscated. One family I visited pointed out their olive grove across the street from their house, a grove no longer accessible to them. As we watched from the roof of their house through the fences enclosing and separating them from their land, a group of perhaps twenty young religious settlers, some carrying rifles, flaunted their presence while the Palestinian family looked on with painful emotion. It is the practice of young religious settlers to visit the compound established by the Levingers in order to justify the

Hadassah, a Jewish clinic until the Arab uprising in 1929. They threw out the Arabs living in Beit Hadassah. By reclaiming it, they asserted that they were wiping out "the shame of 1929," as Miriam Levinger proudly bears witness.[279] There are now as many as 450 persons occupying the compound that has grown up around Beit Hadassah, although Hebron residents do not believe there are that many people in continuous residence. It is perhaps populated with temporary visitors from Jerusalem and elsewhere. Hebron, the second

absurd situation of 5,000 IDF protecting 500 settlers in a Palestinian city of 500,000.

Adjacent to Hebron is the large settlement of Qiryat Arba (Kiryat Arba) with between five and six thousand Israelis living there. Baruch Goldstein was a resident of Qiryat Arba. On another trip to Hebron in 2001, when I visited the shrine to Goldstein in Qiryat Arba, I also visited the shrine in the Ibrahmi Mosque (Cave of the Patriarchs), divided since the Goldstein rampage between Jews and Muslims. I gained *admittance to the Jewish section by insisting to the soldier guarding the entrance that I was entitled as a Jew to do so. The soldier was wary, as my companions were Mary Davies, a missionary, and the director of Wi'am, Zoughbi Zoughbi. Inside, a group of teenagers was attending what appeared to be a class in religious studies. The teacher was apparently discussing the person whose photograph was sitting on a tripod stand. It was a photo of Baruch Goldstein.*

Camp David

Unlike Henry Kissinger and the previous administration, President Carter hoped to achieve a comprehensive settlement of the Arab-Israeli conflict. He was sympathetic to Palestinian aspirations for self-determination and a homeland. Carter maintained the necessity of the Palestinians' acceptance of SC 242, a resolution that made no mention of Palestinians, only of refugee accommodation. The

Moroccan King.[280] Egypt was in the midst of debilitating economic difficulties that were fueling shortages of government subsidies to the population and leading to civil unrest, some of it violent.

Sadat wanted the United States' economic and military support for Egypt. Sadat's proposal was a bold one for a bilateral peace agreement between Egypt and Israel. His rhetoric and perhaps his motivation was for a wider agreement that included withdrawal from all Arab territories captured in 1967. He saw it as a fundamental necessity for peace and the only basis for Israel's security. Sadat promised to accept all international guarantees demanded by Israel. He included the Palestinian issue and considered it essential to any durable and just peace.[281] But he was severely criticized by most other Middle Eastern Arab leadership for breaking ranks. The Arab states and the Palestinians feared that his solo initiative would unwittingly result in a bilateral agreement that would not

Palestinian Liberation Organization could not accept this; as a result, Carter would not open diplomatic conversation with the Palestinians. This fact undermines whatever good intentions Carter had.

Then in November of 1977, Anwar Sadat opened a door. He made a lightning-fast visit to Jerusalem and addressed the Knesset. He had already met with Jimmy Carter in Washington, and there had been secret meetings of Egyptian and Israeli representatives arranged by the

resolve the wider issues. As it turns out, they were correct in their skepticism.

Begin was absolute in his refusal to consider withdrawal from the Golan Heights or any part of the West Bank. Nor would he consider only partial withdrawal from the Sinai in exchange for a peace treaty with Egypt. He increased the building of settlements on both the Golan Heights and the West Bank. Only two months after Sadat's address, in defiance he solidified his position by beginning new construction of Sinai settlements in the illegally held[282] territories. With all of this, Israel was also bolstering support for the Christian militia operations against the PLO leadership in Lebanon. His only concession was what he described as "limited administrative autonomy for the West Bank and Gaza."[283]

In 1978 Carter invited Begin and Sadat to the presidential retreat at Camp David, Maryland. What was so positively lauded in the press at the time was hardly a solution, though it normalized relations between Egypt and Israel and brought substantial US foreign aid to both countries. Israel agreed to leave the Sinai within three years, and Egypt gave Israel free access to the Suez Canal and Gulf of Aqaba. As to the West Bank, the Golan, and the Palestinians, it was the sell-out that the Arab states and the Palestinians had feared. Palestinian aspirations were deferred to the future. "Begin claimed to a frustrated

a retrenchment on Israel's part and an expansion of the Occupation. Israel took deliberate action to transform the political, economic, and demographic character of the Occupied Territories, especially the West Bank.[286] Although autonomy for Palestinians is at the heart of any hope for peace, what transpired was once again a negation of the promise for peace and a failure to pursue an honest resolution of the Palestinian-Israeli conflict.

Failed Initiatives

The events that have followed from the 1980s through 2000 are in alignment with what Camp David represents and with the intentions and policies of Israel since the early days of the Zionist enterprise. United States administrations under George Herbert Walker Bush, Bill Clinton, and now George W. Bush have been a record of apparent US attempts to end the conflict and of Israel's apparent

Carter that at Camp David he had promised only to *negotiate,* not to *agree* to any particular outcome concerning autonomy."[284] It was clearly never Begin's intention to permit real autonomy, whatever he intended to imply. The head of the National Religious Party (NRP) voiced Begin's position following Camp David: "There is a danger of a Palestinian state growing out of autonomy, and it is my task as chair of the Israeli delegation to the autonomy talks to prevent that possibility absolutely."[285] Tragically, this meant

single-minded pursuit of its interests. The actions that culminated in the Madrid Conference of 1991, the Oslo Accords of 1993, and the Camp David talks of 2000, were all part of the same tapestry of failed initiatives. All the while, Israel has continued to absorb the West Bank and Golan Heights with the intention of eradicating Palestinian aspirations and presence.

It has become clear to most of the rest of the world that the foreign policy of the United States has continued to pander to the wavering support of the Arab nations for the Palestinians, meanwhile giving Israel the dollars and diplomatic support for which it asks. It has not been an impartial broker and no doubt has never intended to be, as US interests have aligned themselves for all intents and purposes with the Jewish state. The nascent debate in the United States regarding the lobbying power of pro-Israel Jewish organizations and their influence on United States foreign policy may create some energy to reevaluate whether unwavering support for Israel really serves US interests. As of the summer of 2006, little has changed.

One can only hope that it is becoming increasingly clear to a growing portion of the Israeli population and many of us in the United States that without a just acceptance of a Palestinian state there will never be security for Israel. There have been some positive gains for the Palestinian cause and Palestinian international identity since 1978, but

relationship with its closest neighbors, he rejects Israel's official framing and posits an alternative:

> The re-framing suggested here seeks to address the underlying causes of the conflict between Israel, the Palestinians and the wider Arab world while offering ways out. It might be called a "post-Zionist" approach because the critical Israeli peace camp ("to the left of Peace Now," as we sometimes refer to ourselves) understands that an expanding Jewish state plumped in the middle of a country already inhabited by another people poses fundamental problems of co-existence, human and civil rights, self-determination and justice. It rests on the principle that two peoples live in Israel-Palestine, each possessing rights of self-determination yet capable of finding ways to co-exist. At a minimum it endorses a two-state solution, yet it is open to others as well: the creation of a common bi-national or democratic state encompassing both peoples, a regional confederation, or any other arrangement that respects the parties'

only within the frame of Israel's ongoing march towards what it understands to be its unilateral interests. The bottom line has been and remains the Occupation.

In *Obstacles to Peace: A Critical Re-Framing of the Israeli-Palestinian Conflict,* Jeff Halper, an Israeli who is committed to a just peace, states the viewpoint also expressed here that framing is more important than facts in analyzing the conflict in Israel-Palestine. As an Israeli who believes that Israel's ultimate existence depends on its

human and national rights. Indeed, it argues that only a political solution conforming to human rights and international law will finally meet each people's concern for justice and security. Since it also recognizes the strong and vital cultures of both peoples, the alternative human rights framing relies less on attempts to carve out distinctive Jewish or Palestinian states—an impossible task in a country in which the peoples are so intertwined—as it does on finding a political configuration that affords each its national expression yet preserves the fluidity of residence and movement this shared space requires.

In the end, the reframing offered by the critical Israeli peace camp rejects the fundamental premise of the security paradigm: that Muslims and Arabs as a whole, and Palestinians in particular, are our enemies. We insist that the conflict be conceived as a political one that therefore has a solution. We reject all attempts to mystify it through claims that Jews and Arabs have been enemies "from time immemorial" or that we are involved in a "clash of civilizations." We also reject the notion that terrorism lies at the root of the conflict. While we condemn any attack on civilians, we recognize that such violence is a symptom of intolerable oppression that will end only when the peoples' underlying claims and grievances are resolved.[287]

Halper also points out that although the violence of recent years has obscured gains made over the years, significant progress has been made. At the same time, Halper holds his country accountable for its actions, rejecting the

notion of Israel's expansion into Occupied Territories. His reframing, however, rejects the notion of "both sides" because there is a fundamental asymmetry of power between the sides. In his view, Israel possesses the ability to end the Occupation and will do so "only when it is brought into compliance with internationally accepted standards of human rights and international law—not to mention Jewish morality and values."[288]

The 1987 Intifada

Edward W. Said has written that the Intifada "was surely one of the great anti-colonial insurrections of the modern period."[289] If one measures the Intifada with respect to violence, then Israel was the victor. The destruction of Palestinian life and property was devastating:

> Since the Intifada began in late [December] 1987 until the end of June 1991, 983 have been killed by the Israeli military (this is three times the number of blacks killed by South African troops under *apartheid* for the same length of time); more than 120,000 wounded and beaten, and 15,000 political prisoners in continuous incarceration, most of them without benefit of trial, defense, reprieve, or even a charge; more than 112,000 trees have been uprooted, and 1,882 houses have been punitively demolished; at least 50 percent of Palestinians' land has been confiscated, and more than 220 Israeli settlements established, all by force of Israeli arms, all by official Israeli policy.[290]

Aside from the internal political repercussions for the Palestinian leaders and organizations, what changed (at least at the time) was that perhaps for the first time the world saw the face of Israeli oppression.

There is no need to catalog the atrocities and methods of collective punishments administered during the Intifada. Prime Minister Shamir and his defense minister at the time, Yitzhak Rabin, predicted that the iron fist policy of force, might, and beatings would end the uprising in a matter of weeks or even sooner.[291] But two years later, even Rabin had to acknowledge that he had failed to crush the resistance. Ariel Sharon, another of Shamir's ministers, denounced Rabin for what he termed his misplaced moderation, while Prime Minister Shamir sought cabinet approval for an open-fire policy—authority to shoot stone-throwers on sight. Rabin thought it would only increase the violence and blocked the proposal. It did not stop Shamir and his cabinet from discussing "transfer," that is, the deportation of all Palestinians from the Occupied Territories.[292] Other Israeli leadership, including those in the general staff of the military, began to question the wisdom of the ongoing Occupation of the West Bank and its burden on the army. In one paper, military leaders observed that "3.5 million Israelis cannot keep 1.5 million Palestinians under perpetual curfew."[293]

imagine having the police enter your apartment and close off your bedroom with boards or welded metal, making it literally inaccessible. The inhumanity of such punishments has caused me on subsequent trips to wonder in horrified astonishment what kind of imagination can develop such vengeful deeds. In 1991 after visiting refugee camps and hearing primarily from Palestinians and Israelis opposed to the Occupation, I went on my own into West Jerusalem and met at a café the Israeli-American son of a Jewish friend from the United States who worked as a psychologist in Israel. One of his professional responsibilities was "putting IDF soldiers' psyches back together after service in the Occupied Territories." He shared the pain he felt as he contemplated his son reaching draft age and having to serve in the army. Trying to comprehend what I was seeing and hearing, I said to him out of my own sense of anger and pain that I feared we [Jews] were becoming monsters. His response was, "We have already become monsters."

Personal History: Demolitions

In 1991 when I was visiting the homes of Palestinians in the Jalazon Refugee Camp near Ramallah on the West Bank, I saw some of this destruction firsthand. Besides home demolitions, the IDF also sealed off individual rooms in Palestinian homes so that they could no longer be used by the remaining family members. The occupant of the room that we visited was one of the family's sons who had been arrested and imprisoned. Try to

Palestinian Solidarity

What was accomplished was the organization, empowerment, and solidarity of Palestinians living under Occupation, apart from the PLO. A new voice and a new leadership of opposition to the Occupation began to emerge. In 1988 two important developments were the Palestinian National Council's (PNC) recognition of Israel and Yasser Arafat's Declaration of Independence for the State of Palestine on the West Bank and in Gaza, with East Jerusalem as its capital. Recognition eventually came from over one hundred countries, not including the United States, Western Europe, or Israel. But it was a significant symbolic move forward for Palestinian identity, ultimately changing the focus of the struggle. The denunciation of terrorism by the PNC and the use of violence were to be limited to the Occupied Territories and Israel.

Yasser Arafat requested permission to address the General Assembly of the United Nations in New York. Still

would also renounce resorting to terrorism. The words of these concessions repeated the Secretary of State's phrases almost word for word.[294] George Shultz then appointed an ambassador to be the US contact to the PLO.

Britain followed with a meeting with Arafat in Tunis. With Yitzhak Shamir barely winning another election, the Israelis countered with an escalation in the West Bank and Gaza. They now substituted rubber bullets for batons in assaulting Palestinians. Rubber bullets are steel balls encased in a rubber coating that wound victims rather than immediately kill them.

The first half of 1989 saw the worst violence of the Intifada. Israel sealed off Gaza and denied Palestinian entry into Israel.[295] The US State Department provided statistics (1989) that indicated 366 Palestinians had died, and more than 20,000 had been wounded in the Intifada. The uprising had killed eleven Israelis and wounded eleven hundred.

dismissing such overtures and changes in the Palestinian Liberation Organization, the outgoing Reagan administration in Washington denied Arafat a visa to the United States. Instead, the General Assembly voted to hold its meeting in Geneva, where on December 13 Arafat appealed for peace negotiations. Pressuring Arafat, the outgoing Secretary of State George Shultz extracted from him in his address the acknowledgement that the PLO recognized Israel's right to exist and accepted Resolutions 242 and 338. The PLO

Hamas:

an acronym for the Arabic words that approximate "Movement of the Islamic Resistance." It describes itself as a branch of the Islamic Brotherhood in Egypt.

Ten thousand Palestinians had been imprisoned. It was alleged that some had been tortured.[296]

Hamas

Parenthetically, another outcome was the strengthening of the emerging Islamicist movement Hamas. Ironically, Hamas was supported financially by some Israeli IDF officers as a counter to the PLO during the Intifada in Gaza. Hamas, an acronym for the Arabic words that approximate "Movement of the Islamic Resistance," describes itself as a branch of the Islamic Brotherhood in Egypt and other Jihad groups that find their inspiration in the Palestinian hero Sheikh 'Izz ed-Din al-Qassam.[297]

Another attempt for a peace settlement seemed in the offing. Shamir proposed a plan to the US administration that was inadequate from both the American and the European perspective, as it denied the idea of exchanging

Secretary of Defense Richard Cheney a Memorandum of Understanding was signed with Rabin that gave Israel war materials for research and development. Another agreement followed in which the United States would set aside $100 million worth of military supplies in Israel for their use in a crisis.[299]

In October the United States stopped admitting Russian Jews. This tacitly meant more would immigrate to Israel, another Zionist goal, where they would be resettled in the Occupied Territories. It appeared that Israeli intransigence would once again retard every effort of the Bush White House. James Baker, expressing his anger and frustration with Yitzhak Shamir, was reported to have said, "The White House number is 202-456-1414, and when you are serious about peace, call us."[300] But it was all a prelude to the next venture toward a peace agreement.

land for peace. Rabin served as the Israeli emissary from Shamir to James Baker as the Secretary of State of the new Bush administration. The Americans gave cautious approval, yet expressed the view that the plan did not go far enough. Still in Shamir's cabinet, Ariel Sharon condemned the Prime Minister for "giving too much away."[298] Later that summer Shamir rejected *forever* the idea of a Palestinian state.

Somehow Shamir extracted an increase in military aid and cooperation from Washington, and under United States

The Madrid Peace Conference

All of these events were occurring in the context of other world events that took center stage. In August of 1990, Sadam Hussein's forces invaded Kuwait and occupied Kuwait City. After some diplomatic efforts, a coalition force led by the United States obtained a resolution from the United Nations to "use all necessary means" to force Iraq from Kuwait if Iraq remained in the country after January 15, 1991.[301] On January 12, 1991, President Bush received from the Congress a resolution authorizing the use of force, ending an intense debate (but not the protest) in the country over US participation. With the passing of the UN ultimatum's deadline on January 17, a massive air attack began against Iraqi targets. By the end of February, Iraqi resistance had collapsed and the coalition forces recaptured Kuwait and declared a ceasefire. During the war, Israel did not retaliate against Iraqi missile attacks, partially at the behest of the United States, though it was prepared to do so. Israel was not a member of the coalition forces.

In the midst of the Intifada, Yasser Arafat, in what turned into a major blunder for Palestinians, publicly gave PLO support to Saddam Hussein, who had been the only Arab leader to claim he would fight for Palestinian rights. Iraq also appeared to be the only Arab nation supporting populist Arab efforts against all of the conservative, corrupt, authoritarian oil monarchies. No doubt also contributing

Commonwealth of Independent States with Boris Yeltsin as president. The demise of the Soviet Union effectively removed its influence from the Middle East.

In spite of Arafat's loss of credibility and Shamir's stony defiance, immediately following the Gulf War, George Bush pushed ahead with a peace conference which would include Arab leaders and Palestinian representatives as part of a joint delegation with Jordan, though not officially including members of the PLO. This marked the arrival of the Palestinians, who had long been the missing party, at the Middle East conference table. The conference was carefully stage-managed by the Americans.[302] A precondition for the United States was a freeze on new settlement development in the Occupied Territories. Although Israel had vetoed direct participation of the PLO or residents of East Jerusalem, an advisory group to the Jordanian delegation included Faisal Husseini, with Dr. Haidar Abdel-Shafi

to Arafat's stance was his frustration with Shamir's refusal to make any movement toward legitimizing Palestinian aspirations. Their support was also a reaction to the United States' double standard of supporting Kuwait and turning its back on the Israelis' occupation of Lebanon, the West Bank, and Gaza.

Other dramatic changes were occurring in the international arena. In 1989 the Berlin Wall toppled. In December of 1991, the Soviet Union officially dissolved itself, forming the

from Gaza and Dr. Hanan Ashrawi as a spokesperson. With half the Palestinian delegation made up of doctors and university professors, persons of great dignity, the delegation members presented a new face for the Palestinians. It was in stark contrast to the stereotype many had that all Palestinians were radical terrorists.

Dr. Abdel-Shafi's eloquent speech was deemed the most moderate presentation of the Palestinians' case ever made by an official spokesman since the beginning of the conflict at the end of the nineteenth century.[303] The result was trumpeted in the international media. The basic thrust of his speech was to remind the audience that it was time for the Palestinians to present their own story to the world. It was in stark contrast to Shamir's speech, which proved to be an embarrassment. Its tone in front of an Arab audience was "anachronistic; saturated with the stale rhetoric of the past, and wholly inappropriate for the occasion.... His version of the Arab-Israeli conflict was singularly narrow and blinkered, portraying Israel simply as the victim of Arab aggression and refusing to acknowledge that any evolution had taken place in the Arab or Palestinian attitude to Israel."[304]

Yitzhak Shamir continued to mouth the old saw that all the Arabs wanted was Israel's destruction. He insisted that the cause of the conflict was Arab refusal to recognize the legitimacy of the state of Israel and denied the reality of the

endorsed by the PLO leaders in Tunis, was to convince the people of Israel that the Palestinians were truly committed to peaceful coexistence.[305]

Shlaim comments that former Israeli Ambassador Abba Eban's oft-repeated putdown of the Palestinians that they never missed an opportunity to miss an opportunity for peace "was singularly inappropriate on this occasion and, if anything, could be turned against the Israeli side."[306] The delegation members were remarkably articulate persons who permanently transformed the negative portrayal of Palestinians for everyone with any sensitivity.

With their acceptance of Resolutions 242 and 338 and the proposal of exchanging land for peace, the Palestinians moved closer to American interests at the conference. Israel's refusals were seen for what they were. After the initial presentations, the delegations broke into bilateral conversations. These did not move the

territorial claims. Given that participation in the conference was predicated on the acceptance of SC Resolutions 242 and 338, this was ill-advised at the very least.

Dr. Abdel-Shafi asserted that the Occupation had to end and that Palestinians, who had every right to self-determination, would pursue these rights until they succeeded. He offered the Intifada as the beginning of the establishment of a state, with Palestinian institutions and the necessary infrastructure to take root. The major goal of the speech,

process forward significantly. Internal wrangling beset both the Israeli side and the Arab delegations.

Finding a compromise venue and time to continue the talks was an arduous process. With much consternation on Baker's part, the talks were scheduled to resume in Washington in December. Shamir was opposed to the venue. He asserted that the sole purpose of the Washington meeting should be to establish the ground rules for separate bilateral talks that should be held in the Middle East.

The upshot was that all the Arab delegations arrived in Washington for the talks, but the Israelis were absent.[307]

On the same day, Shamir made a speech once more, "nailing his colors to the mast of Greater Israel and ruling out the return of even one stone in exchange for peace."[308] To punctuate his stubbornness, another settlement was begun near an Arab town on the West Bank.

The distance between the Israelis and Palestinians proved to be much too great. The Palestinians assumed that they had national rights and that the talks were the precursor to an interim period to be followed by independence. The Israelis' position was that the Palestinians were only residing in the territories and had no natural rights at all, certainly not to independence, even after the end of the transitional period.[309] Shamir continued his attempt to convince the Americans that he was serious about reaching an agreement, while telling his right-wing colleagues that he had

no intention of offering meaningful concessions. When accused of dishonesty, Shamir arrogantly replied in a *Ha'aretz* newspaper interview, "for the sake of the Land of Israel, it is permissible to lie."[310]

In the 1992 Israeli elections, the Labor Party, running on a sketchy policy of territorial compromise with the promise to cut spending on settlements, replaced Likud.[311] Yitzhak Rabin replaced Yitzhak Shamir as the Prime Minister.

The Oslo Accords

In the case of the Oslo Accords, it would be accurate simply to state that they were ill-fated from the day Rabin and Arafat engaged in the historical handshake, signing the Declaration of Principles on September 13, 1993. Despite the hope that a real peace accord might be the outcome, it is now clear that the Israeli leadership's principles remained at heart constant, even though two-thirds of the Israeli population

We left Madrid with a

combined sense of euphoria and loss. We felt that we had staked a place for ourselves in this public forum, that we had spoken out as Palestinians. But we also knew this was only the beginning, that the hardest part was yet to be; we

knew that in Madrid the bilateral talks had not actually produced anything, that there was still no concrete engagement.

—Dr. Ashrawi,
This Side of Peace

favored the dismantling of the West Bank and Gaza settlements for peace. With all the criticism of Israeli policies and leadership, Israeli citizens themselves reflect a range of opinions, political beliefs, and outlooks. Israeli citizens have their own hopes for stability and for an end to the perpetual conflict. I was told in 1991 how tense and anxious people were, and that the rates of suicide and domestic abuse had risen dramatically. One easily felt the stress under which people were living. It is hard to be sanguine about such human pain even if one is politically attentive to the causes. Israelis have suggested to me that most Israelis probably neither knew nor cared very much about how crushing the Occupation was for Palestinians. Only a minority of Israelis travel to the Occupied Territories or even to East Jerusalem.

The courageous Israeli reporter Amira Hass has written incisively about the Israeli experience. The following painful and cynical insight comes from a column in *Ha'aretz:*

simply chose not to pay attention to the reality beyond their jobs, their easy commutes on bypass roads, and their subsidized apartments that were superior to housing in Tel Aviv or its suburbs. The same could easily be said about most Americans.

Personal History

With the Oslo process, the Palestinian public was also feeling that some of their expectations were nearing fulfillment. When I visited in the mid-1990s, the change from 1991 was conspicuous and still very positive. I will always recall as a personal symbol seeing the first traffic light installed in Bethlehem in expectation of the tourist crowds that were going to descend during the millennial year. Even Mission Personnel at Global Ministries had assigned a missionary couple to serve the anticipated United Methodists who would journey to the Holy Land during that memorable year.

How perfectly natural that 40,000 people should be subject to a total curfew for more than a month in the Old City of Hebron in order to protect the lives and well-being of 500 Jews. How perfectly natural that almost no Israeli mentions this fact or, for that matter, even knows about it."[312]

In January, I was being guided through the Maal Adumim settlement block by Angela Godfrey-Goldstein, an ICAHD staff person. She told me in conversation that the Israelis living there were just as likely liberal in their outlook and

In contrast to the Israeli leadership, Arafat was willing to do almost anything to gain a concrete agreement, including abandoning most of the principles and aspirations that had held the Palestinians and the Palestinian Liberation Organization together through all of its years of failure, struggle, and hardship. Edward W. Said was one who opposed this strategy from the Palestinian side and understood that it was in fact a capitulation on the part of Arafat. A former member of the PNC feared that after the Madrid Conference the pressure on Arafat and the leadership would be too great to withstand. He noted that after ten rounds of negotiations in Washington, more misery was meted out in the Occupied Territories, more disillusionment set in, and the leadership became more fractious, while Israel still held the cards. Arafat had put his trust in a failing Republican administration, all to the detriment of reaching a just agreement with Israel.[313]

All the Palestinians got from Oslo was an acknowledgment of their existence. The former Secretary of State James Baker said in a television interview in September of 1993 that "Israel has given up nothing, except a bland acceptance of the PLO as the representative of the Palestinian people."[314] Israel retained its occupation of the West Bank and Gaza, even with Arafat's triumphal return to Palestine and the establishment of the Palestinian Authority in Jericho. As it turned out, there was no sovereignty, nor was it intended. Even when I arrived in 1996

to reports from the election polls coming in and the excitement of knowing some of the candidates running for the Palestinian Legislative Council, it was a long way from the birth of a state.

What was created out of the Oslo Accords is an early version of what we see today, a series of cantons (or Bantustans, if one uses the analogy of apartheid South Africa). All access to the land remains in control of the occupiers. Three zones have been designated: Area A (17.2 percent of the West Bank) under sole jurisdiction and security control of the Palestinian Authority, but with Israel in control of movement in and out of the area with its network of checkpoints and barriers; Area B (23.8 percent), with the Palestinian Authority exercising civil authority and responsibility for public order, but with Israel retaining a security presence and overriding security responsibility; and Area C (59 percent), still under total Israeli control.[315]

The Green Line: a term used to refer to the 1949 Armistice lines established between Israel and its opponents (Syria, Jordan, and Egypt) at the end of the 1948 Arab-Israeli War. The Green Line separates Israel not only from these countries but from territories

Israel would later capture in the 1967 Six-Day War, including the West Bank and Gaza Strip. Its name is derived from the green pencil used to draw the line on the map during the talks.

(*Wikipedia,* the Free Encyclopedia, http://en.wikipedia.org)

This means in effect that, with the retention of all the settlements in the West Bank and Gaza (at the time of the accords) and all of the bypass roads that connect the settlements inaccessible to Palestinians, Israel has retained 55 percent of the total land area of the Occupied Territories. Greater Jerusalem alone makes up a huge amount of virtually stolen land, almost 25 percent.[316]

The Separation Barrier

A recent development preventing the possibility of a viable Palestinian state is the construction of Israel's security wall or Separation Barrier, on appropriated Palestinian land basically along the old Green Line, but on the Israel side. It is a massive barrier along almost the entire length of the western West Bank, with a possible extension to the east. Construction of the Barrier began in June 2002. Described as a "defensive fence," it will extend more than 450 miles, encircling 17 percent of the West Bank in a complicated series of secondary barriers. The Barrier is an electronic fence fortified by watchtowers, sniper posts, mine fields, a ditch, barbed wire, security perimeters, surveillance cameras, electronic warning devices, and patrols of killer dogs along most of its length.

Close to Palestinian cities, towns, and neighborhoods, it becomes a wall of solid concrete twenty-four feet high. Built to include the major settlement blocs and Greater Jerusalem (80 percent of the settlers fall on the Israeli side of the Barrier), it will adversely affect 875,000 Palestinians. It will permanently confine 263,000 to small encircled enclaves; 210,000 Palestinian residents of East Jerusalem will be isolated from the rest of West Bank society; 402,000 Palestinians will be enclosed in West Bank cantons. In effect, the Barrier will annex 25-45 percent of the West Bank, including some of its richest agricultural and olive-growing land. One hundred villages will be separated from their agricultural lands. Trapped between the border and the wall, some 350,000 Palestinians face impoverishment, alienation from their land and water, and eventual transfer. Entire cities like Qalqiliya and Tul Karm have been completely encircled. And the Barrier, described by Israel as a "temporary facility," will cost about $2 billion.[317]

Until last year, 30 percent of Gaza was made up of Israeli settlements in one of the most densely populated areas on earth. With Israel's dismantling of the Jewish settlements in Gaza and the brief withdrawal of its forces, Gaza has been turned into what can only be described as a prison camp. As of August 2006, Israel has continued its invasion of Gaza, destroying homes and infrastructure, killing hundreds, and wounding untold numbers more, even while the world's attention was focused on the invasion in Lebanon.

Edward Said says of Oslo:

In addition Israel has tapped into every aquifer on the West Bank and now uses about 80 percent of the water there for the settlements as well as Israel proper. So the domination (if not outright theft) of land and water resources is either overlooked, in the case of water, or postponed, in the case of land, by the Oslo Declaration of Principles.[318]

1996, the third year of the interim period. The remaining issues included the status of Jerusalem, refugees, settlements, security arrangements, borders, relations and cooperation with other neighbors, and other issues of common interest. On May 4, 1999, the interim phase ended with no permanent status agreement in sight. In the Sharm Esh-Sheikh Agreement of September 4, 1999, the beginning of the final status talks was rescheduled for September 13, 1999, with an overall agreement to be reached by September 13, 2000.[319]

In 1999 Ehud Barak, another Israeli general running as the Labor Party candidate, defeated Benjamin Netanyahu, the Likud candidate, in the Israeli parliamentary election. Polls indicated that many Israelis voted for Barak because they believed he would rejuvenate the beleaguered Middle East peace process, which had languished under Netanyahu.[320] His failure led to his defeat in 2000. He was succeeded by Ariel Sharon.

The Clinton-Barak Camp David Final Status Negotiations

The Final Status Negotiations were provided for in the Declaration of Principles (1993) to be the second part of a two-phase timetable, the first part of which was a five-year transitional period in which Israel would withdraw gradually from the West Bank and Gaza Strip Palestinian population centers, transferring power over to the Palestinians. It was intended to begin as soon as possible, but no later than

Barak asked Clinton to convene a meeting representing at least his public interest in reaching an agreement with the PLO to demonstrate Israel's commitment to peace. In July of 2000, President Bill Clinton invited Barak and Yasser Arafat to Camp David for a summit. At a minimum, it was to begin the process of resolving the final status issues between Israel and the Palestinians.

It was not an easy task, not only because of the issues alone, but because Barak, like many of his predecessors, was not really prepared to close a deal. Barak made what the media represented as the most courageous offer ever brought to the negotiating table by an Israeli Prime Minister. According to the Israeli version of the story, Barak offered to return all of the Gaza Strip and 90 percent of the Occupied West Bank to the Palestinians. In return, all he wanted was to annex the 10 percent of the land with the big settlement blocs, where 150,000 Israelis had already established homes. Regarding the most sensitive issue, the city of Jerusalem, to which the Israelis feel particular attachment, he took the enormous risk of agreeing to divide the city and recognize part of it as the capital of the future Palestinian state.[321] In addition, Barak was supposed to have offered to remove the isolated settlements and to substitute other Israeli land in compensation for the retained settlement blocs. And finally he offered religious sovereignty over the Haram Ash-Sharif, the Noble

Categorically it was not true. First, there was no formal declaration. Barak had put nothing in writing to substantiate the substance of the proposals. A year later, Robert Malley, Clinton's special assistant on Arab-Israeli affairs, and Hussein Agah, a veteran of Palestinian-Israeli affairs, published an article in *The New York Review of Books,* which began to debunk the official version. They wrote:

> Israel is said to have made a historic, generous proposal, which the Palestinians, once again seizing the opportunity to miss an opportunity, turned down. In short, the failure to reach a final agreement is attributed, without notable dissent, to Yasser Arafat.
>
> As orthodoxies go, this is a dangerous one. For it has larger ripple effects. Broader conclusions take hold. That there is no peace partner is one. That there is no possible end to the conflict with Arafat is another.
>
> For a process of such complexity, the diagnosis is remarkably shallow. It ignores history, the dynamics of the

Sanctuary, the Temple Mount for Israelis. According to this version of the story, Yasser Arafat rejected the offer and failed to counter with any other proposals. It was claimed that the Palestinians' refusal revealed their underlying rejection of Israel's right to exist. Widely disseminated in the press, Clinton actively supported this version. It has become in the West the accepted version of the substance of the Camp David Summit, known as Barak's Generous Offer.

negotiations, and the relationships among the three parties. In so doing, it fails to capture why what so many viewed as a generous Israeli offer, the Palestinians viewed as neither generous, nor Israeli, nor, indeed, as an offer. Worse, it acts as a harmful constraint on American policy by offering up a single, convenient culprit—Arafat—rather than a more nuanced and realistic analysis.[322]

Barak's central point was that he wanted to come up with a final agreement. Never mind that it discarded the agreements of the Declaration of Principles, which the Israelis had not yet honored. "Precisely because he was willing to move a great distance in a final agreement (on territory or on Jerusalem, for example), he was unwilling to move an inch in the preamble (prisoners, settlements, troop redeployment, Jerusalem villages)."[323]

The pressure was to force Arafat to accept Barak's proposal without any serious negotiation—take it or leave it. Barak manipulated the United States into threatening Arafat with the consequences, which would be laying all of the blame for a failure at his feet. Throughout all the negotiations of Camp David, Barak repeatedly urged the United States to avoid mention of any fall-back options or of the possibility of continuing negotiations if the summit failed.

Arafat was in an extremely difficult position. He no longer had the support of many Palestinians, including the burgeoning Hamas, other Jihad organizations, and Palestinians living in conflict,[325] Arafat would have not only negated the Oslo steps but would in effect have been superceding Resolutions 242 and 338, which had heretofore been the basis of all negotiations and the case for Palestinian international legal standing. This was something he could not do. Once Israel had withdrawn and a state had been formed, the Oslo Accords also gave Palestinians the ability to absorb all the refugees who chose to return to Palestine, and some few to Israel. The rest of the refugees would receive compensation for the loss of their property and for their years of suffering. It was expected that Israel would contribute to this compensation along with other international assistance.[326]

As the years passed after Oslo, it became apparent that Israel did not intend to honor the commitments made there. With the number of settlers having doubled in the intervening years, land was not available to which refugees would be able to return successfully. Israel's attitude had

the Palestinian diaspora. "Barak's stated view that the alternative to an agreement would be a situation far grimmer than the status quo created an atmosphere of pressure that only confirmed Arafat's suspicions—and the greater the pressure, the more stubborn the belief among Palestinians that Barak was trying to dupe them."[324]

Tanya Reinhart fills some of this out and makes another significant point. By insisting on signing a final agreement, accompanied by a Palestinian declaration of an end of the always been that the Palestinians had to keep all of their agreements in Oslo, but that the Israelis did not. In that case, the Palestinians were free to return to the demand that returning refugees could settle anywhere. If the settlers were staying on land in the West Bank and the Gaza Strip, why then should not returning refugees settle wherever they chose? For these and a number of other reasons, Tanya Reinhart concludes: "Based on these facts, the myths and illusions of Camp David are more transparent; one can only conclude that at Camp David Barak was neither aiming for reconciliation nor genuinely attempting to move closer to an end of conflict.[327]

Jeff Halper offers another perspective on Camp David's failure and the less-than-generous Barak offer. He asks us to consider a prison. The inmates possess most of the facility and have the run of the prison. "They have the living areas, the visiting areas, the exercise yard. All the prison authorities have is five percent of the surrounding walls, the cell bars and a few points of control, the keys to the doors."[328]

The Israelis viewed the Intifada as a prison riot and sought to stamp it out as brutally as any prison authorities. The analogy is also frighteningly appropriate with respect to the construction of the Separation Barrier. The overall impression of the Separation Barrier is that the Israelis are creating prisons for the Palestinian residents, prisons from which the Palestinians cannot easily escape.

Halper writes:

Indeed, given the fact that Israel doubled its settler population during the seven years of negotiations, constructed a massive highway system in the Occupied Territories that linked its settlements to Israel proper while creating barriers to Palestinian movement, and imposed an economic closure that impoverished the Palestinian population, no hint is evident "on the ground" that Israel ever contemplated the establishment of a viable Palestinian state.[329]

It is my contention that this has been part of Israeli policy since statehood, through the years of the initial colonization and during the Mandate years. To counter such a persistent policy will surely involve many acts of faith and require significant avenues of activism for justice.

Study Guide
by Sandra Olewine

Introduction

Jesus our brother,
as we dare to follow
in the steps you trod,
be our companion on the way.
May our eyes see not only the stones that saw you
but the people who walk with you now;
may our feet tread
not only the path of your pain
but the streets of a living city;
may our prayers embrace
not only the memory of your presence
but the flesh and blood who jostle us today.
Bless us, with them, and make us long
to do justice, to love mercy,
and to walk humbly with our God.
Amen.

(Janet Morley, *Companions of God: Praying for Peace in the Holy Land,* Beacon Press: London, 1994, p. 2)

For more than ten years I had the privilege and challenge to call the land of Jesus my home. For a little more than nine of those years, I served as the United Methodist Liaison to Jerusalem through the General Board of Global Ministries of The United Methodist Church. I went at a time when there was some expectation that peace was on the horizon (mid-1995) and left when the deadly dance of Occupation, violence, militarism, and extremism grasped firmly the necks of the peoples of that land. As I write this as 2006 draws quickly to a close, I am not optimistic about the future for the people that I leave there, especially the children. But amid the struggles, in the face of overwhelming odds against a just peace, and even with my lack of optimism, I am still hopeful. How can that be? Hope is a theological expression meaning that God is still at work in the broken lives of oppressed people. In the hardest moments of life

in the so-called Holy Land, I experienced an amazing measure of grace and hope, because God *is* still at work in that land through remarkable people who refuse to have their vision limited by the circumstances surrounding their lives. They do not see themselves primarily as victims or as those unable to affect their own future. They see themselves as creative, precious, thoughtful, determined human beings who strive each day to live in the world they believe God desires for all human beings and the breadth of creation. They go against the tide and continue to open spaces where God's in-breaking love has the opportunity to change lives and directions.

The overall goal of this study of Israel-Palestine is to help the people of The United Methodist Church wrestle with the dilemmas, realities, injustices, fears, dreams, and visions of the two peoples of the three faiths who call the land where Jesus walked home. This is often a difficult part of the world to come to terms with. Many people have deep emotions and feelings about this part of the world, even those who know little or nothing about the realities there. Many Christians have romantic notions garnered from Bible stories or images from movies with little grounding in the actual history of the twentieth century. We often forget that the church that had its birth in that land has continued to be in the land and region since the days of Jesus. We may find it startling to realize that Christians spoke Arabic long before they spoke English, and that Arab Christians continue to do so!

Prepare for the Study
Reflect on Your Own Experience
As the author of the study book says, how we frame an understanding of the situation in Israel-Palestine depends on our own experiences and the perceptions that arise out of those experiences. Spend some time reflecting on your own impressions of Israel-Palestine. Consider whose

voices you have heard and what viewpoints have been expressed. Reflect on whose voices have been muffled or absent. How has this affected the way that you view what is happening?

Expand your Perspective

- In advance, read the entire study book. Because the history of the region is so critical to understanding what is happening there now, the writer has focused the book on and made an in-depth examination of the historical context. As you read, consider whose narrative you have heard and whose narrative has been silenced.
- Read through the study guide handouts that express the voices and perspectives of people who live in Israel-Palestine. Reflect on what they are saying to you about the reality of their lives.
- Pray that the Holy Spirit will speak to you through the narratives of people and events. Make one of your prayer petitions be that you will be open to new perspectives and that you will be able to break open the complexities of the situation in Israel-Palestine for the participants in the study.

Develop Session Plans

The study guide includes four sessions, each designed for a two-hour time block.

- Read through the session plans. Decide which activities fit the available time frame and the participants who will be in your group. Adapt the plans to your particular context.
- If you are teaching in a School of Christian Mission, try to obtain the class list in advance. Write to participants and encourage them to read the entire study book in advance of the study. Ask them to collect articles from the newspaper, news magazines, and the internet about the situation in Israel-Palestine.

- Check the list of supplemental resources to see which ones need to be ordered or obtained in advance.

Set Up the Learning Environment
Check Out Your Space

- If possible, find out what kind of learning space will be available to you. If you are teaching in a School of Christian Mission, you may need to adapt some of the learning activities to fit the room. For example, if the room has fixed theater seating, explore other ways to set up learning stations or areas for small group work.
- Find out if you will have access to computers, the internet, and other electronic equipment you may need.
- Check to be sure you are allowed to attach newsprint to the walls. Find out if there are any regulations on what you can use to hang newsprint and/or pictures. (If the newsprint is attached to the wall, make sure ahead of time that your markers don't bleed through the paper and stain the walls.) If you can't use the walls, are there bulletin boards you can attach newsprint on with either staples or push pins? Does the facility have large standing easels on which you could prop the newsprint?

Create a Worship Center

- Use a small table in the middle of the room as a worship center. Or use three or four boxes of various sizes to create a multilevel worship center.
- Cover the table or boxes in colorful cloths if possible.
- Include a large candle (a cross if available) and a stand for the Way of the Cross photos if you aren't projecting the pictures on a wall (see information below).
- Add a crown of thorns (a twisted, dried grapevine wreath available at craft stores), olive branches placed diagonally across the table, a small olive tree or two in a pot, a clear glass jar (or preferably a pitcher) with olive oil, or a bowl with water. If you're making copies of the

Way of the Cross photos, you may want to place the ones you've used around the base of the table as you add each new picture to the table.

The Way of the Cross

This guide is meant to help open the material in the study book in ways that increase understanding, expand dialogue, strengthen commitments, and compel participants to action on behalf of justice and peace. But it is also a study that is set in the context of prayer to remind us to hold those there, as well as ourselves, before the presence and light of God, seeking forgiveness, repentance, renewal, and courage.

Throughout this guide, participants are invited to experience one of the ways of prayer that has become synonymous with a visit to Jerusalem for most Christians—the Stations of the Cross. The Spanish pilgrim Egeria gives us the first record of this practice of walking the Way of the Cross. In 381 and 384, making a Good Friday pilgrimage from the Mount of Olives to the Church of the Holy Sepulchre, she recorded that believers spent three hours in the church listening to Holy Scripture connected with the Passion. While such public processions did not thrive in subsequent times of non-Christian rule in Jerusalem, there is evidence of an ongoing processional route. For example, six liturgical stations on a route from the Mount of Olives to the Church of the Holy Sepulchre were described in tenth century Holy Week records. Records from the fourteenth to the nineteenth centuries indicate that the procession for the Way of the Cross did occur, although there was great variation in the number of stations, the route, and the prayers. The Crusaders even took the idea of the Stations of the Cross back to Europe, "where murderous struggles between Church and State, wars among nations, the plague and famine had given the people of medieval times a new appreciation for Christ's suffering, death and resurrection. These particular attributes of Christ became the principal focus of medieval spirituality. Walking His Way of

the Cross was a meaningful expression of the penitent's pain and of ultimate healing through resurrection."

(John Peterson, *A Walk in Jerusalem: Stations of the Cross,* Harrisburg, Pennsylvania: Morehouse Publishing, 1998, pp. vii-x)

Different names have been given to this spiritual practice of focusing on Jesus' journey towards Calvary and the tomb, with some of the stations coming from the gospel stories. Others came from the medieval European spiritual imagination, such as Jesus' three falls, his meeting his mother, and Veronica wiping his face.

Today, the Stations of the Cross lead right through the busy marketplace of the Old City. All sorts and conditions of people walk this path in prayer amidst the everyday bustle of a teeming city.

In recent years, various Christian communities have used this spiritual practice of reflecting on Jesus' suffering by connecting it with the suffering in today's world, helping us to be mindful that the earth and its peoples still experience life-crushing realities. As those who strive to be faithful to following Christ, we are called to see the places where Christ is still wounded, even crucified, through the pain and struggles in people's lives today; to know that Jesus still weeps over Jerusalem, as over cities and villages around the world, where peace and justice, compassion and mercy, are still unknown. In so doing, we are reminded that those are the places to which we are called to help bring release, healing, hope, and life, through the grace of God.

Therefore, you are invited to "walk" through this study as though you are walking the Way of the Cross and ultimately come to the place where you will be invited "to roll away the stone" so that the reality of new life, resurrection, can come to all the peoples of the land where Jesus lived, loved, died, and rose again.

(Part of the history of the Stations of the Cross is adapted from John Peterson.)

Preparing Pictures for the Way of the Cross

- Download the pictures from http://resources.gbgm
  -umc.org/israelpalestine and arrange to project them
  from your computer using a video projector (LCD
  projector). Or see if there is an overhead projector and
  make transparencies of the pictures. Most copy stores
  can make them for you, or you can buy transparency
  sheets at an office supply store and make transparencies from a computer and printer. If you don't know
  how to do this, ask someone to help you. Make sure
  the room you'll be using can be darkened enough
  so that the projection or overhead can be seen.
  Alternatively, photocopy the downloaded pictures and,
  if possible, enlarge to at least 8"x10". Attach printed
  pictures to a sheet of construction paper. Cut a simple
  cardboard stand to display pictures on the worship
  center table.

Additional Resources

- "The Middle East": two-sided map available from the
  e-store: www.missionresourcecenter.org (#3805)
- *Steps Toward Peace in Israel and Palestine:* Set of
  24 fact sheets on Israel-Palestine developed by the
  Presbyterian Peacemaking Program and available
  online at: www.pcusa.org/worldwide/israelpalestine/
  resources.htm
- *Children of the Nakba* DVD. Order from the
  Mennonite Central Committee, at 888-563-4676
  or go to www.mcc.org/shop (click on MCC Store)

Specific Preparation for Sessions

Session 1

Ask participants to skim the Introduction and Chapters 2
and 3 in the study book. Suggest that they read Chapters
1, 4, 5, and 6 with more attention to detail.

Session 2

If possible, before the study course begins, ask eight
people to prepare to participate in Activity 2 as debaters.
If you are unable to arrange for volunteers in advance, then
ask people as they arrive for the first session in order to
give them enough time to prepare.

Team One

- An Israeli Zionist who believes that all of historic
  Palestine should be under Israel's control and that
  Palestinians should go and live in Jordan or another
  Arab country in order to preserve Israel's Jewish identity.
- An Israeli Zionist who believes that Israel within the
  1948 armistice lines should be a Jewish state, with
  Jerusalem as its capital, and that the West Bank and
  Gaza should be an independent state of Palestine.
- An American Christian Zionist who believes that the
  land was given by God to the Jewish people and that
  when all the Jews are gathered in, the Second Coming
  of Jesus will follow; Palestinians are in the way of
  God's plan.
- A Palestinian who believes that all of historic Palestine
  should be a state of Palestine and that the Jews can
  only stay if they're willing to live in a Palestinian state.

Team Two

- A Palestinian who recognizes the State of Israel
  within the borders of 1948 and believes that all the
  Palestinian land occupied since 1967, including East
  Jerusalem, should be an independent Palestinian state.
  Jerusalem should be an open city to allow movement
  back in forth, particularly in the Old City.
- A US Christian who believes that international law should
  be applied to end the conflict, and that a two-state
  solution is best, with Jerusalem as a shared capital.

- A non-Zionist Israeli who believes there should be one democratic state for all the people and is willing to adjust the name of the state as well as Israel's national anthem.
- A Palestinian who believes that a two-state solution is now impossible because of all the settlements, and that a one-state solution with equal rights of citizenship for all is the only just solution.

Ask the debaters to familiarize themselves with the positions that the other panelists are likely to have. Explain that they'll have exactly two minutes to present their point of view and that later they'll have an opportunity to ask a member of the other team one question. If possible, the teams should meet ahead of time to decide who will ask which member of the other team a question, so that every person gets an opportunity to ask and answer a question. Remind panelists that they'll be given one minute to refute the answer to their question. Debaters can prepare by studying Chapters 2, 3, and 4, pp. 22-93, in the study book.

Session 3
Contact participants in advance of the study and ask them to clip newspaper articles or download articles from the internet about the conflict. If you can't do that, then for a few weeks prior to the course, collect articles that you can give to the participants to use for Activity 4.

Session 4
Learn or ask someone else to learn and lead the new hymn, "Waa Habibi, Waa Habibi." If you have access to someone who speaks Arabic, ask him or her to go over it with you.

Make a large outline map of Israel-Palestine on brown wrapping paper or mural paper (see Session 4 for directions).

Session One

Goals

- To create a sense of community among the participants
- To introduce the ancient spiritual exercise of the Way of the Cross
- To learn about the geography and modern changes in the boundaries of Israel and Palestinian territories
- To grow in understanding about the diverse peoples living in Israel-Palestine today, their cultures and religions

Materials and Supplies

- one copy of Handout 1 (enlarged on copier), copies of Handout 2 for each participant; one copy of Handout 4, "The Peoples of the Land"
- slips of paper
- two copies each of Handouts 3 and 5 (Way of the Cross Meditations)
- five tables and enough chairs for participants (or chairs and space to set up display boards)
- fifteen sheets of poster board (or five three-sided display boards)
- masking tape, colored felt-tipped markers, newsprint
- maps of Israel-Palestine (see Introduction, p. 132)
- copies of pictures for the two Way of the Cross Meditations, or projection equipment

Preparation

- In advance, order copies of "The Middle East" map (#3805) from the e-store.
- Make copies or transparencies of the pictures for the Way of the Cross Meditations, or arrange to project from a computer (see Introduction, p. 132).
- If possible, contact class participants before the study begins and encourage them to skim the Introduction and Chapters 2 and 3 in the study book. Suggest that they read Chapters 1, 4, 5, and 6 with more attention

to detail. Also suggest that they study the timeline in Appendix B.

- Ask four people to lead the group in praying the two Way of the Cross Meditations. Ask two persons to read the titles of the meditations and then read the Scripture text(s). Two additional persons should read the contemporary reflections.
- Make one copy of Handout 1, copies of Handout 2 for each participant, and one copy of Handout 4, "The Peoples of the Land" (cut this up to be distributed to eight people to read in Activity 5).
- On individual small pieces of paper, print the numbers 1 to 5. You'll use these to divide the class into groups. For example, if you have twenty-five participants, you'll need five small pieces of paper with the number 1 on them, five small pieces with number 2, and so forth.
- Place five small tables around the sides of your meeting space with the correct number of chairs needed for each station to evenly divide the class. If it is not possible to locate tables, set up spaces for five groups of chairs around the display boards, or designate five areas if the seating is fixed theater-style.
- Make a three-sided display board for each table by taping three large pieces of poster board together. Lay the boards side by side and place wide masking tape along the seams where the boards touch (or purchase three-sided display boards from a craft store). Attach a map to one of the three panels on each display board. With a wide felt-tipped marker, print the date included on the map somewhere on the same panel.
- Cut Handout 1 into individual information sections. Attach the sections to the poster or display board with the appropriate map. To make these colorful and creative, you might want to print some of the additional pictures in the text to post on the boards. Set up one display board at each workstation.

- For Activity 1, print the following two phrases on separate sheets of newsprint with a colored felt-tipped marker:

    * What was surprising to you?
    * Learning Goals

- For Activity 5, print the discussion questions large enough so everyone will be able to read them.
- Enlarge the timeline in Appendix B and post it where it can be easily seen.

Learning Activities

1. Geography, Maps, and Peoples *(about 40 minutes)*

As participants arrive, give them a copy of Handout 2 and the number of their assigned starting workstation. Be sure to distribute the group evenly between the five stations. Ask participants to fill out the worksheet for their particular station. Once everyone has arrived and filled out the first set of questions, ask them to pair up with someone else in their small group. Tell them that later each person will be asked to introduce someone else in the group to the whole class. Encourage them to find out:

- The person's name
- The person's annual conference, district, or local church
- One thing that the person is hoping to learn from this mission study and whether she/he has ever been to Palestine-Israel

After about five minutes, check in with the groups to see if they've finished their introductions and if they know who is introducing whom later on. If some are not finished, give them several more minutes, but urge them to finish quickly.

Tell participants that they will move clockwise around the room, stopping at each station to answer the appropriate questions on the worksheets. Give participants five minutes at each station. Suggest that at some point they spend a minute or two studying either the posted timeline

or the one in Appendix B of their book.

When all the groups are finished, invite them to turn their chairs toward the center to form a large circle. If the room you are using is large enough to have a table in the center along with the workstations on the sides, then have everyone gather around the table. Ask:

- *What was new to you?*
- *What was a surprise?*

Print their answers on the newsprint you prepared before class. Be sure to write large enough for everyone to see. Take about ten minutes to gather this information.

Say the following or put it into your own words:

The history, geography, peoples, cultures, and religions in this land longing to be holy are complex. One example of that complexity is the way in which Jewish Israelis and Palestinians experience and remember major events very differently. On May 14, 1948, Jews living in historic Palestine declared the State of Israel. The ensuing war is known to them as the War of Independence, a very positive connotation. The same event for Palestinians, whether Christian or Muslim, is known as the al-Nakbah, or the disaster, as over 750,000 Palestinians were displaced from their homes and driven from their land and are not yet being allowed to return sixty years later. A war of independence or the disaster—almost every major historical event will be described in such opposing terms.

Point out that we often bring unstated misconceptions to the study of this issue. Read the quotation from Rev. Alex Awad found in Chapter 2, p. 22, in the study book. Then ask someone to read aloud the paragraph from that chapter that begins "Together, the three Abrahamic religions…." (p. 25) Invite participants to look at the timeline you posted or the one in their study book and to name an event on the timeline that serves as an illustration of coexistence.

Then say:

There are many surprises when we begin to listen to the stories and experiences of everyday people. There are many things we think we know, but then we find out we didn't know enough or that what we knew was wrong. In our upcoming sessions, let's be open to being surprised, willing to hear stories and voices we've never heard before, able to question former ideas and grow in our understanding and concern for this region. Hopefully, we can commit ourselves to holding the peoples living in Israel-Palestine in our prayers, not only through this study but also for the years to come. May we also commit ourselves to standing with those working for a just peace for the peoples of that land as we put our prayers into action.

2. Introductions and Class Procedures *(about 25 minutes)*
Ask members of the group to introduce their partners to the total group. Remember that each person is to be introduced by someone other than her- or himself. On the newsprint headed "Learning Goals," jot down what each person hopes to learn during the study. If something is repeated, put a check mark next to the issue. Be sure to keep this sheet throughout the course so you can check back with the group and discover whether the learning goals are being met.

Keep this process moving. Ask questions if you need clarification, but don't engage in discussion. Help participants to summarize what they want to learn and move along.

- After the group members have finished their introductions, introduce yourself to them. Share your background, why you wanted to facilitate the study on Israel-Palestine, and what your hopes for the course are.
- Call the attention of the group to Chapter 1, "History and Memory," in the study book. Say that the author of the book presents his own personal story to explain the perspective in which he frames the historical events about which he writes. Also refer to "The Holocaust Ideology" (p. 99). Say the writer contends that the perceptions of American Jews about Israel-Palestine have been profoundly shaped by the Holocaust. Invite

participants to consider their personal stories and to reflect throughout the rest of the study about how their own experiences may be shaping their perceptions.

- To ensure that the study will take place in a meaningful and creative environment, establish guidelines for the time together. Print some suggestions on newsprint, for example:
  * Listen courteously to each other.
  * Take turns.
  * Encourage everyone to share, making time for others.
  * Be respectful of each other, even if you disagree.

Then elicit other suggestions from the participants. Post the newsprint where it can be easily seen for the duration of the study.

3. Present the Way of the Cross *(about 5 minutes)*
Acknowledge to the group that discussions about Palestine and Israel often get heated or inflammatory. People can get very emotional, sometimes not even knowing why they feel so strongly. Say that one of the ways that we keep centered and open to each other, that we continue to hold the peoples of the land together in our hearts, and that we strive to grow in our understanding, is through praying together. Say that in each session the group will do a lot of praying, striving throughout to keep focused on Jesus and the suffering of the peoples in Israel and Palestine. In this way participants can learn in an atmosphere of loving concern, repentance, and hope, seeking God's direction and peace.

Before leading them into the Way of the Cross Meditation, summarize in your own words the background information (in the introduction to the study guide) regarding the tradition of the Way of the Cross.

4. Way of the Cross Meditation 1 *(about 5 minutes)*
Either project the first picture or place a copy of it on a

stand on the worship center. Light the candle. Then ask the readers to lead the class in a time of prayerful reflection.

5. The Peoples of the Land (about 40 minutes)
Read or summarize the following:

> *In this special land, we find peoples who have a long history of woundedness, displacement, and loss. Both Palestinians and Israelis have known false accusations, imprisonment, and death at others' hands. Both peoples have experienced the world standing by and doing nothing to stop their experience of devastation. Both have longed to know safety and security for their children and their children's children. Yet, in the midst of such narratives of suffering, Israelis and Palestinians have always been more than victims of their histories. Many of them are creative, loving, hard-working, visionary people. They have different stories, concerns, and dreams. Some are more flexible than others. Just like people all over the world. Neither people are monolithic in their outlook or position. Let us hear from a sampling of peoples of the land.*

- Invite the participants you identified before the session to stand where they are and read the assigned story to the group.
- Post the discussion questions sheet you prepared before class for everyone to see it. Invite the class to quickly divide into small groups of five or six people each and to discuss the questions together. Ask someone in the group to take notes and later share highlights of the group's discussion with the whole class.

  Questions for Discussion:
  1. Are any of the stories new to you? If so, what makes them so?
  2. How does history impact the people's stories?
  3. What role does religious faith play in their lives?
  4. What do you believe are the key issues for each of the people?
  5. Pick two characters. What might you do to help build understanding between them?

After about twenty minutes of sharing, ask each of the groups to share briefly (about two minutes each) the highlights of their discussion.

6. Way of the Cross Meditation 2 (about 5 minutes)
Invite the two volunteers to lead the class in the Third Station. If possible, darken the room again. Either project the Station Three picture or place a copy of it on a stand on the worship center. Ask the readers to begin.

After the prayer, close Session 1 by asking the group to stand (if they are able) and join in singing one of these suggested hymns:
- "Ah, Holy Jesus" (#289, *United Methodist Hymnal*)
- "What Wondrous Love Is This" (#292, *United Methodist Hymnal*)
- "Guide My Feet, Lord" (#2208, *The Faith We Sing*)
- "Faith Is Patience in the Night" (#2211, *The Faith We Sing*)

Assignments for Next Session
1. Ask participants to reread Chapters 4, 5, and 6 in the study book.
2. Remind the eight people you recruited before the course or ask eight people now to prepare for the role-play debate.

Looking Ahead: Ask a volunteer to prepare a short reflection, about five to seven minutes, for the Way of the Cross Meditation in Session 3. Give this person a copy of the contemporary reading and ask her or him to consider what emotions the reading stirs up, in light of Jesus' command to love our neighbors as ourselves and our enemies as our neighbors. What challenges and opportunities does this put before us in the world we inhabit today, no matter where we live?

Session Two

Goals

- To analyze the complexities of land issues, border disputes, and questions of statehood between Israelis and Palestinians.
- To explore how religion is used positively and negatively in both the Middle East and in the United States when it comes to the questions concerning Palestine and Israel.
- To research the impact of the conflict in the Holy Land on women and children.
- To continue praying the Way of the Cross.

Materials and Supplies

- copies of the prayer from Handout 1 or newsprint sheet with prayer
- two copies each of Handouts 1 and 2
- copies of Appendix C: "Women and Children in Israel and Palestine" for participants
- copies of pictures for the Way of the Cross Meditations, or projection equipment
- signs for the debate (see Preparation)
- tables and chairs for debate activity
- cards with #1 and #10 printed on them and clear space for Activity #3
- stopwatch or watch with second hand

Preparation

- Make copies of the prayer from Handout 1 to be read in unison by everyone or print it in very large letters on newsprint and hang it in a place where everyone can read it easily. Also make two copies of Handouts 1 and 3 for the readers.
- Before the session, ask four people to lead the class in praying the two Way of the Cross Meditations. Two persons will read the titles of the meditations and the Scripture texts. A third person will read the contemporary reflection in the first meditation and a fourth will

lead "A Litany for Jerusalem" in the second meditation.
- Copy the pictures for the meditations, make transparencies of them, or arrange to project them from a computer.
- Make copies of Appendix C: "Women and Children in Israel and Palestine" for participants.
- Check to see that the eight people you asked to participate in the debate in Activity 2 are prepared for the activity.
- Use a colored felt-tipped marker on construction paper to make the following time signs for the debate: 1 minute, 30 seconds, 10 seconds, STOP. Make sure you have a stopwatch or a watch with a second hand so you can time the speakers.
- Before class, set two tables, each with four chairs, on one side at the front of the room with a space between them. Place the table and chairs at an angle toward each other, but so the rest of the class can see them. Leave enough room between the tables for you to stand to act as the moderator of the debate.
- Clear an area in the room with about a ten-to-fifteen-foot-long space upon which you can have the group stand in a straight line. Use masking tape or yarn to mark the line. At one end of the line on the wall or the floor, post a card with #1, and on the other end a card with #10.

Learning Activities

1. The Way of the Cross Meditation 3
(about 5 minutes)

Darken the room slightly if possible. Project the transparency of the picture or place the copy on the worship table. Light the candle. When everyone has gathered, have the group sing one of the following suggested hymns:

- "I Surrender All" (#354, *United Methodist Hymnal*)
- "He Touched Me" (#367, *United Methodist Hymnal*)

- "I Have Decided to Follow Jesus" (#2129, *The Faith We Sing*)
- "Jesus Walked This Lonesome Valley" (#2112, *The Faith We Sing*)
- "The Lone, Wild Bird" (#2052, *The Faith We Sing*)

Summarize the following:

> *In the traditional Stations of the Cross, the gospel accounts provide the background for most of the fourteen stations. But some stations come from the traditions of the early church and the experiences of early pilgrims to Jerusalem. The story of Veronica is from the early apocryphal writings. According to an early version of Acts of Pilate, a woman named Veronica was the same woman Jesus cured of a disorder of the blood, and she came to his trial to proclaim his innocence. A later version of the story recounts that Veronica had in her possession a cloth with the imprint of the face of Jesus. Supposedly Veronica wiped Jesus' face with a cloth on his journey to Calvary.*
>
> *Women played a key role in the whole story of Jesus' passion, steadfastly remaining with him through his crucifixion, attending his burial and anointing his body. This traditional account focuses on Veronica's solidarity and acts of compassion.*

Ask the volunteers to lead the class in the Way of the Cross Meditation.

2. Debate Show *(about 40 minutes)*

- Invite the debaters to sit at the two tables as divided in the pre-assignment descriptions.
- Once everyone is in place, welcome everyone to the debate. Share with the group that there are many things that keep us from being able to do as Veronica did. Our ideologies, our dogmas, our fears, and our positions can all keep us from seeing the need or humanity in others' faces. In Palestine and Israel, competing ideas about how the land should be exclusively held, divided, or shared often create seemingly insurmountable obstacles on a road to justice and

peace. Say that today we're going to try to grow in our understanding of some of the positions held by people concerned about how this conflict will finally be settled. By listening carefully to each panelist, we'll try to "have ears that hear" even those positions that we find objectionable. Such listening is an act of compassion and recognition of the dignity of the one speaking. It is one of the foundations upon which life-giving community can be founded.

Remind everyone of the rules of the debate. Each panelist will be given two minutes to explain her or his position on land, borders, and statehood. After each panelist's opening statement, a panelist on one side will be allowed to challenge one member of the other team. The challenged panelist will have one minute to answer the questioner, who will in turn have one minute to refute the answer. The challenges will go back and forth between the sides until all panelists have had a chance to ask a question of a member of the other team.

- Begin the debate and watch the time carefully. Alert presenters when they have one minute left, thirty seconds left, and ten seconds left by holding up the pre-made signs. Stop them at exactly two minutes. Go back and forth between the two teams until all eight panelists have had their opening arguments. Remind the panelists that the questions they direct to the opposing team members should be clear and concise.
- Begin the challenge-and-answer section. Remind panelists when they have thirty seconds left and when they have ten seconds left. Stop them after one minute has elapsed.
- Thank the debaters for their work and participation. Then open a general discussion for approximately ten minutes with the whole group, using some of the following questions:

* With which positions were you familiar before the debate? Which positions were new to you?
* Did any of the positions surprise you? Why or why not? Do any seem insupportable? Why?
* What solution seems most likely to lead to a just and durable peace?

3. Continuum Choices *(about 30 minutes)*

- Ask the group to distribute themselves evenly along the line between #1 and #10. Be sure they have some room around them.
- Tell participants that you are going to read a series of statements about the impact of religion on the conflict. After each statement, everyone should move up or down the line in accordance with how much they agree or disagree with the statement read, with #1 being "strongly disagree" and #10 being "strongly agree." For example, if the statement is "Christians disagree a lot about the impact of religion on the conflict" and someone strongly agrees, that person would move toward #10; if people moderately agree, they should move toward the middle of the line; and if they really disagree, they should move to #1. Encourage them to try to avoid choosing the middle of the line too often.
- After you read each statement and participants arrange themselves on the line, ask one or two people to share briefly why they are standing where they are.

    Statements:
    1. Jerusalem is equally important to Jews, Christians, and Muslims.
    2. The conflict in the Holy Land is rooted primarily in religious ideologies.
    3. The commonalities among the three Abraham/Sarah/Hagar traditions can help create a vision for a just peace in Israel-Palestine.
    4. Christian Zionism plays a significant role in shaping US foreign policy in this conflict.
    5. Many Christians feel the conflict is between Jews and Muslims.
    6. Biblical Israel is equivalent to the modern State of Israel, and therefore the land belongs to the Jewish people.
    7. Palestinians are paying the price for Western Christian anti-Semitism.
    8. Religion is a hindrance to finding a peace settlement for the conflict.
    9. Criticism of policies of the State of Israel is the same as anti-Semitism.
    10. The conflict is a political one over land and who controls it, not primarily one about religion.

- After the last statement and explanation, invite participants to form groups of three or four with those standing closest to them. Ask them to spend about ten minutes discussing what they learned from the study book about the positive and negative impacts of religion in this conflict.

4. The Impact on Women and Children
(about 35 minutes)

Invite the small groups to combine into four groups by numbering off from one to four and move around tables to work. Each table will be asked to research the impact that the conflict has had on the women and children using Appendix C: "Women and Children in Israel and Palestine." Ask Table 1 to look at Israeli women, and Table 2 at Palestinian women. Table 3 should research the impact on Israeli children, and Table 4 on Palestinian children. Give each group newsprint and a marker to jot down in short sentences or phrases what they discover. Ask the group to designate someone to present the final list to the whole group. Give the groups about fifteen minutes to work, then give them a five-minute warning. After the five minutes, call everyone back to the total group. Invite each group to post its list and give each one about three minutes to share the results of their research.

5. Way of the Cross Meditation 4

(about 10 minutes)

If possible, darken the room a little. Either project the picture or place a copy of it on a stand on the worship center. Ask two volunteers to lead the class in the time of prayerful reflection.

Close by singing one of the following hymns:

- "When Cross the Crowded Ways of Life" (#427, *United Methodist Hymnal*)
- "All Who Love and Serve Your City" (#433, *United Methodist Hymnal*)
- "The Servant Song" (#2222, *The Faith We Sing*)
- "Sent Out in Jesus' Name" (#2184, *The Faith We Sing*)

Assignments for Next Session

1. Remind participants to bring to the next session the newspaper or internet articles that they located about the conflict. If they haven't yet found any, suggest they research current newspapers and internet sites between now and the next session.

2. Remind the person who volunteered to give a personal reflection on the contemporary reading in the Way of the Cross Meditation to be prepared.

3. Ask for volunteer(s) to read the online resource "Why Divestment? And Why Now?" (http://resources.gbgm -umc.org/israelpalestine) and be prepared to summarize the ideas and discuss it.

Session Three

Goals

- To examine current issues of racism, terrorism, Occupation, refugees, and liberation
- To examine the role of media in reporting the Israel-Palestine conflict and the myths of Israel-Palestine that have developed in US culture
- To explore the Israel and Palestine communities in the United States and the influence or lack thereof on US policies
- To continue praying the Way of the Cross

Materials and Supplies

- copies of reflection pictures for Way of the Cross Meditations, or projection equipment
- copies of Handout 4 Session 1, Handout 2 Session 2, and fact sheets (see Preparation)
- copies of "Walls That Divide Are Broken Down" (http://resources.gbgm-umc.org/israelpalestine)
- five to seven orange or green cards (3" x 5" cards or small Post-it® notes) and enough blue cards for the rest of the participants
- cardboard boxes or building blocks and tables, or clothesline, tape, and newsprint
- newspaper or internet articles on the crisis in Israel-Palestine
- two copies each of Handouts 1 and 2 (Way of the Cross Meditations 5 and 6) and copies of Handouts 3, 4, and 5 for participants
- copy of DVD *Children of the Nakba* and DVD player
- newsprint and markers, a chalkboard and chalk, or white board and markers

Preparation

- Before class, place five to seven chairs in the back of the room facing towards a wall away from the rest of the group, preferably with their backs to the rest of the group. If possible, place some sort of barrier between the chairs and the rest of the room. If there are moveable display boards or chalkboards, you could use those to really separate the chairs from the rest of the room.
- Gather five to seven orange or green cards (3" x 5" cards or small Post-it® notes). There should be enough blue cards for the rest of the participants to have one. On three of the blue cards, make a dot with a felt-tipped marker.
- Collect boxes or ask each participant to bring a box, or obtain cardboard building bricks from a children's educational supply store. Set up tables down the middle of the room on which to put the blocks. This will provide enough height to block the view from one side to the other. Or simply use sheets of newsprint taped to clothesline stretched between the walls.
- Collect some newspaper or internet articles that you can give to participants who don't have them to use for Activity 4.
- Download and make copies of the following fact sheets from http://www.pcusa.org/worldwide/israelpalestine/resources.htm#sheets: "Occupation," "Home Demolitions," "Settlements," "The Separation Barrier – The Security Barrier – The Wall"
- Ask four volunteers to lead the class in praying the two Way of the Cross Meditations. Two persons will read the meditation titles and the Scripture texts. The other two will read the contemporary reflections. Check with the person giving a personal reflection on the reading for Way of the Cross Meditation 5 to be sure he or she is prepared.
- Obtain a copy of the DVD *Children of the Nakba,* a DVD player and monitor. On newsprint or a chalk/white board, print the discussion questions listed in the activity.
- Make copies of the handouts.

Learning Activities

1. The Wall: Security or Apartheid *(about 40 minutes)*

- As participants arrive, invite them to choose from a box or basket one of the colored cards that you prepared. Those who receive the blue cards will sit in the chairs set up for the regular class. Direct anyone who chooses an orange or green card to go and sit in one of the chairs at the back of the room.

- When you're ready to begin, ask the persons whose blue cards have a dot to go to the back of the room. Their job is to make sure none of the participants at the back with the orange or green cards leave their chairs or turn them around to face the rest of the room for any reason.

- Some participants may ask why folks are in the back. Some in the back may get frustrated and even angry. Explain that those at the back of the room don't have the appropriate ID cards and do not have permission to be in the rest of the room. The room is only for blue-card holders. That is just the way it is—they are there and we are here. (Note: This can be difficult for the leader! But this is an important simulation exercise to help the group begin to wrestle with the impact of the Occupation on Palestinians' lives. Try not to give in to people and instead get on with the exercise. There will be time later on for people to talk about what they were experiencing.)

- Divide the remaining participants into four small groups. Give participants copies of Handout 3, "Fact Sheet: Palestinian Right of Return for Refugees" and the two handouts from previous sessions. Also make available some of the fact sheets you downloaded. Ask them to think about the issues or situations named in the study book, handouts, and fact sheets that would likely lead to a wall between peoples, and to print each of their ideas on a separate block or piece of newsprint. Give them about ten minutes and then ask them to bring their blocks or newsprint to the center, standing around the tables there. They should each read what is written on their block or paper. If using blocks, invite them to place their blocks one at a time on the table to build a wall dividing the group. If using newsprint, instruct them to tape the newsprint papers to the clothesline. Be sure part of the group is on one side of the wall and part on the other. When all have added their blocks or sheets, ask:
  - *Do walls make good neighbors?*
  - *Why do these issues lead toward the building of destructive walls?*
  - *Do you like being separated by the wall?*

- Invite the group to sing "Walls That Divide Are Broken Down" (http://resources.gbgm-umc.org/israelpalestine). As they are singing, have them dismantle the wall between them. Do not invite those at the back of the room to participate in this. Some of the main group may go back and take the wall down there, too. If they do, that's okay. Don't stop it, but allow it to happen spontaneously.

- At the end of the exercise, invite the people sitting in the back to bring their chairs and join the group. Help the group debrief the experience of excluding some of the class. Ask:
  - *Did any of those in the back try to get up or turn their chairs around?*
  - *Did the monitors talk to those in the back? Was there any negotiation going on?*
  - *How did those segregated in the back feel? Did it make them angry to be excluded?*
  - *How did the monitors feel having to keep people in the back?*
  - *How did those in the main group feel? Once they got into the exercise, were they conscious that people were in the back?*

* What was this exercise meant to help the group experience?

- (Optional) Ask the person who volunteered in the last session to summarize the ideas in the online resource "Why Divestment? And Why Now?" (http://resources .gbgm-umc.org/israelpalestine). Invite participants to respond.

2. Way of the Cross Meditation 5 *(about 15 minutes)*
Invite the group to move into a big circle. Remind them that the previous exercise offers just a brief glance into the lives of those who are excluded on the basis of their nationality, religion, and other reasons. Exclusion is a very painful experience, especially when it impacts one's ability to work, learn, pray, receive medical care, and so forth. Say that we Christians tragically still exclude people—at personal, national, and global levels. We sometimes think we're not like "those" other people who are violent or militant. Yet we fail to see the brokenness and violence in our own hearts. Invite participants as they move into the Way of the Cross Meditation to be mindful of their own brokenness and our personal and corporate sin, seeking forgiveness from the Prince of Peace.

- Say that the Kyrie Eleison, "Lord have mercy," is an ancient plea of the Christian community. In light of the violence, militarism, and state and insurgent terrorism in our world today, and in recognition that we have contributed to the growth of the destruction either by acts of omission or commission, we need to cry out to God for mercy and forgiveness, for hearts turned toward the Giver of Life and Love that we might have strength and vision to work for a different future for all of creation. Say that the litany they are about to share was written by a Palestinian Christian, a Syrian Orthodox Christian layperson who had resided his entire life in Jerusalem and lived through the many periods of violence and distrust.

- Divide the class into two groups (right and left sides, men and women, youth and adults, or some other division). Then teach the Kyrie Eleison. Sing it through once yourself or ask someone else to do so, and then invite the group to sing along. Sing it two or three times until you think the group feels comfortable with it. Don't rush. Let it be sung prayerfully.

- Ask the two readers and the person giving a personal reflection to lead the group in experiencing the Way of the Cross Meditation.

3. Children of the Nakba *(about 40 minutes)*
Invite the class to watch the DVD *Children of the Nakba* (28 minutes). After watching the DVD, discuss the following questions:

- Mr. Laham, an 86-year-old man, was not allowed to return to visit his land for a day without applying for special permission, when it was only a few miles away. Consider how his village is linked to his past and to his identity. How has your identity been shaped by a town, state, province, or country? How is that place accessible to you and what would it mean for you if it was inaccessible?

- According to Israel's Law of Return, any Jew can come to live as a citizen in the State of Israel, some even receiving financial benefits (including tax exemptions and free benefits such as plane tickets, housing, medical insurance, and language study). Compare this with Israel's refusal to allow Palestinian refugees who wish to live in peace with their neighbors to return (as stipulated in UN General Assembly Resolution 194). What is Israel's responsibility to Palestinian refugees? How could the dialogue between residents of Kibbutz Baram and refugees from Bir'im village in the video be a starting point?

- When Na'im returned to Beit 'Itab, the land was empty.

Na'im states, "No one lives here. I must live here." The land of most of the more than 500 villages destroyed in 1948 also does not house Israeli communities. In some instances, however, the village's former land is now used for Israeli agriculture, and in others Israeli Jews now live in former Palestinian homes. What prevents Palestinian refugees returning home to the sites of destroyed villages when the land is empty? What are creative ways to think about return in instances when there are new inhabitants in refugees' homes?

- At this point in history, there are Israeli citizens who know no other home than Israel. How does their new identity compare to that of the children in the Dheisheh refugee camp who consider themselves to be from Beit 'Itab? How does the work of the Zochrot Association bring the stories of both groups together?

- In Colossians 3:9-11, we read that when we align ourselves with the image of our Creator, we understand that God intends that all people be equal (Jew and Greek, circumcised and uncircumcised, slave and free). How can this call to align ourselves with our Creator shape our perspective on the situation in Palestine and Israel, and how we should see and love the "Other"?

4. Angles of Vision: Media and our Perceptions
(about 30 minutes)
Say that media plays a significant role in shaping the public perception. The issues and personalities presented affect the search for a just peace throughout the region and especially in Israel and Palestine. People with various perspectives on the conflict feel "their side" is unfairly represented. Many groups have worked on preparing guidelines to help outsiders get a handle on how well the information is shared.

- Divide the group into small groups of four or five people to explore articles about the issues. Make sure they have brought articles with them or that you have given them copies of articles on the conflict. Ask the groups to read the articles and then to go through the questions in Handout 4 to assess how the story was told. Ask them to consider the following questions:
  * *What did you discover?*
  * *What perceptions do you have about how the conflict is usually covered?*
  * *How are Israelis often portrayed in stories about the conflict?*
  * *How are Palestinians portrayed?*
  After twenty minutes, bring the groups back together and discuss in the total group what they discovered, what questions they still have, and so forth.

- Suggest to participants that they look at Handout 5 for some sources where they might get coverage on the conflict with perspectives different from what they usually get. If you have access to computers at your teaching site, you might even have them go to the computer lab to go online to see what the current stories are.

5. Way of the Cross Meditation 6 *(about 5 minutes)*
Invite the volunteers to lead the group in praying the Way of the Cross Meditation. Ask one of the volunteers to lead the closing prayer, or do it yourself.

Sing one of the following hymns as you depart:
- "Let There be Peace on Earth" (#431, *United Methodist Hymnal*)
- "Help Us Accept Each Other" (#560, *United Methodist Hymnal*)
- "The Spirit Sends Us Forth to Serve" (#2241, *The Faith We Sing*)
- "They'll Know We are Christians by Our Love" (#2223, *The Faith We Sing*)

Session Four

Goals

- To explore the stance of The United Methodist Church during the ongoing Israeli-Palestinian conflict.
- To network with existing organizations to achieve lasting peace in the region.
- To continue to pray the Way of the Cross.
- To develop action plans that will lead participants to influence US policy to achieve justice and peace for Palestine and Israel and to live out the gospel and be in solidarity with one another.

Materials and Supplies

- copies of reflection pictures for the Way of the Cross Meditations, or projection equipment
- newsprint and markers
- one copy of Handouts 1 and 2
- copies of Handouts 3 and 4 for each participant
- index cards or paper and pencils or pens
- self-addressed stamped envelopes
- map outline on brown package wrapping paper or mural paper
- kneeling cushions or small pillows (optional)
- five containers of sand (see Preparation) and taper candles for each participant, or tea lights; matches
- flashlights
- large standing cross or flat cross

Preparation

- Learn or ask someone else to learn and lead the new hymn, "Waa Habibi, Waa Habibi." If you have access to someone who speaks Arabic, ask them to go over it with you. If you don't feel comfortable with this or don't have anyone who can lead the hymn, plan to use "When I Survey the Wondrous Cross" (#298, *United Methodist Hymnal*).
- Make a copy of Handout 2, "Who Will Roll the Stone Away?" Before class, assign one of the boxes to each of the seven people to read. Also ask two other people to read "Stories of Hope" (Appendix A).
- Obtain sheets of newsprint and markers for Activity 3.
- For Activity 4, make copies of Handouts 2 and 3 for each participant. You'll also need index cards or paper and pencils or pens. If possible, before the session, ask each person to bring a self-addressed stamped envelope. If you can't contact them beforehand, have envelopes and stamps available. Don't be afraid to ask for donations to cover the costs of the stamps if you don't have a fund to draw from for this.
- Before the session, ask someone to lead the class in the Way of the Cross Meditation, reading the title "Jesus is Laid in the Tomb," and then the Scripture passage.
- Make an outline of the map of Israel-Palestine on a large sheet of paper for Activity 5. It should be large enough that participants would have room to stand, sit, or kneel around it. Brown package wrapping paper or mural paper works well. You can tape two sheets together to make it wide enough. The map doesn't have to be exact, but it should be recognizable. You will place the map on the floor near the worship center, along with kneeling cushions or small pillows if they are available. Fill three to five containers (such as six-inch plastic flower pots) about three-quarters with sand and place around the map. Place thin taper-style candles for each participant in piles near the containers. Another option is to use tea light candles. Obtain a couple of flashlights for the readers.
- Ask someone to practice the chant to use throughout the service. Or as a last resort, teach the words to the group and have everyone say it together rather than sing it. If possible, place a standing cross on the map. You could also place a cross flat across the map.

Learning Activities

1. Jesus Is Laid in the Tomb *(about 5 minutes)*

If possible, darken the room a little. Either project the picture for the station or place a copy of it on a stand on the worship center. Light the candle.

If you are singing the suggested hymn, try to sing at least the chorus in Arabic, following the phonetic pronunciation. This is one of the favorite Arabic hymns for Holy Week all across the Middle East. It has a haunting melody.

2. Palestinians and Israelis Work for Peace *(about 20 minutes)*

Summarize the following:

> Our concern for peace and justice in Palestine and Israel does not grow out of a vacuum. The pleas from the Christian heads of churches in Jerusalem in the early 1980s really challenged the churches in the West to become more active in our solidarity and action. Millions of Christians from all over the world were visiting the Holy Land every year. Unfortunately, too many went to that broken land and treated it like a museum. In many pilgrimages, Christians have run where Jesus walked, rushing from holy site to holy site. Often folks have had a deeply spiritual individual or communal experience with companions, but usually got back on the plane and flew home, unaware that Christians were struggling under the impact of Occupation. We never worried about Israelis or Palestinians who were mourning loved ones killed by the terror of the other. The heads of churches said that because we didn't know anything of the current context, we were ill-equipped to help the peoples of the land who were searching for a just and sustainable way out of the conflict.

Invite volunteers to tell briefly about the author's experience of being on a tour of the Holy Land in 1980 (Chapter 1, pp. 19-20). If you haven't asked before, check to see if any of the participants have been on such a tour. Ask:

- *Did you run where Jesus walked?*
- *Did you think much about the people you saw?*

- *What might have been different if you had walked and talked and listened to the peoples of the land as part of the visit?*
- *Have any of you been on a different kind of visit where you did meet with the people? What did that add to your experience?*

Summarize:

> Too often, what we do know about the conflict is usually limited to sound bites about some violent event. We seldom hear the voices of those peoples of the land who are committed to a different future for the region. They are the silenced or ignored members of both communities. But their efforts and tenacity keep the conflict from completely going out of control. They are ones who are rolling the stone away, letting light into dark places, bringing hope to despairing people.

Ask the volunteers to read the stories on Handout 2, "Who Will Roll the Stone Away?" (pp. 202-206) and the two "Stories of Hope" (Appendix A, pp. 159-163). Invite them to stand where they are, if they are able, and remind them to read loudly enough so everyone can hear them. After all the stories have been read, ask:

- *Did anything surprise you?*
- *How would you describe the work that these organizations do?*
- *Is there a common denominator among them?*
- *What do you think are the guiding principles of their work that allow these organizations to be peacebuilders in a context of fear, hatred, and violence?*
- *Do you know of groups doing similar work for peace and justice in your area?*
- *What essential commonalities are there in the core guiding principles?*

3. Peace and Justice Through the Church's Work *(about 30 minutes)*

Summarize for participants:

> The United Methodist Church is committed to a just and durable peace with security and hope for all the peoples of Israel-Palestine. Our Book of Resolutions from General Conference includes a number of resolutions calling on United Methodists to participate in acts that will help build a culture of justice and peace in the region.

Ask participants to turn to the online resource "United Methodist Resolutions" (http://resources.gbgm-umc.org/ israelpalestine) to see current resolutions of the church. Ask them to list the key points of each resolution, working through them one at a time. List their responses on newsprint or chalk/white board. Then ask questions such as the following:

- *What commonalities do you notice between resolutions of The United Methodist Church and the actions of the Israeli and Palestinian groups?*
- *What differences are there?*
- *Do you believe that as United Methodists we are helping to roll the stone away? If so, how? If not, what might we be doing?*

4. What Can We Do to Roll the Stone Away?

(about 45 minutes)

Divide the class into groups of five or six people. Make sure everyone has a copy of Handout 3: "Solidarity: Creating a Circle of Concern" and Handout 4: "Places to Connect." Give each group newsprint and markers. Ask the groups to take about twenty-five minutes to review the two handouts and to discuss practical ways they can become peace-with-justice evangelists for Israel-Palestine. Ask them to identify someone who can record their suggestions and present them to the whole group.

- Gather the group back together and spend about ten minutes sharing the lists.
- When all groups have shared their ideas, pass out

index cards or paper. Ask participants to take a few minutes to think through all the suggestions that have been made and to enter into a time of reflection about what they will commit to do. Invite them to write down at least one thing they will commit to do for justice and peace. They should put the card or paper in the self-addressed and stamped envelope. During the closing worship, there will be a time to offer their envelopes in prayer. After the service, collect the envelopes and tell participants that you will mail the envelopes to them in three months as a reminder about their commitments. (Note: Please don't forget to mail these commitment cards to participants.)

5. Closing Worship *(about 20 minutes)*

Explain that you're going to make some adjustments in the room in order to get prepared for the closing worship time. Before you close, however, thank the participants for their energy, input, and commitment. Give them the opportunity to thank you as well. Then ask them to help you make the necessary adjustments in the room for the service below. (Note: This worship experience is paperless. Only the leaders have the order of service.)

Preparation

- Before beginning, teach the repetitive chant, "Christ Is Our Peace." Explain that there is no need for them to have anything to read; this is a time of prayerful reflection. Move the chairs into a large circle around your worship center. Place the large map of Israel-Palestine on the floor. Set the pots of sand at different places around the map with taper candles lying by the pots, or distribute the tea lights around the map.
- This service is in the dark, or as dark as possible with minimal lighting so that people can see where they're going. Dim the lights once you have everything prepared and you have rehearsed the chants.

Worship Service

Reader 1: As we prepare to leave one another's presence, we do so mindful of the wounded world, and confess our complicity in its wounding. We come to the cross to pray for the end of hostility and hatred and the fear that divides nations, destroys communities, and sows the seeds of death in our own hearts. We come to hear God's promise to pardon, strengthen, and heal us, and to be gathered again into the blessed, broken body of Christ who is our peace. We come to join those who would roll the stones away so that life might dance forth.

There will be a time during our prayers when you may come forward to the cross at the center of the map of Israel-Palestine. You may sit or kneel to pray at any place around the map and light a candle (secure tapers in one of the pots of sand), remaining as long as you desire. You are invited to bring your envelope with your commitment card and place it on the map as well.

Proclamation of Praise

Reader 1: Blessed be God, who forgives our sin, heals every illness, saves us from death, enfolds us with tender care, and crowns us with steadfast love. *(See Psalm 103:2-4.)*

All: **Amen.**

Chant: *(During this time, the cross is brought out and put in place.)*

Reader 2: The grace of the Lord Jesus, the love of God, and the communion of the Holy Spirit be with you all.

All: **And also with you.**

Reader 2: Let us pray (*pause*). Holy God, out of your great love for the world, your Word became flesh to live among us and to reconcile us to you and to one another. Rekindle among us the gift of your Spirit that we might live as one new humanity in Christ, dismantling the walls that divide, ending the hostility among us, and proclaiming peace to those who are far off and to those who are near, through Christ Jesus in whom we all have access in the one Spirit to you, both now and forever. *(See Ephesians 2:14-18.)*

All: **Amen.**

Antiphon: *(sung by cantor first, then by all):*
Christ, our peace, you break down the walls that divide us:
Christ, our peace, bring us together in you.*

Reader 3: This morning, Tuesday, June 27, 2006, the Israeli bulldozers guarded with armed personnel started cutting and uprooting olive trees in the Cremisan area of Beit Jala, just west of Bethlehem, in preparation for the construction of the Segregation Wall. The Cremisan area has the only remaining forest in the city, and the most fertile agricultural land, which is the main source of income to many farmers in the city. The project Open Bethlehem's chief executive, Leila Sansour, says: "At a time when the US Congress is considering the plight of Palestinian Christians, we are witnessing the destruction of this community's land, heritage, and livelihood. The people of Bethlehem are united in their message to the international community: If you want to help us, stop the construction of Israel's Wall."

Reader 1: A reading from the prophet Isaiah:
Do not fear, for I am with you; be not afraid, for I am your God: I will strengthen you, I will help you, I will uphold you with my right hand. (Isaiah 41:10)

Antiphon: *(sung by cantor first, then by all):*

Christer, our peace, you break down the walls that divide us:

Christ, our peace, bring us together in you.

Reader 2: Since the isolation of Jerusalem behind the Apartheid Wall, entering the city is impossible without a permit from the Israeli Occupation forces. Abed el-Fatah sent his medical file with the application for a permit through the Red Crescent. A week after applying for the permit he received a paper telling him that his application was refused for "security reasons." Abed, whose medical case was critical, could not wait for approval. He took the decision to enter Jerusalem by jumping over the Apartheid Wall in Abu Dis area. Abed said: "Although my case is critical and the reality is that I need an ambulance to reach the hospital, I had to jump over the wall to make my surgery.
(http://stopthewall.org/latestnews/1317.shtml)

Reader 1: Do not fear for I have redeemed you; I have called you by name, you are mine. When you pass through waters, I will be with you; and through the rivers, they shall not overwhelm you; when you walk through fire you shall not be burned, and the flame shall not consume you. (Isaiah 43:1-2)

Antiphon: *(sung by cantor first, then by all):*

Christ, our peace, you break down the walls that divide us:

Christ, our peace, bring us together in you.

Reader 3: For the last two years, the Occupation and its Wall have made life increasingly impossible for us. They are literally expelling us from our land. This year the Occupation permitted us to spend just four days planting and cultivating our fields. What can we do with just four days? How can we plant seeds or cultivate the land? There was no time for anything. They banned us from using tractors and machinery—they said everything must be done with animals. Everybody worked solidly for the four days. We tried, but in the end we had to leave most of the land uncultivated. They are forcing us and our animals out.
(http://stopthewall.org/communityvoices/1187.shtml)

Reader 1: A reading from the prophet Isaiah:
Do not fear, for I am with you; I will bring your offspring from the east, and from the west I will gather you; I will say to the north, "Give them up," and to the south, "Do not withhold; bring my sons from far away and my daughters from the end of the earth—everyone who is called by my name, whom I created for my glory, whom I formed and made." (Isaiah 43:5-7)

Antiphon: *(sung by cantor first, then by all):*

Christ, our peace, you break down the walls that divide us:

Christ, our peace, bring us together in you.

Reader 2: The Israeli Committee Against House Demolition members physically block bulldozers sent to demolish Palestinian homes. We also mobilize hundreds of Israelis and Palestinians to rebuild them as acts of resistance. In addition to its effectiveness as a means of raising awareness of the workings of the Occupation, house rebuilding has proven to be an effective vehicle of grassroots peace-making.

Reader 1: A reading from the prophet Isaiah:
"You are my servant, I have chosen you, and

not cast you off"; do not fear, for I am with you; be not afraid, for I am your God; I will strengthen you, I will help you, I will uphold you with my right hand. (Isaiah 41:9b-10)

Invitation

Reader 2: Jesus says, "Come to me all who are weary and carrying heavy burdens, and I will give you rest."

Reader 3: Come, you who feel far from God's embrace: a stranger to God's promises, unsure of God's love.

Reader 1: Come from behind the walls that surround you: hostility that consumes, fear that entombs, and pride that divides and destroys.

Reader 2: Come, you who long for peace on earth: peace among nations and between peoples, peace in your homes and in your hearts.

Reader 3: Come, you who seek healing in the world: freedom for the captive and for the captor, hope for the hungry and for the greedy.

Reader 1: Do not fear. Come to the cross of Christ Jesus, where, lifted up, he gathers all people to himself, ending our divisions, becoming our peace, and granting us God's abundant life. *(Pause briefly.)*

Reader 2: When the music begins, come as you are drawn—to stand, sit, or kneel to pray. Light a candle, stay as long as you desire, returning to your seat when you are ready. Bring your commitment envelope with you and place it on the map. If you choose to remain seated, you are invited to lift your prayers in silence and in song and to place your envelope on the map when you leave.

(Softly sing "Christ, Our Peace.")

Closing Collect
(When the prayers at the cross have come to a natural end, and participants have returned to their chairs, continue.)

Reader 1: Gathering our many prayers into one, let us pray *(pause)*. O God, rich in mercy, when we were dead through our sin, out of your great love, you raised us up and made us alive together with Christ. Receive the prayers of your people; by your grace save us, heal our divisions, and make us one in Christ Jesus, your Son, our Peace. *(See Ephesians 2:4-6.)*

All: **Amen.**

Sending
(Blessing)

Reader 3: Go now into the world! May Christ dwell in your hearts through faith, as you are being rooted and grounded in love, strengthened by the Spirit, and filled with the fullness of God. *(See Ephesians 3:16-19.)*

All: **Amen.**

(The closing worship moment is based on a service written by Rev. Susan Briehl, Spokane, Washington, for the Evangelical Lutheran Church of America's 2005 Global Mission Event.)

Two-Hour Session

One-Session Study

Four two-hour sessions offer the opportunity to explore more thoroughly the content of this study, but sometimes it is necessary to provide a shorter class. This session provides a guide to which activities would help introduce and expose participants to the peoples of the land, its history, and the hopes for the future if you only have a two-hour block of time available. This will allow only a taste of the material, but it is hoped participants will be eager to know more and commit to further study at a later date.

Goals

- To introduce the ancient spiritual exercise of the Way of the Cross
- To begin to grow in understanding about the diverse peoples living in Israel-Palestine today, their cultures, and religions
- To develop action plans that will lead participants to influence US policy to achieve justice and peace for Palestine and Israel and to live out the gospel and be in solidarity with one another.

Materials and Supplies

- (choice of one activity) for Activity 1, Session 1: five tables and enough chairs for participants (or chairs and space to set up display boards); fifteen sheets of poster board (or five three-sided display boards); masking tape, colored felt-tipped markers, newsprint; maps of Israel-Palestine (see Introduction, p. 132). For Activity 3, Session 3: copy of DVD *Children of the Nakba,* a DVD player, and a TV/monitor.
- worship table, candle, and matches
- copies of pictures for Way of the Cross Meditations, or equipment to project them
- copies of handouts from various sessions (see activities below)

- index card or paper and pens or pencils

Preparation

- The leader has a choice between two different exercises to open the session. See Session 1 (p. 134) for the set-up for Activity 1. If you choose to use the alternative Activity 3 from Chapter 3, obtain a copy of the DVD *Children of the Nakba,* a DVD player, and a TV/monitor. Ask someone to show you how to use or run the equipment if you are not familiar with it.
- Copy or arrange to project the reflection picture for the Way of the Cross Meditation (see Introduction, p. 132).
- Set up a worship center using the instructions in the Introduction (p. 130).
- Ask four people to lead the group in praying the two Way of the Cross Meditations. Ask two persons to read the titles of the meditations and then read the Scripture text(s). Two additional persons should read the contemporary reflections.
- Learn or ask someone to lead the new hymn in Activity 1. If you don't feel comfortable with this or don't have anyone who can lead the hymn, you can use #298 (*United Methodist Hymnal*) "When I Survey the Wondrous Cross."
- Depending on what choice you make for Activity 4, either ask seven people before class to be ready to read the information on the Handout "Who Will Roll the Stone Away?" from Session 4 (pp. 202-206), or if you choose to use Activity 4, Session 4 (p. 148), make copies of the Handouts (pp. 207-209 and 210-213) for each participant. You'll also need index cards or paper and pencils or pens.

Learning Activities

1. Option A: Geography, Maps, and Peoples
(about 30 minutes)

As participants arrive, give them a copy of Handout 2 from Session 1 (p. 184) and the number of their assigned starting workstation. Be sure to distribute the group evenly among the five stations. Ask participants to fill out the worksheet for their particular station. Once everyone has arrived and filled out the first set of questions, ask each one to pair up with someone else in their small group. Tell them that later each person will be asked to introduce someone else in the group to the whole class. Encourage them to find out:

- The person's name
- The person's annual conference, district, or local church
- One thing that the person is hoping to learn from this mission study and whether she/he has ever been to Palestine-Israel.

After about five minutes, check in with the groups to see if they've finished their introductions and know who is introducing whom later on. If some are not finished, give them an additional couple of minutes, but urge them to finish quickly.

Tell participants that they will move clockwise around the room, stopping at each station to answer the appropriate questions on the worksheets. Give participants five minutes at each station. Suggest that at some point they spend a minute or two studying either the posted timeline or the one in Appendix B of their book.

When all the groups are finished, invite them to turn their chairs toward the center to form a large circle. If the room you are using is large enough to have a table in the center along with the workstations on the sides, then have everyone gather around the table. Ask:

- *What was new to you?*
- *What was a surprise?*

Print their answers on the newsprint you prepared before class. Be sure to write large enough for everyone to see. Take about ten minutes to gather this information.

Say the following or put it into your own words:

The history, geography, peoples, cultures, and religions in this land longing to be holy are complex. One example of that complexity is the way in which Jewish Israelis and Palestinians experience and remember major events very differently. On May 14, 1948, Jews living in historic Palestine declared the State of Israel, and the ensuing war is known to them as the War of Independence, a very positive connotation. The same event for Palestinians, whether Christian or Muslim, is known as the al-Nakbah, or the disaster, as over 750,000 Palestinians were displaced from their homes and driven from their land, and are not yet being allowed to return sixty years later. Almost every major historical event will be described in such opposing terms.

Point out that we often bring unstated misconceptions to the study of this issue. Read the quotation from Rev. Alex Awad found in Chapter 2 (p. 22) in the study book. Then ask someone to read aloud the paragraph from that chapter that begins "Together, the three Abrahamic religions..." (p. 25). Invite participants to look at the timeline you posted or the one in Appendix B and to name an event on the timeline that serves as an illustration of coexistence. Then say:

There are many surprises when we begin to listen to the stories and experiences of everyday people. In our upcoming sessions, let's be willing to hear stories and voices we've never heard before. Let's be open to questioning former ideas and to growing in our understanding and concern for this region. Let's commit to holding the peoples living in Israel-Palestine in our prayers, not only through this study but from now on. Let's commit to putting our prayers into action by working for a just peace.

Option B: Children of the Nakba *(about 30 minutes)*
Invite the class to watch the DVD *Children of the Nakba* (28 minutes). Discuss the following questions:

- Mr. Laham, an 86-year-old man, was not allowed to return to visit his land for a day without applying for special permission, when it was only a few miles away. Consider how his village is linked to his past and to his identity. How has your identity been shaped by a town, state, province, or country? How is that place accessible to you and what would it mean for you if it was inaccessible?

- According to Israel's Law of Return, any Jew can come to live as a citizen in the State of Israel, some even receiving financial benefits (including tax exemptions and free benefits such as plane tickets, housing, medical insurance, and language study). Compare this with Israel's refusal to allow Palestinian refugees who wish to live in peace with their neighbors to return (as stipulated in UN General Assembly Resolution 194). What is Israel's responsibility to Palestinian refugees? How could the dialogue between residents of Kibbutz Baram and refugees from Bir'im village in the video be a starting point?

- When Na'im returned to Beit 'Itab, the land was empty. Na'im states, "No one lives here. I must live here." The land of most of the more than 500 villages destroyed in 1948 also does not house Israeli communities. In some instances, however, the village's former land is now used for Israeli agriculture, and in others Israeli Jews now live in former Palestinian homes. What prevents Palestinian refugees from returning home to the sites of destroyed villages when the land is empty? What are creative ways to think about return in instances when there are new inhabitants in refugees' homes?

- At this point in history, there are Israeli citizens who know no other home than Israel. How does their new identity compare to that of the children in the Dheisheh refugee camp who consider themselves to be from Beit 'Itab? How does the work of the Zochrot Association bring the stories of both groups together?

- In Colossians 3:9-11, we read that when we align ourselves with the image of our Creator, we understand that God intends that all people be equal (Jew and Greek, circumcised and uncircumcised, slave and free). How can this call to align ourselves with our Creator shape our perspective of the situation in Palestine and Israel, and how we should see and love the "Other"?

2. Introductions and Class Procedures *(about 15 minutes)*
Ask members of the group to introduce their partners to the total group. Then introduce yourself to them. Share your background, why you wanted to facilitate this study session on Israel-Palestine, and what your hopes for the session are.

Call the attention of the group to Chapter 1, "History and Memory," in the study book. Say that the author of the book presents his own personal story to explain the perspective in which he frames the historical events about which he writes. Invite participants to consider their own personal stories and to reflect throughout the rest of the study about how their own experiences may be shaping their perceptions.

3. Way of the Cross Meditation *(about 5 minutes)*
Summarize in your own words the background information in the introduction to the study guide about the tradition of the Way of the Cross (p. 131). Either project the first picture or place a copy of it on a stand on the worship center. Light the candle. Then ask the readers to lead the class in the time of prayerful reflection using Handout 3 Session 1 (p. 185).

4. The Peoples of the Land *(about 40 minutes)*
Read or summarize the following:
> *In this special land, we find peoples who have a long*

history of woundedness, displacement, and loss. Both Palestinians and Israelis have known false accusations, imprisonment, and death at others' hands. Both peoples have experienced the world standing by and doing nothing to stop their experience of devastation. Both have longed to know safety and security for their children and their children's children. Yet, in the midst of such narratives of suffering, Israelis and Palestinians have always been more than victims of their histories. Many of them are creative, loving, hard-working, visionary people. They have different stories, concerns, and dreams. Some are more flexible than others. Just like people all over the world. Neither people are monolithic in their outlook or position. Let us hear from a sampling of peoples of the land.

Use either the stories of the peoples of the land found in Session 1 (Handout 4, "The Peoples of the Land") or the stories on the impact of the conflict on women and children (Appendix C: "Women and Children in Israel and Palestine"). Depending on which activity you choose, follow the suggestions for that activity found in the appropriate chapter.

5. Way of the Cross Meditation *(about 5 minutes)*

Either project the first picture or place a copy of it on a stand on the worship center. Light the candle. If you are singing the suggested hymn, try to sing at least the chorus in Arabic, following the phonetic pronunciation. This is one of the most favorite Arabic hymns for Holy Week all across the Middle East. It has a haunting melody.

Ask the readers to lead the class in the time of prayerful reflection using Handout 1 Session 4 (p. 201).

Summarize the following:

Our concern for peace and justice in Palestine and Israel does not grow out of a vacuum. It was the pleas from the Christian heads of churches in Jerusalem in the early 1980s that really challenged the churches in the West to become more active in our solidarity and action.

Millions of Christians from all over the world were visiting the Holy Land every year. Unfortunately, too many went to that broken land and treated it like a museum. In many pilgrimages, Christians have run where Jesus walked, rushing from holy site to holy site. Often folks have had a deeply spiritual individual or communal experience with companions, but usually got back on the plane and flew home, unaware that Christians were struggling under the impact of Occupation. We never worried about Israelis or Palestinians who were mourning loved ones killed by the terror of the other. The heads of churches said that because we didn't know anything of the current context, we were ill-equipped to help the peoples of the land who were searching for a just and sustainable way out of the conflict.

Invite volunteers to tell briefly about the author's experience of being on a tour of the Holy Land in 1980 (Chapter 1, pp. 19-20). If you haven't asked before, check to see if any of the participants have been on such a tour. Ask:

- *Did you run where Jesus walked?*
- *Did you think much about the people you saw?*
- *What might have been different if you had walked and talked and listened to the peoples of the land as part of the visit?*
- *Have any of you been on a different kind of visit where you did meet with the people? What did that add to your experience?*

Summarize:

Too often, what we do know about the conflict is usually limited to sound bites about some violent event. We seldom hear the voices of those peoples of the land who are committed to a different future for the region. They are the silenced or ignored members of both communities. But their efforts and tenacity keep the conflict from completely going out of control. They are ones who are rolling the stone away, letting light into dark places, bringing hope to despairing people.

- Ask the volunteers to read the stories on Handout 2, "Who Will Roll the Stone Away?" and the two "Stories of Hope" (Appendix A). Invite them to stand where they are, if they are able, and remind them to read loudly enough so everyone can hear them.

After all the stories have been read, ask:
- *Did anything surprise you?*
- *How would you describe the work that these organizations do?*
- *Is there a common denominator among them?*
- *What do you think are the guiding principles of their work that allow these organizations to be peace-builders in a context of fear, hatred, and violence?*
- *Do you know of groups doing similar work for peace and justice in your area?*
- *What essential commonalities are there in the core guiding principles?*

6. What Can We Do to Roll the Stone Away?
(about 20 minutes)
Divide the class into groups of five or six people. Make sure everyone has a copy of Handout 3: "Solidarity: Building a Circle of Concern" and Handout 4: "Places to Connect." Give each group newsprint and markers. Ask the groups to quickly review the two handouts and to discuss practical ways they can become peace-with-justice evangelists for Israel-Palestine. Ask them to identify someone who can record their suggestions on newsprint and post the sheets on the wall. Then ask participants to take about five minutes going around the room reading the newsprint sheets.

Call the group together and pass out index cards or paper. Ask participants to take a few minutes to think through all the suggestions that have been made and to enter into a time of reflection about what they will commit to do. Invite them to write down at least one thing they will commit to do for justice and peace.

7. Closing *(about 5 minutes)*
Thank the participants for coming. Encourage them to take home the index cards on which they recorded personal commitments. Also invite them to read the entire study book. Remind them that we are called to pray and act to help build peace at home and in Israel-Palestine as well.

Sing the chant in Activity 5 (p. 149):
Christ, our peace, you break down the walls that divide us:
Christ, our peace, bring us together in you.

Appendix A
Stories of Hope

Ashley Wilkinson

Ashley Wilkinson is a Mission Intern with the General Board of Global Ministries. She works at the Wi'am Palestinian Conflict Resolution Center. The Center blends a traditional Arabic method of conflict mediation (Sulha) with Western techniques to offer mediation services to the Bethlehem community. The Center also provides trauma-coping programs for children and youth, job-creation programs, women's initiatives, and exchange opportunities with international groups, such as the International Fellowship of Reconciliation (IFOR).

I am no longer my own but yours.
Put me to what you will; rank me with whom you will.
Put me to doing; put me to suffering.
Let me be employed for you, or laid aside for you; exalted for you, or brought low for you.
Let me be full; let me be empty.
Let me have all things; let me have nothing.
I freely and wholeheartedly yield all things to your pleasure and disposal.
And now, glorious and blessed G-d, Father, Son, and Holy Spirit, you are mine and I am yours. So be it. And the covenant which I have made on Earth, let it be ratified in Heaven. Amen.

When I was commissioned as a mission intern with Global Ministries nearly one year ago, I never could have imagined the ramifications of praying John Wesley's Covenant Prayer. I trembled with fear as I read it with my fellow interns, knowing full well that we would each face life-altering experiences in the near future. I still tremble as I read these words and clumsily try to discern what they mean both in my Bethlehem context and in my "back-home" context. Thankfully there are faithful people on both sides of the ocean who teach me how to pray this prayer.

I am no longer my own but yours. I work at the Wi'am Palestinian Conflict Resolution Center. It is in this place that I learn from my colleagues just what it means to give up my life, my time, and my agenda in order to serve G-d and neighbor. Wi'am is a grassroots organization that strives alongside other democratic forces present in the larger Bethlehem community to build a democratic and just society. The Center aims to improve the quality of relationships by: addressing injustices rather than avenging them, dignifying persons on both sides of the conflict, promoting human rights, and advocating for peace among all people.

People in the Bethlehem community know that Wi'am is the place to go when you need your neighbor most. During the day people constantly come to the office, and during the night they go to the homes of the Wi'am caseworkers. My colleagues listen compassionately to the struggles that face each person, and then they work to restore dignity and improve the quality of relationships among the people here. They practice every moment of every day what it means to no longer belong to their own hearts or desires. They teach me to belong to G-d, to be about what G-d is about, to surrender each moment to G-d's will instead of my own.

Put me to what you will; rank me with whom you will. Living in Bethlehem means living in a constant state of change. Working at an NGO just about anywhere means cultivating a personal and organizational adaptability to change. At Wi'am, we do whatever needs to be done. Wi'am does not only help people work through their conflicts, but they also empower people to determine their own futures. Oftentimes, this means that Wi'am is ranked with the marginalized of society—the women, the children, the youth, the unemployed, the hungry, the imprisoned, and the weary. My colleagues provide space for kids to be kids, to give them the space and time in which to deal with the ongoing trauma of living in an unstable environment. They inspire women to discuss, determine, and define their roles in society. They give work to the unemployed, food and love to the hungry, and they help seek justice for those who have been wronged. Jesus walks into this office each day—and my colleagues remind me to welcome Him in the face of the child, woman, man—they teach me to find Him in every situation. And they love to be ranked with Him, no matter in what form He comes.

Put me to doing; put me to suffering. Let me be employed for you, or laid aside for you; exalted for you, or brought low for you. One aspect of my work with which I struggle the most is identifying just what it is that I am doing here in Bethlehem. As human beings, I think it is natural for us to want to do many things. As Christians, it is often difficult to avoid developing a savior complex. We want to help. We want to heal. We want to fix. We want to make a difference. But at the end of the day, we cannot save people. For that is not our role. In the short time I have been here, I am learning to recognize the times when G-d puts me to doing, along with the times I am employed and laid aside for G-d. I am beginning to realize that often when we are laid aside, it is not so much because we are not capable of doing or effecting change. Rather, G-d does not desire us to do these things on our own. We do not save others, and it is often in the vacuum of doing, in the vacuum of employment that we stop looking at our own work and start looking at G-d's work. Being available to people is equally as important as doing good things for people. My colleagues teach me this lesson continually when they drop their "work" in the middle of the day in order to attend a funeral or celebrate the birth of a baby with the people in this community. They teach me how to "do" what G-d does, how to "suffer" the way G-d suffers, how to be "employed" for G-d, how to be "laid aside" for G-d.

And as I stumble around in proverbial cultural education, I am learning what it means to be brought low for G-d.

My colleagues and friends are patient and loving, forgiving and kind, despite my many missteps and blunders. I am learning to say I am sorry. And more importantly I am learning that true repentance is not just speaking remorse, but also changing my heart and changing my behavior. It is not so much that my feelings and my heart remain neutral whether I am exalted or brought low, but I am learning to accept both with humility, recognizing that no matter what place G-d would have me in, I always belong to G-d. The core of who I am is rooted in G-d's love and gift of grace to me. When I am confident of this identity, then it is possible for both triumphs and failures to be seen as opportunities for me to learn and grow. Whether I am exalted or low is not essential. That I belong to G-d is what is paramount.

Let me be full; let me be empty. Let me have all things; let me have nothing. I am in between. Many historians describe this land as the land between. This area has always been between superpowers and the local people have (for the majority of their history) lived under occupation by outside forces. There is great attachment to the land here. There is also a great attachment to the community. People here are dedicated and loyal, and they have a passion for the land and for their neighbors that I have never before experienced. Such existence leaves me feeling so full I often feel I might burst. There is so much to be joyful about here! Strong families, committed community, passion for a better life, excellent food, and the fabulous ability to laugh and enjoy the people close at hand. Yet there is so much to mourn here as well: lack of freedom, dehumanization, trauma from past violence, a sense of helplessness regarding any desire to bring about helpful change.

I am in between. I feel overwhelmed and drained all at once; courageous and fearful of the effects of my actions; full of life and hope, yet despairing and weary, thinking that no one outside this place cares. I feel hyphenated. I am American, but one who has lived and experienced a different culture. I do not feel un-American, nor do I feel American in the way I had previously understood. I feel divided and yet rooted in this newly unfolding self.

I am in between. I feel I have all that I need and nothing that I want. I need love. I need family. I need people to support me and yet love me enough that they will challenge me to be the woman G-d has called me to be. I need change and challenge and growth. But I do not always want them. To be in between means cultivating the capacity to be faithful throughout change, throughout growth, throughout all the painful experiences of life.

I am in between. I am full and I am empty. I have all things and I have nothing. I learn from this land and this people to be fully present where I am—to be true to what and where G-d has called me. I am in between.

I freely and wholeheartedly yield all things to your pleasure and disposal. In the past, I might have understood this to mean a yielding of material comforts or treasures to G-d in exchange for a humble and simple lifestyle. While I do not rule out that understanding now, I realize that to yield freely and wholeheartedly is to give up so much more than possessions or comforts. It is also yielding the familiar, yielding future plans, yielding expectations, yielding all your preconceived notions, your heart, and even your body to the disposal of the only One who can direct all of these in a way that will allow you to be the most true form of yourself. It is only when we yield all of our lives to G-d that we even begin to see ourselves as we truly are. Broken and brave, doubting and faithful, selfish and loving…we must yield in order to be transformed. Such yielding will look different for each person, but yield we must if we are ever going to live. I realize too that in this place people are often forced to yield involuntarily. They yield their freedom as they encounter walls and checkpoints. They yield their humanity as they are harassed in their homes and in the streets. They yield their security, living in the constant awareness that the military could enter their homes and communities at any minute. Often they even yield their hope for the future because history has taught them to do so. But yielding to G-d is different, isn't it? I believe it is. G-d does not ask us to yield our freedom because G-d gives the only true freedom we will ever know. G-d does not ask us to yield our humanity because G-d created us in G-d's image. G-d does not ask us to yield our security because G-d is the only real security we have. And G-d would never ask us to yield our hope. Hope is the heart of resurrection.

And now, glorious and blessed G-d, Father, Son, and Holy Spirit, you are mine and I am yours. So be it. And the covenant which I have made on Earth, let it be ratified in Heaven. Amen.

Zoughbi Zoughbi

Zoughbi Zoughbi is the Director and Founder of the Wi'am Palestinian Conflict Resolution Center in Bethlehem, Palestine. Zoughbi has worked in the fields of conflict transformation and peace-building in the Palestinian community for over twenty-five years. He actively participates in peace initiatives with locals and the international community, and in his work as an educator, trainer, peace activist, lecturer, facilitator, and mediator, he speaks from a unique and faithful perspective.

I feel it is important to talk about partnership. I believe that without this partnership, without the possibility of celebrating family members' relationships across different areas and different nations, we will not be able to deliver the good news.

It is very important for us who live in this part of the Middle East, where things are not going in the right direction, where there is always conflict, to have partnership. We feel the partnership among The United Methodist Church, the local people, and churches in Palestine has had a positive impact on all of us. This partnership also has an impact on the mission and message we deliver to the people. We are members of the same body of Christ, with different tasks, responsibilities, and gifts. Through partnership, we can feel that we are not left alone.

This unique partnership has led us to be proactive and not to be at the receiving end all the time. When the Oklahoma tornado occurred, one of our volunteers flew to the States to be in solidarity with the people there. Waseem assisted in many different ways. We need to find ways to have partnerships and to understand that this is a two-way street with multi-lanes. Using this approach, we will be nourished and transformed. We will grow and we will be changed. This will help us to shift from blame, victimhood, and finger-pointing to responsibility.

Thank you for giving us the space, time, opportunity, and synergy to assume with you our collective responsibility toward the issues of the whole world. As the Rev. Dr. Martin Luther King, Jr., said, "Injustice anywhere is a threat to justice everywhere."

I believe that everyone suffers in his or her own way. It is not possible to have a monopoly over suffering. At the same time, one of the most important things in human nature is to believe that we belong to a bigger community. When we believe this and feel ourselves to be part of that bigger community, then suffering will not be as intense; and in one way or another, this community will help create a healthy atmosphere for all of us. This is especially helpful for the psychology of the oppressed, to remind them that they are not alone. Experiencing a sense of the larger community also serves as a remedy for the temptation to perpetuate victimhood.

I see the churches in the United States as having potential for change, and this is often where I find hope. I have a dream for the church in the States, because without such a change, without such depth in the relationship you have with us here, we cannot see any positive outcome on the horizon.

And of course this could not be done without hope. I see hope in those people who come as interns, volunteers, and staff workers into this area where there is protracted violence and conflict. Each of these people has a choice, and anytime you have a choice, you take a risk. Coming here can be a very risky mission. At the same time, plans and hopes are everywhere. We receive hope since you, our international brothers and sisters in Christ, are here to hear us. Through your compassionate listening, we are redeemed. We are healed. You create a healthy atmosphere for us to air out our frustration and anger, to channel it in a more positive way, and to transform it. We are then able to create a different scenario.

As a Christian, I am always hopeful. But I cannot be hopeful without my brothers and sisters in Christ in other countries. Hope is a matter of choice. Hope is not only an emotional thing but also a reasonable approach to fight against hopelessness and frustration, which will lead only to hate. Hope is the nonviolent approach to struggle that will not demonize the other but will *invite* the other to join. Hope is an oasis of interactions of people from different backgrounds and walks of life to see new possibilities. Hope allows people to adopt different approaches to create a healthy atmosphere. Hope is the gift of uplifting the spirits of the people who are paying a heavy price in pain. Hope is to walk with them, to share with them, and of course to help them see the possibility of a different reality. Through the work of Wi'am and through our partners, we see that hope truly soars even in the midst of trauma and injustice.

I remember the siege of Bethlehem for forty days in May and June of 2002. One of our many friends is the Rev. Sandra Olewine. Many times we would call each other and say: "What is going on? Did you hear that? Is it a bomb? A shell? Where did it land?" Sandra was living in Bethlehem, near some Palestinian official offices, and facing Beit Jala. This was a very risky area. People were always in danger. We tried to talk to her about moving, but Sandra insisted on staying put and going to work on foot.

If I walk to work during curfew, it is courageous and risky. But I was born here, and I am stuck without options. So to see a Methodist minister from the United States, walking at that time to the place where she works, risking her life—moving not only from her office or home but from Bethlehem—gives me insight. It empowers my walk. And it creates in me a different approach. Many times when we would call each other or when we would meet after the lifting of curfew, I was shivering with hope. During the times when I felt down, I would say, "G-d, where are you? Don't forsake us." And I could hear a gentle voice, a human voice, a blessed presence in response.

This not only gives you hope but plants hope: the seeds of love, the seeds of agape. The message of the good news travels through people like Rev. Sandra. They walk in our shoes and also live with us in terrible times. Enduring the rough times and challenges as a single person in a strange land during a hostile Occupation, she was still giving.

People were lacking food and security. And we saw that Sandra was sharing with the people around her whatever was left. She was able to keep a smile on her face and to resist the paranoia. And she was able to resist the false god of this or that voice telling her that she ought to leave. She insisted she would stay. I was really humbled. Many times I see that that situation was amazing. G-d is there when I see Sandra and people like her—those who by choice come to this part of the world knowing it is risky, knowing it is not going to be a vacation. I see Christ in their faces. I see Christ's wounds and at the same time I see Christ's transfiguration. I see a Christ transformed in their social gospel, and of course for me this is a big source of hope.

This hope speaks to me whenever I doubt that there is a G-d. I see hope in my friends, colleagues, and partners. When I doubt justice, I see that some people are struggling for and willing to pay a price for it. When I question authority and see someone giving an unexpected answer to create a different synergy and thereby enrich and empower people—this hope enhances the walk that we adopt.

Despite all of the doubts.

Appendix B
A Timeline of Israel and Palestine

B.C.E.

ca. 1300–931 Hebrew tribes and Philistines migrate into Canaan. The Hebrew tribes defeat the Canaanites and, after a struggle, the Philistines. The kingdom of Israel is established with Saul as the first king. King David establishes Jerusalem as the capital, and King Solomon builds the first Temple there.

ca. 931 The kingdom splits into the Northern Kingdom (Israel) and the Southern Kingdom (Judah).

ca. 721 Northern Kingdom falls to Assyria.

ca. 587/586 Southern Kingdom falls to Babylon, which destroys the Temple and takes many into exile.

ca. 539 Babylonian Empire falls to the Persian Empire. Persian emperor Cyrus allows some Jews to return from exile.

ca. 520–515 Temple in Jerusalem is rebuilt as the Second Temple.

ca. 331 Alexander the Great defeats the Persian Empire. Following his death, the land is subject to rule by Egypt and Syria.

ca. 166–160 Maccabeans lead a revolt against the ruling Syrian Hellenists because of restrictions on the practice of Judaism, the desecration of the Temple, and the imposition of Greek religion.

ca. 142 Hasmoneans (Maccabeans) begin a period of Jewish rule.

ca. 63–61 Romans conquer Jerusalem.

ca. 20 Herod begins improvements on the Temple in Jerusalem.

ca. 4 Jesus is born. He is crucified by Rome between 31 and 33 C.E.

C.E.

66–73 First Jewish Revolt against Rome takes place. Jerusalem and the Second Temple are destroyed in 70.

133–135 The Second Jewish Revolt against Rome occurs. Roman forces crush the rebellion. The emperor Hadrian renames the province Syria Judea as Syria Palaestina and forbids Jews to dwell in Jerusalem.

313 Emperor Constantine recognizes Christianity as the official religion of the Roman Empire. Throughout the period of the Roman Empire, Jews are periodically subjected to varying degrees of persecution.

570 The prophet Mohammed is born.

ca. 638 Muslims from the Arabian Peninsula conquer Jerusalem. Caliph Omar provides the Christians of Jerusalem with a covenant guaranteeing their protection and allows Jews to return to Jerusalem.

705 The Dome of the Rock mosque is completed by Caliph Abd al-Malik ibn Marwan.

715 The Al-Aqsa Mosque is built by Caliph Walid.

1071 The Seljuk Turks invade and capture Jerusalem.

1096 Participants in the First Crusade massacre Jews as they pass through several European cities. Over the next centuries Jews face persecution to varying degrees in various European countries including restrictive laws, pogroms, and expulsions.

1099 Crusaders conquer Jerusalem, killing many Jewish and Moslem inhabitants and expelling surviving Jews.

1187 Muslims under Saladin conquer Jerusalem.

1291 Crusaders are evicted from Palestine.

1517 Ottoman Empire conquers Palestine. Small Jewish communities flourish.

1537–1541 Under Suleiman the Magnificent, walls are built around Jerusalem.

1843 First writings of modern Zionism appear.

1856 Ottoman Empire requires people to register land and pay taxes.

1860 Mishkenot Sha'ananim, first modern Jewish settlement outside the walls of Jerusalem, is built.

1878 Petah Tikvah, first Zionist settlement, is built.

1897 First Zionist Congress meets in Basel, Switzerland.

1908 *Al-Karmil,* first Arabic newspaper in Haifa, popularizes opposition to selling land to Zionists.

1909 First kibbutz, Degania, is founded. Tel Aviv is founded as a Hebrew-speaking Jewish city. Hashomer, first Jewish self-defense organization, is founded.

1914 World War I begins. Ottoman Empire enters the war on the side of Germany.

1916 The Sykes-Picot Agreement divides the Ottoman lands into French and British spheres of influence.

1917 Britain signs Balfour Declaration supporting the "establishment of the Jewish national home…and safeguarding the civil and religious rights of all the inhabitants of Palestine."

1918 World War I ends, bringing defeat of the Ottoman Empire.

1919 First Palestinian Congress advocates incorporation of Palestine into greater Syria.

1920 League of Nations divides lands of Ottoman Empire into entities called Mandates that are intended to lead to the creation of nation states. Britain accepts Mandate for Palestine. Haganah is organized for Jewish self-defense.

1933 Hitler rises to power in Germany.

1936–1939 While previous incidents of violence have occurred, the Arab Revolt is first major outbreak of Arab-Jewish hostilities.

1939–1945 The Holocaust takes place during World War II. Jewish migration into Palestine increases.

1942 Zionist leaders meet to discuss postwar plans with the aim of founding a Jewish commonwealth.

1944 Arab leaders meet to discuss postwar plans for independence and ways to prevent implementation of Jewish control over Palestine.

1945 Palestinians receive representation in newly formed League of Arab States.

1947 United Nations General Assembly passes Resolution 181, which would partition Palestine into Jewish and Arab states and establish Greater Jerusalem as an international city. The Jewish state would receive 56.47 percent of the land of the Palestine Mandate, the Arab state about 43.53 percent. Numerous skirmishes, road ambushes, riots, and bombings take place, organized by both Jews and Palestinians.

1948 Violence escalates. British Mandate ends. Israel declares statehood on May 14. Egypt, Syria, Iraq, Lebanon, Jordan, and Saudi Arabia declare war on Israel. The war results in a divided Jerusalem and some 650,000 to 750,000 Palestinian refugees. The UN General Assembly passes Resolution 194 calling for the cessation of hostilities and establishing the Right of Return for refugees who wish to live in peace.

1949–1950 At war's end, Israel holds about 78 percent of the territory of the Palestine Mandate. The Green Line, set at the 1949 armistice, establishes borders between Israel and Arab lands. Jordan annexes East Jerusalem and West Bank. Egypt controls Gaza Strip. UN Relief and Works Agency is established to care for Palestinian refugees until they can return home.

1950 Israel enacts Law of Return stating that every Jew has the right to become a citizen.

1964 Palestine Liberation Organization (PLO) is established. At the time, its aim is to destroy Israel. Leaders of Arab states largely control PLO, which operates out of Gaza Strip.

1967 Six-Day War. Israel conquers Gaza Strip, West Bank, East Jerusalem, the Sinai, and Golan Heights, creating more Palestinian refugees. PLO headquarters move to Jordan. UN Security Council passes Resolution 242 calling for Israeli withdrawal establishes "land for peace" principle.

1968–1969 Fatah gains formal control of the PLO, and Yasser Arafat becomes chair of the PLO.

1969–1970 The War of Attrition takes place between Egypt and Israel. Jordan moves against the PLO, whose members flee to Lebanon. Israel begins the policy of establishing settlements.

1973 Egypt and Syria attack Israel, beginning Yom Kippur War. Israel pushes back both armies.

1974 Arab League declares the PLO to be the only legitimate representative of the Palestinian people. The UN recognizes the Palestinians' right to sovereignty and grants observer status to the PLO.

1978 Egypt and Israel agree to the Camp David Accords, which create peace, provide for the return of the Sinai to Egypt in exchange for recognition of Israel, and set a framework for settling the Israeli-Palestinian conflict. Israel invades Lebanon, occupying its southern border in response to the violence of the PLO.

1980 Israel declares Jerusalem its eternal, undivided capital, affirming the annexation of East Jerusalem.

1981 Israel annexes the Golan Heights.

1982 Israel invades Lebanon a second time, laying siege to Beirut. PLO moves its headquarters to Tunis.

1985 Israeli government orders withdrawal of its troops from most of Lebanon.

1987 An *Intifada,* a Palestinian popular uprising, begins in Gaza and spreads to the West Bank. Stone-throwing Palestinian teens attack Israeli soldiers.

1988 PLO accepts UN Security Council Resolutions 242 and 338, implicitly recognizing Israel. The United States opens dialogue with the PLO. Hamas Islamic Brotherhood is founded with a charter based on forged anti-Semitic Protocols of the Elders of Zion and advocating destruction of Israel.

1992 President George H. W. Bush's administration holds up $10 billion in US loan guarantees to Israel (fiscal years 1993 to 1997) in attempt to limit Israeli settlement building.

1993 Israel and PLO sign Oslo Declaration of Principles, providing for mutual recognition. PLO renounces violence and use of terrorism and agrees to revise the PLO Charter to remove chapters referring to destruction of Israel.

1994 Palestinian National Authority (PNA) is established in Gaza and the West Bank. PLO and Yasser Arafat arrive in Gaza. Jordan and Israel sign peace treaty.

1995 Oslo Accords establish three areas of control in the West Bank: Area A under Palestinian control, Area B under Palestinian civilian control and Israeli security control, and Area C under exclusive Israeli control. Prime Minister Rabin is assassinated in Tel Aviv.

1997 Israel and PLO sign Hebron Protocol dividing the city of Hebron. Israel starts building a settlement, Har Homa, on a hill overlooking East Jerusalem, resulting in widespread protests. Israel imposes closures on Palestinian communities in the West Bank and Gaza.

2000 Israeli Prime Minister Ehud Barak, Palestinian Chairman Yasser Arafat, and US President Bill Clinton meet at Camp David in failed attempt to negotiate a settlement on final status issues. The Al-Aqsa Intifada begins, following a visit to Temple Mount/Haram al-Sharif by Israeli opposition leader Ariel Sharon. Violence escalates rapidly and continues, involving rock-throwing, machine gun and mortar fire, suicide bombings, and road ambushes.

2002 In retaliation for a series of suicide bombings, Israeli army reoccupies Palestinian areas. Yasser Arafat is placed under house arrest. Saudi Crown Prince Abdullah proposes a peace plan, endorsed by the Arab League, promising recognition of Israel for ending the Occupation. UN Security Council passes Resolution 1397 affirming a two-state solution. President George W. Bush declares a vision for a "viable Palestinian state next to a secure Israel." Israel begins construction of security barrier in the West Bank.

2003 The United States, the European Union, the UN, and Russia release the Road Map to Peace, which contains a process to guide Israelis and Palestinians toward peace. Israelis and Palestinians acting as individuals, and not as representatives of any government, release the Geneva Initiative, containing a vision for a two-state peace.

2004 The International Court of Justice (ICJ) rules that the Israeli security barrier violates international law. UN General Assembly votes to order Israel to dismantle the barrier. Israel announces that it will ignore the ruling but changes the barrier route according to rulings of the Israeli High Court. Yasser Arafat dies.

2005 Mahmoud Abbas is elected president of PNA. Israeli settlers and troops evacuate Gaza Strip and four settlements in West Bank. Ariel Sharon quits Likud Party to form a new party, Kadima.

First Months of 2006 Ariel Sharon suffers massive stroke, and Deputy Prime Minister Ehud Olmert assumes power. Hamas, which is on US State Department's list of terrorist organizations, wins majority in Palestinian Legislative Council elections.

July 2006 Israel-Lebanon Conflict: Hezbollah launches Katyusha rockets over border into Israel on July 12 as a diversion; crosses border and kidnaps two Israeli soldiers and kills three. Israel attempts rescue; five more killed. In retaliation, Israel launches massive artillery and airstrikes against Lebanese civilian infrastructure and invades southern Lebanon. Hezbolllah responds with rocket launches and guerrilla warfare. Fifteen hundred killed, mostly Lebanese civilians. About 900,000 Lebanese and 300,000 Israelis internally displaced. Much of South Lebanon rendered uninhabitable due to unexploded cluster bombs.

August 11, 2006 UN Security Council unanimously approves Resolution 1701 in an effort to end the hostilities.

August 17, 2006 Lebanese army begins deployment in southern Lebanon.

September 8, 2006 Blockade lifted.

October 1, 2006 Israel army reports withdrawal, but some troops remain near the border. Israel continues jet fly-overs.

December 1, 2006 Kofi Annan reports to the Security Council evidence of unauthorized assets, weapons, and armed personnel in Lebanon.

Presbyterian Church (USA) • 100 Witherspoon Street Louisville, KY 40202-1396 • 800-872-3283
Resource Sheet 1: Developed February 2005, updated March 2006, adapted December 1, 2006
www.pcusa.org/worldwide/israelpalestine/resources.htm

Sources

1. Jewish Virtual Library, *Timeline for the History of Judaism,* www.jewishvirtuallibrary.org/jsource/History/timclinc.html
2. MidEast Web, *Timeline of Palestinian Israeli History and the Israel-Arab Conflict,* www.mideastweb.org/timeline.htm
3. Churches for Middle East Peace, *Timeline of the Israeli-Arab Conflict,* www.cmep.org/documents/Timeline.htm
4. Palestine History, *Palestine Quick Timeline, 1900-2004,* www.palestinehistory.com/history/quicktime/quicktime.htm
5. Palestine Remembered, *Palestinian History: A Chronology,* www.palestineremembered.com/Acre/Palestine-Remembered/Story564.html
6. Wikipedia Free Encyclopedia

Women and Children in Israel and Palestine

Introduction

In every conflict the world over, the most vulnerable in society face the greatest challenges and dangers. In Israel-Palestine, the spiraling violence in Israel and the Occupied Territories since 2000 has brought untold suffering to the Palestinian and Israeli civilian populations. At the beginning of 2007, more than 3,500 Palestinians, including more than 600 children and more than 150 women, have been killed by Israeli forces, and more than 1,000 Israelis, including more than 100 children and some 300 women, were killed by Palestinian armed groups. Most of the victims were unarmed civilians who were not taking part in any armed confrontations. Tens of thousands of Palestinians and thousands of Israelis have been injured, many maimed for life. Palestinians do not feel safe either in the street or in their homes, as Israeli army aircraft, helicopter gunships, and tanks frequently shell Palestinian refugee camps and densely populated residential areas. Israelis also do not feel safe when they leave their homes, as Palestinian armed groups deliberately target Israeli civilians in suicide bombings and other attacks on buses, restaurants, and other public places.

The militarization of the conflict since 2000 is primarily responsible for these realities. From the first days, the Israeli army abandoned policing and law enforcement tactics and adopted military measures generally used in armed conflict. They routinely use excessive and disproportionate force against civilians, including the above-mentioned bombings and shelling, as well as the large-scale destruction of Palestinian homes, land, and infrastructure, and the imposition of military blockades and prolonged curfews that keep the Palestinian population imprisoned in their homes. Armed Palestinian attacks against Israeli civilians, which were sporadic before the *Intifada,* have become a frequent occurrence, including suicide bombings, shootings, and other attacks on buses, cafes, and public places.

—Excerpted from *Israel and the Occupied Territories: Conflict, Occupation and Patriarchy: Women Carry the Burden* (March 31, 2005) Amnesty International Report (http://web.amnesty.org/library/index/engmde150162005)

Despite all the complexities and difficulties faced by the women and children in this land, there are many who refuse to be silent in the face of oppression, who refuse to grow hard-hearted due to their own loss and trauma, who refuse to give up hope for a better world for themselves, their children, and others' children. What follows does not communicate every story or every reality. Rather, it serves as an invitation to study and read more to discover other stories and realities.

An analogy can be drawn between the psychological experience of a nation under siege and that of a woman living in an abusive relationship…. This poses a potentially dangerous situation for women, who will fall victim to a three-tiered process of violation. At present, they are victimized by the political violence, living in perpetual fear for their safety and that of their families, while bearing the additional burdens imposed on them under harrowing conditions, such as the destruction of homes, the razing of agricultural property, the uprooting of trees, and rampant unemployment. Additionally, they are victims of heightened violence within the home but are unable to express any of their suffering or anxiety, as they are forced into silence for fear of being blamed at the public level for being selfish and inconsiderate given the national emergency the whole society is undergoing, and at the private level from being blamed for their own victimization—a vicious circle.

—Maha Abu-Dayyeh Shamas, Women's Centre for Legal Aid and Counseling (http://web.amnesty.org/library/index/engmde150162005)

Status of Women in Israel

Since its establishment in 1948, the state of Israel has had the image of a country in which women enjoy full equality. But there are many areas in which traditions, social institutions, religious rules, and even laws have kept women at a disadvantage: in the workplace, in divorce proceedings, and as victims of violence. Changes in the political and economic climate, such as the Middle East conflict and the influx of thousands of guest workers, have created new problems. The widening economic gap in Israeli society along ethnic and geographical lines points to the entrenchment of poverty and disadvantage in particular groups. Old women, single mothers, Arab women, immigrants from Ethiopia and the former Soviet Union, and foreign workers (with or without work permits) are most vulnerable to poverty, health problems, and the abuse of basic rights. Women as a group are disadvantaged in the labor market, the health system, education, the courts, and religious institutions and are subject to harassment and violence.

Social and Historical Factors

The status of women in Israel has been influenced by several social and historical factors. Though the founding fathers of the state were mostly oriented towards a secular and liberal or socialist ideology, they assigned to the religious institutions all matters concerning personal status, such as marriage, conversion, divorce, burial, and so forth. Acting in accordance to Jewish religious law, the Orthodox stream of Judaism virtually obtained a monopoly over official Jewish religious life and personal status.

Another factor influencing the status of women is the centrality of the IDF (Israel Defense Forces). Though women have always served in the IDF, the army offers a predominantly male environment that spills over into civilian society by means of the "old boys' network." Finally, even though the Proclamation of the Establishment of the State of Israel declares equality between the sexes, so far none of the Basic Laws, which in the absence of a constitution form the country's normative rules, incorporates this principle, due mainly to the unresolved relationship between religion and the state.

Women's Work

In general, women work mostly in lower-paying jobs, in services, education, health, welfare, and clerical positions. They are significantly less represented in prestigious and lucrative occupations such as hi-tech, management, and engineering. For example, while 57 percent of all academic degrees are earned by women, and 46 percent of doctoral students are women, only 22 percent of senior faculty members and 7.8 percent of full professors are women.

—R. Werczberger, Research and Information Center, The Knesset "The Advancement of the Status of Women—Israel 2001" (http://www.mfa.gov.il/MFA/MFAArchive/2000_2009/2001/8/)

Status of Women in Palestine

The large-scale destruction by the Israeli army of Palestinian homes, land, and properties has made tens of thousands of Palestinians homeless and destitute. The imposition by the Israeli army of curfews and blockades throughout the Occupied Territories has impeded movement and restricted access for 3,500,000 Palestinians to work, education and medical facilities, and other crucial services. The continuous expansion of Israeli settlements and related infrastructure on occupied Palestinian land has deprived Palestinians of key resources such as land and water. As a result, the Palestinian economy has been virtually destroyed, unemployment and poverty have spiraled, and health and education have been negatively affected.

Stresses on Women

The resulting damage to the fabric of Palestinian society has deeply affected women, who have been placed at the receiving end of increased pressures and violence in the family and in society. They have faced increased demands as caregivers and providers while at the same time their freedom of movement and action has been curtailed, and they have borne the brunt of the anger and frustration of male relatives who feel humiliated because they cannot fulfill their traditional role as providers. The escalation of violence and the deterioration of the situation in recent years have occurred in the context of Israel's thirty-eight-year military Occupation of the West Bank and Gaza Strip, which has had a serious impact on many aspects of Palestinian women's lives.

Women as Caregivers

Palestinian women have also had to shoulder most of the burden of caring for tens of thousands of men and children who have been injured in the past four-and-a-half years. Their task has been made more difficult due to the limits of Palestinian medical facilities, Israeli army blockades which hamper access for Palestinians to hospitals in the Occupied Territories and travel abroad, and increased poverty among Palestinians. Similar difficulties also affect the wives and mothers of thousands of Palestinians who have been killed or who are detained in Israeli prisons. In the absence of a social security system in the Occupied Territories, thousands of women whose husbands have been killed or imprisoned are forced to depend on relatives and charity organizations for survival. In the current situation of widespread poverty and unemployment, such dependence leaves these women particularly vulnerable to pressures and control by the male relatives on whom they depend for their survival and the survival of their children.

Impact of Violence on Israelis

Israelis are tired of the violence, observed Zeev Wiener. "Most victims will recover in a couple of weeks and go back to their normal lives," he said, "but some will have post-traumatic stress disorder." The psychiatric condition provokes unwanted memories of the bombings—sometimes down to details like the smells that surrounded the scene—months or even years after an attack, he said.

Wiener said that stress disorders, anxiety, and depression are common among those who have experienced bombing attacks or who have lost loved ones in the conflict. He believes that almost half the population of Israel suffers from some post-traumatic symptoms and that 10 percent has full-blown post-traumatic stress disorder.

The effects have reverberated throughout Israeli society beyond the initial violence. "When you send an eighteen-year-old boy or girl to war and put them in impossible situations, then bounce them back to Israeli society, you have problems," he said. "The impact [of violence] is not just because of suicide bombing but because of the whole conflict."

Israeli society has witnessed increasing civil violence, widening social gaps, declining patriotism, and increasing distrust of Israeli leadership, he said. "Society does not trust the establishment, including the law and police," Wiener said. "People feel helpless, and they get used to feeling that way."

—Excerpted from Zeev Wiener, April 2004, *Harvard Public Health Now* (http://www.hsph.harvard.edu/now/apr2/doctors.html)

The Least of the Least

Palestinian Arab women and girls account for 572,000 of Israel's citizens. They are the most disadvantaged sector of the population, facing double discrimination both as Arabs within the Israeli state, and women within Palestinian society. These combine to make Palestinian Arab women in Israel the poorest, least paid, least educated portion of the community who are subject to forms of legal abuse, with inadequate protection by the courts. Their situation is made worse by their lack of political representation and lack of access to decision-making and positions of power. As a consequence, their perspectives and needs are continually neglected.

(http://www.arabhra.org/factsheets/factsheet5.htm)

Barriers to Palestinian Family Reunification

For more than five and a half years, Israel has prevented family unification between Palestinian residents of the Occupied Territories and their spouses from abroad. Israel also prohibits the foreign family members from visiting the West Bank or the Gaza Strip.

Since the beginning of the second Intifada, Palestinians have submitted more than 120,000 requests for family unification, which Israel has refused to process. Only in rare instances, which Israel deems "exceptional humanitarian cases," have state authorities processed the requests.

The freeze on processing family unification requests has created a harsh reality for tens of thousands of Palestinian families: spouses are unable to live under the same roof; children are forced to grow up in single-parent families though their parents want to live together; people do not leave the Occupied Territories to go abroad for medical treatment because Israel will not issue them a new visitor's permit; tens of thousands of women live in the Occupied Territories with no legal status and thus face the constant threat of deportation, become prisoners in their homes, and are unable to live a normal life.

(www.btselem.org/english/Publications/Summaries/200607_Perpetual _Limbo.asp)

One Family's Story

Hassan Ribhi Hassan Yihya, 39, married and father of three, is a greengrocer and a resident of al-Bira, Ramallah district. His testimony was given to Iyad Haddad in al-Bira on 2 August 2005.

In September 1997, I got engaged to my cousin, 'Abir Mahmud Abu Nasreh. She was then seventeen and was living with her family in Amman. We were engaged for about a year, during which I went to visit her in Jordan to get to know her better, until we decided to marry. I submitted a request for a visitor's permit for her and her parents so they could enter the West Bank. They received the permits in August 1998. They stayed here for a month and we got married in September. We live in al-Bira. Her parents returned to Jordan.

Three months after we got married, 'Abir's visitor's permit expired. I did not renew the permit, and she became a "person staying illegally" in the area. About a year after we got married, I submitted a request for family unification on her behalf. I made the request to the Israeli Civil Administration via the Palestinian Ministry for Civil Affairs. The officials at the ministry told me it would take time for my request to be considered, and I knew there were thousands of such requests.

I made sure that she didn't leave Ramallah so that the soldiers would not arrest and deport her. I preferred that she stay inside the city, because if they deported her, she wouldn't be able to return. She couldn't visit her parents in Jordan, and they kept in touch only by telephone. When she spoke with them, I felt how much she suffered from not being able to see them. She was worried and sad all the time. Even if I wanted to pamper her, I couldn't take her on trips outside of town because she did not have a permit. She did not have relatives in the West Bank other than one uncle who lives in Bil'in. He came to visit her on special occasions and holidays. The visits made things easier for her and raised her spirits.

Our three children also gave her some consolation. Our eldest child, our daughter Alaa, was born on 10 June 1999. Our second child, Ribhi, a boy, was born on 22 January 2001, and our son 'Omer was born on 1 February 2004.

Every time I went to the ministry to check on the request, they told me there was still no answer or there was nothing new and that everything was awaiting decision by the Israelis.

When the second Intifada began, the Israelis froze the handling of requests for family unification. We lived our lives in the normal manner, for better or worse, like everyone else. But recently the situation became intolerable. 'Abir was in a terrible emotional state. I would come home from work at the vegetable market and see her crying or brooding. She yearned to be with her parents and was tense all the time. About three months ago, I came home and she told me that she had packed her clothes and that if I wanted to go to Amman with her, I could come. About a month later, she went to Amman. She left on 6 June 2005, without notice. I was really angry. I realized that she was hurt and things were bad for her, but what did the children do? They remained with me. The smallest child is eighteen months old, still an infant. I spoke with her by phone and told her that I was angry over what she had done. She said that she wanted to see her parents and go to the wedding of her brother, who was the only boy among ten children. She cried and felt bad that she left the children. She said she was very sorry and that it was clear to her that she had almost no chance to return to the West Bank.

I checked again about the request for family unification at the ministry in Ramallah and they told me the same thing—that it depended on the political situation, and that family unification would be possible when the Jews allowed it. They said that I also didn't have any chance in obtaining a permit for her to enter the West Bank for a visit.

Now I live alone with the children. I didn't even know how to prepare bread or milk for the infant. I didn't know how to change diapers or to do other things one has to do when taking care of infants. My wife did everything. I had to take the children to my mother to live, even though she is sixty years

old and has arthritis in her legs. She can barely take care of herself, but we have no choice. I went to live with my parents to be with the children. My life changed completely. In the past, I would come home from work, shower, and eat with my wife and children. Then I would play with them, or we would go out to do something and have fun in all kinds of places. I got into a routine of "from home to work and from work to home." I am frustrated and depressed. When I return home at night, the children are sleeping, and when I get up in the morning, I barely see them. When I look at the children, I feel sad, especially when one of the children wakes up at night and asks for his mother.

Also, I don't have a wife to share my problems with, or who can help me. When I talk with 'Abir by telephone, she begins to cry. She regrets that she left and wants me to do everything I can to enable her to see our children. Her sister told me that she holes up in the house and cries when she sees small children. I don't have the words to describe how bad the situation is. I also worry about my mother's condition, and what would happen if she were unable to continue to take care of the children. What would I do in that case? Stop work and take care of them? And how would I support them?

(www.btselem.org/english/Testimonies/20050802_Hassan_Yihya _Family_Separation.asp)

A Different Voice from Sderot

Early last week, I threw open the metal cover of my "security room," which had been sealed shut for many months. The room, which is both my work area and my "protected space," filled up with sunlight at once. It was a huge relief. Within minutes and over the next two days, Qassam missiles landed around us, but something in our consciousness was already more calm and optimistic. Thus began the ceasefire.

For most of you here tonight, the ceasefire is an important political event. For us, adults and children in Sderot and the adjacent villages, and for those in the Gaza Strip as well, it is the simple human act of opening a window (if you have one at all), and a release, if only for a moment, from the chronic fear and oppressed uncertainty that have become our constant companions. It is called: normal life.

Allow me to share with you some personal insights and feelings of the past year. I have been living in Sderot for almost twenty years. For five and a half years I have been "breathing" Qassams. Some of them fell a few meters from my home, and for the first time in my life I comprehended the emotional meaning of the expression "victims of shock and anxiety." All the daily worries that were generously exported to the public are familiar to me, too. All the rituals that emerged around the anxieties: to jump in response to any unusual noise, to watch the sky while walking in the city, to bolt out of bed like an automaton at three in the morning and run to the security room, to wait tensely for the boom, to verify that everybody is okay, and so on again.

Nevertheless, I want to sound a slightly different voice. Let me start by saying that the repeated calls "to destroy Beit Hannon," "to raze Gaza," "to black out cities," and to "turn off the water" horrify me when they are uttered by a frustrated public. They are even more horrifying when they are stated by public figures, ministers, and journalists who are expressing empathy with the people of Sderot. These are calls for which there cannot be empathy! When one repeats the same call so many times, it inadvertently becomes legitimate, part of the daily agenda. What singed the ear five years ago is suddenly transformed into acceptable music and then to sweet music. One gets habituated. This process of habituation scares me even more than the Qassams.

Sderot is a multicultural city, multi-tribal. Journalists must be extra cautious when they presume to reflect the "Feelings of the Residents." Not all the residents of Sderot seek revenge. Not all the residents of Sderot wish to "Raze Beit Hannon." Not all wish to be rejuvenated by rivers of Palestinian blood. We have enough on this account—too many years, too much blood.

—"A Different Voice from Sderot / Nomika Zion" (http://coalitionofwomen.org/home/english/articles)

Children and Youth in Palestine

The Palestinian society is a very young one. Children and youth under twenty-five make up 66.7 percent of the population in the Occupied Palestinian territory. Adolescents whose ages range between ten and nineteen constitute 23 percent of the total Palestinian population. The psychosocial situation among adolescents worsened during the past five years of conflict. Children and adolescents are suffering from emotional problems such as headaches, sleeping disorders, violent acts, loss of appetite. Adolescents (aged thirteen to eighteen) are becoming more vulnerable than other children to aggression, rebellion, risk-taking behavior, helplessness, frustration, and withdrawal.

Many schoolchildren witnessed their school besieged by Israeli troops and had seen their school exposed to firing or shelling. A considerable number of children had been witnesses to a killing by Israeli troops of a student from their school or seen the killing of a teacher in school.

As a result, many schoolchildren were exposed to physical violence and had even used physical violence against their schoolmates. Teachers also reported that they had used physical punishment against students; with 77 percent of them having used verbal punishment. Domestic violence is another challenge faced by Palestinian children. The initial results of the study of domestic violence note that fathers and mothers resort to physical punishment of their children.

At Sharja primary school in Qalqilya, a town in the northern West Bank entirely encircled by the barrier separating Israel from the occupied Palestinian territory, the students said they wanted to do something about the way the ongoing violence was making itself felt in their schools and on their education. According to a 2006 study, almost half (45 percent) of Palestinian students are exposed to violence in schools.

"The external violence is affecting relationships in schools, between teachers and students and between students themselves," said Hasem Alshair, a trainer and former school counselor. Teachers themselves were overwhelmed by conflict-induced stress, and were behaving aggressively with students. "It's hurting children," Alshair said.

Ibraham Jameel said up to a third of students at his school in the nearby town of Khalet Yaseem were dropping out, with violence as the key cause, after poverty.

"Even verbal violence" could really damage children, said Lamees Moeen, sixteen. "Are we here to learn or to be insulted?"

Dana Smeek, seventeen and in her final year, said a number of students had lost their fathers in the fighting. Many more parents were unemployed, and some families could not afford the cost of school fees and supplies, particularly if there was more than one child. Poorer students were often excluded or marginalized, which hurt their grades, she said.

"New graduates are having a hard time finding jobs—but that doesn't change the importance of getting an education," Smeek said.

(http://www.unicef.org/oPt/voices_children_2823.html)

Impact on Palestinian Children

Constituting over half the population, and as the most vulnerable and dependent sector of society, Palestinian children are disproportionately affected by Israeli policies. Inability to access medical care, poverty levels that affect nutritional intake, and interruptions in some immunization programs have all led to an overall decrease in the status of children's health and an increase in malnutrition and anemia

rates. Spiraling poverty, curfews and closures, the devastation of basic infrastructure, the ever-present threat of violence, and the deliberate destruction of homes and schools have provoked a serious decline in the quality of education and the loss of school days.

—Defense for Children International, September 28, 2004 (http://www.palestinemonitor.org/nueva_web)

Impact on School Children of Israel: One Story

To the children of Sderot (Israel) and the western Negev, life in the shadow of Qassams (rockets) has been a traumatic experience for a long time; so much so that some of them even say that they don't remember life without them. The Committee for Children's Rights heard testimonies Tuesday from the mouths of some of those kids who have been under constant threat of rocket attacks.

"We have no normal life. We never know what will happen the next hour when Qassams fall; we are not only afraid for ourselves, but also for our families. It's traumatic to think that someone close to us will get hurt. It's just terrible," said Bar, one of the children who testified before the committee.

The children said that because of the Qassams they have problems in studying, concentrating, and they are lagging behind compared to other children of the country. "I have a hard time concentrating in school, and the Qassams affect my entire life," said Niv. "Every time I want to do something, I give up because I think that the alarm will go off at any moment. I can't study and I can't even play soccer," he added.

Niv's classmate Gon explained their learning conditions in recent times: "Because not all of our classrooms are protected, we have to study in shifts. We have no gym class because there is no safe place to practice, and the Yitzhak Rabin ceremony was also not conducted as planned. During the night we can't fall asleep because of the drones and helicopters flying overhead, and during the day we can't concentrate because we are too tired."

Liza from Sderot can't remember life without Qassams, but she remembers the day she started being afraid that something will happen to her or one of her friends. It was the day a girl she knew was killed by a Qassam rocket.

—"Sderot Kids: Can't Remember Life without Qassams"
Children of Sderot, western Negev, speak in front of Children's Rights Committee in Knesset.
(http://www.ynetnews.com/articles/0,7340,L-3325250,00.html)

Declaration from Israeli Women in War

A war is being waged in the north and south of Israel—a war that invades our private as well as public space. Our homes are no longer protected, but exposed to risk on many levels—national, economic, social, family, and emotional. In this war, hundreds of thousands of civilians, including children, are under attack in Israel, Lebanon, and Gaza.

This war mixes a "military" with a "civilian" reality, breaking down the distinctions between army and society, political and personal, strength and weakness, military and social allocations. In this war, the home front is being asked to show strength, but not asked its opinion. In the media, the masculine-military discourse is the only one heard. This language does not express our lives.

As activists in feminist organizations, we call attention to the population that has been abandoned at the home front—many of them women and children who lack all protection. These include Mizrahi, Arab, and immigrant women with no resources and support networks, many of them single mothers, some whose lives were already troubled by violence. This war has had a special impact on women.

Decisions are being made about military and political measures that bring massive harm to the civilian population, but there is no real examination of non-military alternatives,

no representation of women, no attention to the civilian and gender considerations, and no discussion of the ethical and humanitarian implications of war policies on civilians in Israel and beyond its borders.

We call upon the Israeli authorities:

Regarding compensation for loss of income: To recognize that most women who remain in the war zone are those lacking the means to leave and struggling with difficult circumstances. These women need immediate and ongoing assistance and should be included in all decisions regarding compensation for their loss of income as a direct and indirect result of the war. This compensation must be accomplished rapidly, without undue bureaucracy, and with dignity.

Regarding violence against women during war: To recognize that war situations increase the incidence of gender violence against women and girls, and to undertake to prevent and deal with this violence. The security of women is jeopardized by a discourse of national security that fails to include the security of women.

Regarding assistance to families: To provide material and emotional support to women and families in their shelters and homes—food, medical attention, emotional support, communication tools, police responsiveness.

Regarding Arab citizens of Israel: The state of Israel must provide equal services to its Arab citizens—accessible help, infrastructure, and information—to create physical, social, and economic security to all its citizens. Arab women are particularly vulnerable to the economic and social repercussions of war, which should be addressed.

—*Declaration from Israeli Women in War,* August 16, 2006
(http://coalitionofwomen.org/home/english/articles/declaration_from_israeli/)

Not In My Son's Name

[A]ll women on the roundtable discussion, including the Israeli women, some of whom were having their first visit to

Ramallah, started fantasizing about a different role women can forge: Gilad's mother mobilizing other Israeli mothers to march in the streets of Israel with one major slogan: "Not in the name of my son."

Like all mothers of the world, we recognize Aviva Gilad's agony and feelings, and fully understand her desire for his safe return. We imagine that, like all mothers, she won't accept that her son's liberty be on the account of Palestinian blood, mainly the blood of the children in the Gaza Strip.

Therefore, I decided to write my appeal to Aviva Shalit. "Can we appeal to you today to get your moral voice for the sake of humanity? Do you accept the collective punishment policies your government is executing in the name of your son?

"Your son's name will be remembered by all Palestinian children for generations to come as a curse for the bloodshed. I am sure you want a different remembrance of your son's name. A happy ending story with his safe return and, with him, the return of all children and women imprisoned in Israeli jails. Like a mother waiting impatiently for the safe return of her son, hundreds of Palestinian mothers are waiting for the moment to hug their children released from Israeli prisons."

I know many will say that, as women, we cannot have an impact on the current military madness. I do not believe that. On the contrary, we women can make a real difference. Didn't the Four Mothers' movement in Israel make a huge difference in the Israeli public during the Lebanon war? Why don't we women, who are often portrayed as victims, start receiving some recognition for our actual and potential roles in attaining peace and promoting security?"

I am a woman and a mother who believes in the politics of small things. I believe that we women and mothers can make a difference in the lives of our countries even with small initiatives. So let us not wait. Let our voice of reason be heard. Let our voice of passion for humanity be heard. We women, give life…we'd better protect it!

I assure you, the day you march calling for the safe return of your son, the day you march to call for an end to the Israeli collective punishment against the Palestinian people living under brutal occupation of your government, the day you cry out to your government that their attacks in the Gaza Strip will not bring them closer to gaining your son' safe release…we women in the Occupied Territories will be marching to support your call for a safe return of your son…we will be calling for the respect of international law…we will be calling for the respect of the human rights of both peoples in the Holy Land.…

Together we can make a difference in our countries. Together we can push forward a different peace agenda that is based on a negotiated and just settlement, and not on unilateralism or convergence. Peace can never be imposed by one party of the conflict. Peace can only be negotiated by both parties.

Together we can raise our voices against the Israeli Occupation that has brought insecurity and instability to both Palestinians and Israelis. Together, we can make a difference in the lives of our children and grandchildren.

—"Not In My Son's Name: An Appeal to Aviva Shalit,"
Terry Boullata, Occupied East Jerusalem, a mother of two children
December 7, 2006
(http://coalitionofwomen.org/home/english/articles/120706_e/)

Yali Hashash

My name is Yali Hashash. I represent the women's Coalition for Peace in Israel, the feminist organization I belong to. My organization is called Ahoti (sister) and it stands for social justice, peace, and ethnic equality for women.

Previous attempts to achieve stability in the region, whether in the north through peace negotiations with Syria and Lebanon, or whether through peace settlements with the Palestinians, have all failed so far. It is my belief that one of the main reasons for that failure is that these attempts have failed to take into account any considerations of economic security for the vast population on all sides of the conflict. In Ahoti—my organization—we strongly believe that any discussion of peace in the Middle East is futile unless it gives people a sense of future prospects, both of physical safety, but also of economic stability.

Peace agreement attempts seem to fail in gaining large supporters from all sides partly because they seem to deteriorate rather [than improve] the economic security of large populations. Factories at the periphery in Israel have been shut and moved to Jordan and Egypt for low-cost labor, making the periphery pay for the peace costs. The Oslo Agreement suggested solving most territorial issues, yet offered no economic future prospects for Palestinians. Thus, support for militaristic action at least gives a sense of belonging and solidarity, and perhaps a hope for social mobility to people, which peace as practiced so far has failed to do.

So today, while opposing the aggression against civilians in northern Israel and southern Lebanon, and Israel's disproportionate retaliation against the civilian population,

I wish to remind you that a temporary ceasefire or even a peace agreement is not enough. Only massive investments in local economy throughout the Middle East, while opposing a neo-liberal economy, can recruit people once again into believing that peace holds any future for them and their children. Indeed, only a strong alternative to the American "new order" policy, an alternative that promotes coexistence rather than constant forcing of a neocolonial order, can bring true peace to the region.

Unfortunately, some leaders in my country have adopted the "evil axis" rhetoric promoted by Bush. It is a rhetoric that leads to a dead end and goes against all that we know about true negotiation. Jews and Arabs have long rich traditions of negotiating. Both have been the carriers of goods, knowledge, and culture to the whole world, using negotiation as a skill that is crucial for survival in a heterogeneous reality, and developed it to an art. Given the right economic terms, I am confident that negotiating peace in the Middle East is not beyond us.

—Excerpted from an address by Yali Hashash to a rally for peace in Copenhagen on August 7, 2006.
(http://coalitionofwomen.org/home/english/articles/070806)

Appendix D
Session Handouts

Handout 1 Session 1
Workstation Display Boards

(Enlarge this handout on a copier and make one copy. Cut up the information by the major time blocks to create the study board workstations.)

Display Board One
British Mandate Map (1917-1947) *(refer to Chapter 3, pp. 44-61 in study book)*

The League of Nations gave Mandates over territories of the former Ottoman Empire to the French and British with the understanding that these territories would establish statehood in a *short* period of time. The French mandated Syria and Lebanon, the British Palestine and Iraq. Syria achieved independence in 1936 and Lebanon in 1941. Iraq declared its independence in 1931. The story of Israel-Palestine begins here.

The **Balfour Declaration (1917)** was written to Lord Rothschild by Arthur James Balfour.

> *I have much pleasure in conveying to you, on behalf of His Majesty's Government, the following declaration of sympathy with Jewish Zionist aspirations which has been submitted to, and approved by, the Cabinet: His Majesty's Government view with favor the establishment in Palestine of a national home for the Jewish people, and will use their best endeavors to facilitate the achievement of this object, it being clearly understood that nothing shall be done which may prejudice the civil and religious rights of existing non-Jewish communities in Palestine, or the rights and political status enjoyed by Jews in any other country. I should be grateful if you would bring this declaration to the knowledge of the Zionist Federation.*

The Mandate provisions were met with outright rejection by the Arab delegation. They felt slighted and betrayed by the British, who they believed had not been forthright in their promises during the war. Pasha al-Husseini had expected that there would be areas within Palestine where Arabs would be autonomous, as well as other benefits for Arabs who chose to live within the Jewish homeland. Both T. E. Lawrence and Sir Henry McMahon had made such promises to secure Arab military support in the war. The Arabs had no purchase for Jewish expansion of any description.

(David Fromkin, *A Peace to End All Peace: The Fall of the Ottoman Empire and the Creation of the Modern Middle East,* New York: Avon Books, 1989, p. 521)

Dr. Samih K. Farsoun *(see Endnote 71, p. 216)*, Palestinian professor who taught at American University in Washington, describes the history we are considering:

> *"During the last years of the Ottoman era, Palestinians and other Arab leaders lobbied the Ottoman authorities against the Zionist project. Intellectuals' criticisms of Zionism and peasant resistance to evictions from land purchased by Zionist Jewish agencies indicated concern about the threat of Zionism and presaged the character of the forthcoming resistance. Concern turned into alarm, anger, and hostility…"* against the pro-Zionist provisions of the Mandate, the Jewish immigration, and the land purchases. *"In short, Palestinian actions against both Zionism and the British Mandate became highly politicized. Small seemingly social and religious incidents quickly erupted into major political confrontations between Palestinians and Jewish immigrant-settlers. By the 1930s the clashes and riots targeted the British authorities of the Palestinian Mandate government as well."*

The Arabs did dissent. With their legitimate grievances and the compliance of the British government with Zionist aims, the "Arab Revolt" broke out in April of 1936. One additional factor of major significance that contributed to the boiling over of hostility was the sudden "spectacular rise of Jewish immigration into the country in the first half of the 1930s." In spite of the recommendations of one British commission after another to reduce immigration in accordance with the nebulous policy that numbers would bear some relation to the economic "'absorptive capacity,' tens of thousands of Jews poured into Palestine, the rise of Nazism in Germany having pushed them out of central Europe. Only 4,075 immigrated into Palestine in 1931 and 9,553 in 1932, but the numbers soared to 30,327 in 1933, 42,359 in 1934, and 61,854 in 1935." The ratio of Jews to Arabs grew from "16 percent in 1931 to 28 percent in 1936."

After an exhausting five years of war, Britain was eager to escape from its seemingly intractable involvement with Palestine. She therefore advised the United Nations that she was passing responsibility for the Palestine Mandate over to the international body. So on November 29, 1947, the fifty-six mostly Western member states of the UN, adopted a resolution to partition the land of Palestine.... When the UN's partition resolution was adopted, the population of Palestine was close to one million. Sixty-nine percent were Arabs who owned more than 90 percent of Palestine's 10,500 square miles (about the size of Maryland). Thirty-one percent of the population were Jews who owned *five percent* of the land. Yet despite these verifiable facts compiled by the British, the partition resolution assigned 52 percent of the land to [what was soon to become] the new State of Israel and 48 percent to the Palestinian Arabs.

In 1880, there were approximately 456,000 Arabs and 24,000 Jews living in historic Palestine. By 1914, the Jewish population had increased to about 60,000, nearing 9 percent of the population. By 1947, Jewish immigration had climbed to almost 600,000, making them 39 percent of the population.

Display Board Two

UN Partition Map / Post-1948 War Map *(refer to Chapter 4, pp. 62-93 in the study book)*

1. Summarize UN Resolution 181 *(refer to UN Resolutions at http://resources.gbgm-umc.org/israelpalestine)*.

2. In the months prior to the declaration of statehood by the Jewish residents of Mandate Palestine, approximately 300,000 Arab Palestinians were displaced from their homes, and another 450,000 were displaced during the war. UN Resolution 194 resolves that the refugees wishing to return to their homes and live at peace with their neighbors should be permitted to do so at the earliest practical date, and that compensation should be paid for the property of those choosing not to return and for loss of or damage to property which, under principles of international law or in equity, should be made good by the governments or authorities responsible. This resolution has yet to be implemented, although this was a condition of Israel's recognition as a state and acceptance as a member of the UN.

3. At the ceasefire, the Gaza Strip came under Egyptian administration, and what became known as the West Bank (because it was the west bank of the Jordan River) came under Jordanian administration. Most of Jerusalem was under Jordanian control, with a small section under Israeli control. In the partition plan, the Jewish state was to have 56 percent of the land. At the end of the war, they had control over 78 percent of historic Palestine.

Display Board Three

Map After War of 1967 (Six-Day War, June 5-10, 1967) *(refer to Chapter 5, pp. 94-105 in the study book)*

1. Impact of War
   - Israel launches preemptive strike against Egyptian Air Force.
   - The West Bank, including East Jerusalem, is captured from Jordan and occupied.
   - The Golan Heights is captured from Syria and occupied.
   - The Gaza Strip and Sinai Peninsula are captured from Egypt and occupied.

2. UN Security Council Resolution 242, passed by the Security Council of the United Nations on November 22, 1967, demands the withdrawal from the "areas which were occupied during the most recent conflict," and the right of all states in the region to "live in peace within

secure and recognized boundaries." To this day, Israel has yet to establish officially its borders, except for its northern border with Lebanon created in May 2000 when the Israel Defense Forces (IDF) withdrew after 18 years of occupying southern Lebanon.

3. Israel constructs colonies across the West Bank, including East Jerusalem and Gaza, in violation of Fourth Geneva Convention.

4. Phases of Palestinian Resistance to the Israeli Occupation:

   - Non-Cooperation (1967-1970) – general strikes; in 1968 the Palestine Liberation Organization adopts its national charter, insisting the Palestinians have a right to their own homeland. In 1969 Yasser Arafat is elected chairman of the PLO.

   - Steadfastness (1970-1982) – maintenance of the status quo and resistance. After three passenger airlines are hijacked to Jordan in 1971, Jordan's King Hussein orders his army to destroy the PLO and the leadership is driven out to Lebanon. This event is known as Black September, leaving some 2,000 dead.

   - Isolation (1982-1987) – PLO is exiled from Lebanon to Tunis.

   - Intifada (1987-1990) – A generation of Palestinian youth confront Israeli soldiers with stones, seeking to "shake off" twenty years of Israeli military Occupation.

   - Casualties (Palestinian):
     * 1,600 Palestinians killed (130 women and 490 children included in this total)
     * 175,000 Palestinians arrested and detained
     * 100,000 Palestinians injured, 40 percent of whom suffer permanent physical disabilities

   - Casualties (Israeli):
     * 401 Israelis killed

   - Negotiation (1990-1993) – Negotiation, recognition, and "reconciliation"

   - Oslo Period (1993-September 2000)
   - 2nd Intifada (September 29, 2000-now) – called by some the Al-Aqsa Intifada, due to opening clashes occurring on the Haram al-Sharif, following Ariel Sharon's "visit" on September 28, 2000.

5. UN Security Council Resolution 338, passed on October 22, 1973, called on all parties to the present fighting to cease all firing and terminate all military activity immediately, and called upon all parties concerned to start immediately after the ceasefire the implementation of UN Security Council Resolution 242.

6. Immigration of one million Russian Jews as well as Ethiopian Jews into Israel; emigration of Palestinian Christians and increased Muslim birth rate in Palestine.

7. Hamas, an acronym for the Arabic words that approximate "Movement of the Islamic Resistance," describes itself as a branch of the Islamic Brotherhood in Egypt. Hamas was supported financially by some Israeli IDF officers as a counter to the PLO during the Intifada in Gaza. Along with other Jihad groups, Hamas found its inspiration in the Palestinian hero Sheikh 'Izz ed-Din al-Qassam.

8. In 1988 two important developments were the PLO's recognition of Israel and Yasser Arafat's "Declaration of Independence for the State of Palestine" on the West Bank and in Gaza, with East Jerusalem as its capital. Recognition eventually came from over one hundred countries, not including the United States, Western Europe, and Israel. But it was a significant symbolic move forward for Palestinian identity, ultimately changing the focus of the struggle. The denunciation of terrorism by the PLO and the use of violence were to be limited to the Occupied Territories and Israel.

   Yasser Arafat requested permission to address the General Assembly of the United Nations in New York. Still dismissing such overtures and changes in the Palestinian Liberation Organization, the outgoing Reagan administration in Washington denied Arafat a visa to the United States. Instead, the General Assembly voted to hold its meeting in Geneva, where on December 13 Arafat appealed for peace negotiations. Pressuring Arafat, the outgoing Secretary of State George Shultz extracted from him in his address the acknowledgement that the PLO recognized Israel's right to exist and accepted Resolutions 242 and 338. The PLO would also renounce resorting to terrorism. These concessions repeated the Secretary of State's phrases almost word for word. George Shultz then appointed an ambassador to be the US contact to the PLO.

Display Board Four

Initial Oslo Map – 2003 *(refer to Chapter 6, pp. 106-127 in the study book)*

1. September 13, 1993 – The Declaration of Principles (DOP) are signed in Washington, DC. Palestinian Interim Self-Government Arrangements (Oslo):

   - Called for "direct, free and general political elections" for the Palestinians.
   - Called for beginning of a five-year transitional period following Israeli withdrawal from the Gaza Strip and Jericho areas, to be completed by May 1999.
   - Called for permanent status negotiations to begin "not later than the third year of the interim period."
   - "The two sides (Israel and the Palestinians) view the West Bank and the Gaza Strip as a single territorial unit, whose integrity will be preserved during the interim period."
   - "The two parties agree that the outcome of the permanent status negotiations should not be prejudiced or preempted by agreements reached during the interim period."

2. Oslo II – Palestinian-Israeli Interim Agreement on the West Bank and Gaza Strip (Washington, DC – September 28, 1995):

   - Security arrangements and Israeli redeployment from seven West Bank towns and cities, including: Jenin, Tulkarem, Kalkilya, Nablus, Bethlehem, Ramallah, Hebron
   - The West Bank is divided into Areas A, B, and C:
     - **A** = areas that are exclusively under Palestinian military and civil control (around 9 percent)
     - **B** = areas that are under Palestinian civil control, but Israel maintains overriding security control (around 30 percent)
     - **C** = areas that are fully under Israeli military and civil control: Israeli settlements, military installations, etc. (around 60 percent)
   - Calls to open a Safe Passage Route for Palestinians traveling between the West Bank and Gaza Strip
   - Calls for the opening of a Seaport/Harbor in Gaza

3. Oslo III – Final Status Talks. Issues include:
   - Jerusalem
   - Refugees — either Right of Return and/or compensation for lost property
   - Israeli Settlements
   - Water
   - Borders/Security
   - Release of Political Prisoners/ Administrative Detainees

4. Assassination of Prime Minister Rabin by Orthodox Jew, multiple changes in Israeli governments, stagnation of the Palestinian Legislative council by Arafat, bombings by Hamas and Islamic Jihad.

5. The number of Jewish settlers living in Occupied East Jerusalem, the West Bank, and the Gaza Strip doubled during the active phase of the Oslo process. In late 2000, there were approximately 200,000 Israelis living in the settlements in the West Bank and the Gaza Strip and another 200,000 living in the settlements in East Jerusalem.

Display Board Five

Today's Map *(refer to pp. 124-127 in the study book)*

1. September 28, 2000 — Right Wing Opposition Party Leader (Likud) Ariel Sharon visits the Haram al-Sharif/ Temple Mount area accompanied by thousands of Israeli police and military. His attempted visit sparks massive riots and protests following Friday prayers on September 29, 2000. The "Al Aqsa Intifada" begins.

UN Security Council Resolution 1322, adopted on October 7, 2000, "condemns acts of violence, especially the excessive use of force against Palestinians, resulting in injury and loss of human life" and "calls upon Israel, the occupying Power, to abide scrupulously by its legal obligations and its responsibilities under the Fourth Geneva Convention relative to the Protection of Civilian Persons in Time of War of 12 August 1949." The vote was 14 in favor, 0 against, and 1 abstention—the United States.

2. Spring 2002 — Israel begins its construction of the Wall in the West Bank and East Jerusalem. It will eventually be over 450 miles long, separating Palestinians from their fields, work, school, places of worship, and medical care. International Court of Justice rules the Wall is illegal under International Law, Summer 2003, as it cuts deeply into Palestinian territory, ignoring the Green Line of 1948.

The reality of checkpoints, gates, and barriers across West Bank and East Jerusalem sets in. Several hundred such barriers exist, making direct passage anywhere in the Palestinian territories impossible.

3. August 2005 — Israel unilaterally removes settlers and settlements from Gaza and four small settlements in the West Bank; Israel still controls borders, air space, and water resources; as such, it is still considered Occupied Territory; settlement expansion continues in the West Bank and East Jerusalem.

History Questions

(Use the information on the various display boards to answer the questions below. You will not visit the boards in sequence, so be sure to check at which workstation you are, in order to find the answers to the questions under each section.)

Historic Palestine — British Mandate (1917-1948)

1. Why did the British have control of historic Palestine?
2. What were the key points of the Balfour Declaration?
3. Was the Mandate period a peaceful one? Why or why not?
4. What was the population and what percentage were the different religious groups?

UN Partition Plan and 1948 War

1. What is UN Resolution 181? How would the partition plan change the map?
2. Did the Arab and Jewish parties agree to it? Why or why not?
3. When did Palestinians begin to be refugees? How many refugees were created prior to the war in May 1948, and how many as a result of the war?
4. At the end of the war, how much of historic Palestine did the new State of Israel control?

Six-Day War (June 5-12, 1967)

1. What areas did Israel occupy and control at the end of the Six-Day War?

2. What is UN Security Council Resolution 242? Has it been implemented?
3. What is Occupation and how does the Fourth Geneva Convention apply?
4. When did Hamas come into being and what is this group?
5. What are Israeli settlements/colonies? How many were there in September 1993?

Oslo Process (September 1993 – September 2000)

1. Who signed the Oslo Agreement and when?
2. What were the primary changes that were to happen under this agreement?
3. Who was assassinated in November 1995 and by whom?
4. What were some of the key changes during this period?

2006

1. Does the current map give you hope that a two-state solution is possible? Why or why not?
2. What impact does the Wall have on Palestinian society? What is the argument the Israeli government makes for why the Wall is necessary?
3. What did the International Court of Justice decision say about the Wall in the ruling of Summer 2004?
4. How many checkpoints, roadblocks, and barriers are there across the West Bank and East Jerusalem?

Jesus Is Condemned to Death

A reading from Matthew 27:24, 26:

When Pilate saw that he was getting nowhere, but that instead an uproar was starting, he took water and washed his hands in front of the crowd. "I am innocent of this man's blood," he said. "It is your responsibility!" Then he released Barabbas to them. But he had Jesus flogged and handed him over to be crucified.

A reading from Matthew 5:11:

Blessed are you when people insult you, persecute you, and falsely say all kinds of evil against you because of me.

Listen as we hear a contemporary reflection by Palestinian poet, Mahmoud Darwish:

Poem of the Land

A small evening

A neglected village

Two sleeping eyes

Thirty years

Five wars

I witness that time hides for me an ear of wheat

The singer sings of fire and strangers

Evening was evening

The singer was singing

And they questioned him

Why do you sing?

He answers them as they seize him

Because I sing

And they have searched him:

    In his breast only his heart

    In his heart only his people

    In his voice only his sorrow

    In his sorrow only his prison

And they have searched his prison

To find only themselves in chains

(Mahmoud Darwish, "Poem of the Land V," *Modern Anthology of Palestinian Literature,* ed. Salma Khadra Jayyusi, New York: Columbia University Press, 1992, p. 149)

A Time of Prayer

After each set of petitions, let us join in saying:

Lord have mercy,
Christ have mercy,
Lord have mercy.

Let us pray: *(Allow for silence before each set of petitions.)*

For politicians, statespersons, government officials, leaders, especially those in our own countries, that they may seek the common good—peace, equity, and justice;

For judges and magistrates, that they may administer true justice impartially and with mercy;

For those who possess the power over life and death over others;

For every occasion when human beings use their skill to hurt and kill;

Lord have mercy.
Christ have mercy.
Lord have mercy.

For those condemned to death for whatever reason;

For those imprisoned, lawfully and unlawfully, justly and unjustly;

For those serving very long or indeterminate sentences;

Lord have mercy.
Christ have mercy.
Lord have mercy.

For ourselves;

When we judge others, and for those we condemn;

When we stand judged or condemned, rightly or wrongly;

That we may know the witness and humility of Christ;

Lord have mercy.
Christ have mercy.
Lord have mercy.

(John Peterson, *A Walk in Jerusalem: Stations of the Cross,* Harrisburg, Pennsylvania: Morehouse Publishing, 1998, p. 4.)

The Peoples of the Land

Moshe

I am one of the first generation of native-born Israelis, born in 1952. My mother was a Holocaust survivor from Hungary. My father's parents immigrated to Palestine in the 1920s, and he was born here shortly afterwards. He too is a native, but his first ID card issued by the British authorities was as a Palestinian, not an Israeli. We native-born Jews are called Sabras. The *sabra* is a native cactus. Its fruit is very prickly on the outside but very sweet on the inside—just like us! My wife and I have five children, and we are a modern Orthodox family living in Jerusalem. We keep a kosher home, observe Shabbat (Sabbath), and are dedicated to having our children know who they are as Jews in this world. I was raised as and continue to be a Zionist. I believe in Israel as a Jewish state that is necessary for the preservation, protection, and flourishing of the Jewish people. Finally, we have control over our own futures, can protect ourselves, and can make our own mistakes. We have tried many times to make peace with the Arabs here, but they continuously choose the path of violence. So we have to keep a strong army in which I proudly served, as do all young Israelis. Someday, maybe there will be peace. I have come to accept that Palestinians have a right to a state. I'm willing to give up part of Israel to work toward a two-state solution. I believe, though, that the founding of the state was a divine act, bringing us home after 2,000 years of exile. I will always support Israel as a Jewish state because that is as it is supposed to be. As a Jew and an Israeli, I feel strongly that we should strive to make the world a better place. So as a physician, I donate many hours a year to work with the poor and serve as part of our nation's rescue teams that are sent to other places in the world when disaster strikes. In this way, I work to fulfill our Jewish injunction to help heal the world and make Israel a caring nation.

Benyamin

I am a Jewish Israeli just finishing high school. I was born in Tel Aviv. Like everyone my age, I am scheduled to begin my military service now. But I'm a part of a small but growing number of students who do not want to do military service. I'm happy to serve my country in some sort of community service that builds the country up, but I object to military conscription, particularly as the army mostly now serves as an Occupation police force that has little to do with Israeli security. I've already spent three months in jail for refusing to show up at my induction, because I haven't been granted status as a conscientious objector—a very difficult status to get in Israel. I guess I'd describe myself as a secular Jew. I'm not religiously observant but culturally I'm Jewish. I love Israel but think we need to move beyond Zionism or at least redefine it. It is time to build one state for Jews and Palestinians and for others who want to come here. We live in too small a place to set up boundaries and borders between us. In the twenty-first century, it is hard to argue for a state that wants to be a mono-nation. It really isn't realistic or helpful at this point in our world. We need to focus more on what draws us together than what keeps us apart. I work with a number of Israeli organizations that are trying to bring not just some enforced calm but a real peace, based on recognizing everyone's dignity and humanity. For me, that is what being Jewish is about.

Jennifer

I am one of millions of Israelis born somewhere else in the world but have made *aliyah* ("come up") to Israel to become a citizen. I am from the United States, but immigrants come from countries all over the world. The largest single block of Jewish immigrants is from the former Soviet Union. I was raised in a reformed Jewish household in the United States where my parents raised us to care about the state of the world and to be active in our Jewish community and faith.

We always talked about the need for a two-state solution so that the peoples in the land could live in freedom and security. I traveled to Israel while I was in college on a Birthright Tour. We went all over the country to connect to different periods of history and to meet Israelis from all walks of life. We didn't spend much time with Arab Israelis and none with Palestinians, which bothered me some. It was sort of like they didn't exist. But I loved being in a place where being Jewish was so much a part of the daily culture, where the rhythm of life was shaped by our tradition. Having lived in the US, I had never experienced being part of the majority. It was such an exhilarating experience that I decided once I finished graduate school to make *aliyah*. I was trained as a lawyer and started work in Haifa. From my work at a women's center there, I began to see how invisible Palestinians were, whether they had Israeli citizenship or lived in the Occupied Territories. I have slowly become more and more involved in joint Jewish and Palestinian Israeli women's peace work in the north. I still think that a two-state solution is the best. I believe that Israel can be a Jewish state and a full democracy, but only if we give up our control over the lives of the three million Palestinians living in Gaza, the West Bank, and East Jerusalem. My new country needs to go back to the pre-1967 borders and share Jerusalem as a capital for both nations. If we can do that, I believe that peace is possible for us all.

Rachel

I am an Orthodox Jewish woman, married with eight children. I came to Eretz Israel (the Land of Israel) when I was six years old. My family came from Australia to live in the land that God set aside for us and to reclaim it for the Jewish people. My family lived in a neighborhood in Jerusalem until the disaster of the Oslo peace process and our government's decision to give some of our land to the Palestinians. Clearly, this is against the divine mandate, and we, like thousands of others, moved to one of the Jewish communities (others call them settlements) in Samaria (called the West Bank by some) so that we could make sure that Jews were not uprooted from biblical Israel ever again. It hasn't been easy for us. To travel from our home to Jerusalem for work or school or to visit family means we have to travel on roads where we're subject to shooting by Palestinians. Especially since 2001, life has been hard. A Palestinian blew himself up at the gate of our community. Luckily no one else was injured or killed. It isn't easy to stay here, but we feel called by our faith to protect this land. We are glad to face the dangers because it is what being a faithful Jew is all about. People say Palestinians have a right to a state. I don't know about that—at least not here. Why can't they just go to Jordan? Sixty percent of the people living in Jordan now are Palestinian. They could have that country. It's huge. They have over twenty Arab nations to go live in. We have one little Jewish state. Our leaders are really betraying the Jewish people worldwide when they negotiate over this land. It isn't ours to negotiate with—it is a covenant from G-d. Some others in our community are willing to take up arms against our government if they try to move us. We're not. But we would use all means of protest, legal avenues, and persuasion to make sure we never leave the Promised Land again. I love my family and I can give them no greater gift than to appreciate our connection to this land and the covenant we have from G-d. We won't give up the fight.

Ibrahim

I am an old man now, born in the 1920s in a small village near Jaffa. My family has been farmers for centuries. Our land was bountiful in oranges, olives, and grapes. I was in my mid-twenties when the al-Nakbah came, the disaster in 1948. Fighting was fierce near us. We made the decision to take the family south to get away from the fighting. We had to leave everything behind, taking only what we could carry. We thought we would be back in a few days at most. About 750,000 people thought they'd be back in a few days. Funny, days gave way to weeks, then months, then years. A few days have become almost sixty years. Now there are over five million Palestinian refugees worldwide. We ended up near Gaza City. We couldn't get any farther because Egypt had closed the passage to the Sinai. We set up camp with others from our village. Day after day thousands more came. The 10,000 residents of Gaza soon became almost 40,000 as refugees like us poured in from all over the rest of Palestine. Finally in 1949, the United Nations came and helped to organize the camps, giving us some food, helping us construct temporary shelters. Everyone assumed we'd be going home soon. But, thanks be to God, we survived. We made the most of the little square block room with its tin roof. There was no land to tend, although I tried to grow a little orange tree to keep our hope alive. I made sure my children went to school so they would have opportunities for a better life when we finally got to go back home. I drew a picture of the village—every house, every tree. I shared this with my children as time went on so they wouldn't forget, so they would know where they came from, who they were, what our land looked like. The key to the front door hangs on the block wall over the mat I sleep on at night. Now, I take out the ragged piece of paper and share the drawing with my great grandchildren. Telling our stories of where we come from and who we are is important. We have our faith. Allah has kept us strong. I pray five times a day, but I long to go to Jerusalem to pray at Al-Aqsa Mosque one more time before I die. We live in very hard conditions. Our camp now is over 90,000 people. It is crowded, hot, dusty. But my orange tree still grows. My grandson had a permit to get out of the Gaza Strip, so he went to our village. He told me the land is vacant. The ruins of a lot of the homes can be found under the brush. Even part of the mosque is still there. If no one is

there, why can't we go back? I want to see my land again before I die. I will live with the Jews, my children and grand-children will live with the Jews, if we're allowed to return. Why not? We lived together before the al-Nakbah. No one should want to take all the land for themselves. It isn't right. People talk about one state, two states. What does it matter, as long as I can go back to my land? Then there will be peace for us all.

Ahmed

I was born in Jerusalem in the Old City in early 1967. I don't remember the Six-Day War. I was only an infant, but my mother tells me fighting was fierce near us. She kept me and my sister under the stairwell while the fighting went on outside. My father was in Amman at the time and wasn't able to get back to us right away. Luckily for us, he did get back to us when the Israeli government gave out our new IDs. Others weren't so lucky and couldn't get back. Even though my grandparents, parents, and my sister and I were born in Jerusalem, our new IDs from the Israelis stated we were alien residents. As I grew up and began to under-stand the reality around me, I began to ask, "What? Did I suddenly drop down from the moon? Who was the alien in the city?" My father is a religious man, going to the Haraam al-Sharif for prayers every Friday, doing his daily prayers five times a day, fasting during the holy month of Ramadan. Just two years ago he was able to make the Haj, the pilgrimage to Mecca. I'm not so observant, I guess. I believe in God. But all religions just seem to be part of the problem here. God is always on "our" side, no matter what side we're on—guess that means God is always fighting himself! Maybe without all of our religious baggage, we could find ways to live in this place without killing each other. What I'm interested in is justice. I want to go where I want, when I want. I want my family members who were trapped in Amman in 1967 to be able to return home. I want to have a passport that says I'm a Palestinian, not some travel document that I have to get from the Israeli authorities every time I want to leave. I want to get married, but there is no place in Jerusalem for us to live. If we move outside the city, the Israeli authorities will take my ID from me, saying I'm no longer a resident of Jerusalem. If that happens, I lose my national insurance and my right to live in Jerusalem. Israelis can move around in the country, even out of the country, and don't lose their right to live in Jerusalem. But if I do, even though I was born here, I can lose that right. This place is enough to make anyone insane.

Nour

Many people outside think I'm an atypical Muslim woman. I am faithful to the tenets of our faith and I wear a *hijab* and modest dress. But that doesn't mean I'm subservient to anyone or that my husband sees me as less than he. That is not what Islam is about—women had social rights, particularly around divorce and inheritance laws, through Islam much sooner than women in Judaism or Christianity did. I hold a Ph.D. in English literature from Oxford University and teach at a university in the West Bank. My family has lived in Nablus for generations. During the first Intifada, my husband, like many of our men, was rounded up and put in prison. There was never a charge against him—"administrative detention" it was called. I became very active in the women's organizations that worked to continue the struggle against the Occupation. I am a fighter—I will not acquiesce to Israel taking our land. I want to live in peace. I want my children to know peace, but not a peace at any cost, especially the cost of our dignity, humanity, and land. I supported the movement in Palestine to accept two states. But now? With the settlements everywhere, the Israeli-only bypass roads, the Wall and checkpoints, we live in a piece of Swiss cheese. There is no state possible here now, except the state of apartheid. It is unacceptable. So now I am

pushing for a one-state solution. I want full rights as a human being in this land. I will not accept living in a jail-like reality. I would rather die fighting than to accept such an indignity for myself and my children. It used to take me thirty-five minutes to reach my work. Today, if I can make it at all, it can take three or six hours or all day, depending on how many checkpoints and the mood of the soldiers there. This is no way to live.

Hanan

I am one of the invisible people in this land. I'm a Christian Palestinian who has an Israeli passport. As a Christian, most folks outside don't even know I exist. When I meet Christians from around the world, they always ask when I converted, assuming I must have been Muslim or Jewish. When I tell them my family became Christian in 33 AD, they're taken aback. Christians forget that the church that began in this land never stopped being in this land, and as Palestinian Christians we have helped keep the faith alive here since the days of Jesus. As a Palestinian living inside what became the State of Israel, people don't know what to make of me. If I'm Israeli, I must be Jewish. Well, 20 percent of Israelis are Palestinian, either Muslim or Christian. In the country, I'm usually described by Jewish Israelis as an Arab Israeli. I think it is a way to try to erase the reality that there was a Palestinian consciousness prior to the founding of the State of Israel. As if all of us who are ethnically Arab here were just aimlessly wandering the landscape when the war broke out. If we called them Palestinian Israelis, then it might disturb one of the foundational myths that this was a land with no people for a people with no land. But growing up inside Israel means my life has been quite different from Palestinians living in the West Bank and Gaza. My soul is often divided. I don't have a desire to go live in another part of Palestine, even if a Palestinian state were actually to emerge. My family has lived in Nazareth for centuries. This is home, no matter what the name of the country. Yet I live in a country that continually says it is a Jewish state whose symbols, songs, and culture are centered around Jewish identity. Every day I am reminded that I'm not really wanted here! At best, I'm tolerated as a Palestinian, but I'll never be a "real Israeli" in many people's eyes. But I continue to work for the development and advancement of Palestinians in Israeli society, through education to strengthen our young people in their sense of identity, dignity, and purpose.

Jesus Falls for the First Time

A reading from Isaiah 53:4-5:

Surely he took up our infirmities and carried our sorrows, yet we considered him stricken by God, smitten by him, and afflicted. But he was pierced for our transgressions, he was crushed for our iniquities; the punishment that brought us peace was upon him, and by his wounds we are healed.

A reading from Matthew 26:40-41:

Then he returned to his disciples and found them sleeping. "Could you not keep watch with me for one hour?" he asked Peter. "Watch and pray so that you will not fall into temptation. The spirit is willing, but the body is weak."

Listen as we hear a contemporary reflection by Palestinian poet Siham 'Arda:

Whispers from the Jail

From me in the jail
From the innermost darkness
From among the groans of the fifth intern
I disclose my pains to you darling.
I long for your beautiful, sleepy eyes.
Do you feel sorrow for me, my darling?
…
Do you silently read my verse,
Or do you suppress your sorrow?
You're my solace in my loneliness.
Darling, don't panic,
Despite beating my feet, my back, my side
    with their sticks, I'm fine.
And despite stretching my body,
And despite my oppressor's cruelty,
I'll be fine.
As long as my faith in the justice of my case

is deep and the friend will remain a friend.
Despite the oppressor's cunning,
I'll be fine.

Yesterday, they beat my leg, electrified my
    body, and they tied me up with iron chains,
And I, motionless, resisted pain.
Their wires injured my body
And blood gushed from my wounds
And my soul suffered Christ's pains.
My screams shook the prison
They scare my oppressor.
They closed my mouth with their fists
To silence the voice.
The voice died away in me
And I'm still fine.

Tell mom I'm adamant.
She heals my wounds
And her wishes in the silent darkness
Have reached my soul.
Tell her, as long as I see her angelic face,
I'll be fine.

(Siham 'Arda, "Whispers from Jail")

A Time of Prayer

O Lord, visit your peoples, both Palestinian and Israeli. Manifest yourself to them in your rich mercies, give showers to the earth that they may bring forth fruit. Comfort the heart of all that mourn and lift up the downcast. Be with those in prison and in hospitals, with the persecuted and oppressed; strengthen the weak and give food to the hungry. Defend those who have none to argue their case, and raise up your justice in the land. Amen.

Veronica Wipes the Face of Jesus

A reading from Isaiah 53:2-3:

For he grew up before him like a tender shoot, and like a root out of dry ground. He had no form or majesty that we should look at him, nothing in his appearance that we should desire him. He was despised and rejected by others; a man of sorrows, and acquainted with infirmity; and as one from whom others hide their faces he was despised, and we held him of no account.

Listen as we hear a contemporary reflection by Janet Morley, who works with Christian Aid in Britain:

The Kingdom of God isn't announced with handshakes (however momentous), political flourishes, or speeches that move the heart. As in this place, it will be known in thorough healing work: painstaking attention to particular bodies, committed lives, strategic actions; the binding and silencing of demons of hatred and injustice that will not want to leave or lose their grip—the mighty works, in daily life of flourishing community.

(Janet Morley, *Companions of God,* UK: Beacon Press, 1994, p. 38)

The handshakes took place in September 1993 when Prime Minister Yitzhak Rabin, Chairman Yasser Arafat, and President Bill Clinton signed the Oslo Agreements.

A Time of Prayer

Invite participants to pray together:

O God, as we stand in this place, we remember Veronica's act of compassion to our Lord Jesus. We celebrate her courage to reach beyond the constraints of social, religious, and political barriers in order to offer a loving touch. Help us, O Lord, to be people with similar courage, to participate in the healing of the world through our actions. Equip us to cross the barriers erected by human actions that stand in the way of compassion, mercy, healing, and love. In Christ's name we pray. Amen.

Jesus Meets the Women of Jerusalem

A reading from Luke 23:27-31:

A great number of the people followed him, and among them were women who were beating their breasts and wailing for him. But Jesus turned to them and said, "Daughters of Jerusalem, do not weep for me, but weep for yourselves and for your children. For the days are surely coming when they will say, 'Blessed are the barren, and the wombs that never bore, and the breasts that never nursed.' Then they will begin to say to the mountains, 'Fall on us'; and to the hills, 'Cover us.' For if they do this when the wood is green, what will happen when it is dry?"

Let us hear a contemporary reading from a Jewish Israeli peace activist:

The predominant voice heard in Israel these days is that of the extreme right wing, and their latest slogan is "Let the IDF win." Other voices are also heard, especially that of the women's peace camp. Yesterday, in an astounding show of unity, Jewish and Palestinian women—all Israeli citizens—held a joint peace action in the Arab heart of Israel, Wadi Ara. The demonstration yesterday was a brilliant show of the unity of women for peace, with some five hundred Jewish and Arab women coming from all parts of Israel. Signs ranged from the demand for equality for Israel's Arab citizens, to ending police brutality, to stopping the Israeli Occupation across the "Green Line" (1948 border). My favorite banner was, "We refuse to be enemies."

After the street protest, the women jammed a hall in Umm al-Fahem, the focus of the prior unrest. Outside, the destruction of the previous month was still starkly visible—broken street and traffic lights, debris everywhere. But inside, the Arab proprietor donated coffee and baklava to the whole crowd, and we listened to speeches in Arabic and Hebrew by women committed to equality and a just peace, and pledging to instill these values in our children. It was a sweet moment of reconciliation for us all, and we are determined to nurture it into a fully blossomed peace.

(Gila Svirsky, Jerusalem, November 22, 2000, http://www.joannestle.com/livingrm/gila/gila001122werefuse.html)

Let us join together in "A Litany for Jerusalem":

One: Let us pray for the city of Jerusalem.

All: Lord Jesus Christ, today we share your tears for the cities of the world. Still we have not loved the things that make for peace. We weep for the divided cities, especially for the city of Jerusalem; where brother fights brother and sister with sister; where anger feeds on hatred, where prejudice blinds the eye to compassion, and even religion divides, where children are taught to hate, and old people relish ancient wrongs.

One: We weep for the cities of oppression and especially for the city of Jerusalem:

All: Where iron law imprisons freedom, where thought is curbed and consciences stifled, where the questioning spirit is a traitor, where art and civilizing truth grow barren, and diversity is shackled.

One: We weep for our cities, especially the city of Jerusalem, and we weep for ourselves; we have not learned the things that make for peace.

All: Lord, turn tears into love and love into work. Turn work into justice and all that makes for peace. In the name of Christ, we pray. Amen.

(Sabeel Ecumenical Liberation Theology Center, *Worship Book,* 1996 International Conference on Jerusalem)

Jesus Is Stripped of His Garments

A reading from John 19:23-25a:

When the soldiers had crucified Jesus, they took his clothes and divided them into four parts, one for each soldier. They also took his tunic; now the tunic was seamless, woven in one piece from the top. So they said to one another, "Let us not tear it, but cast lots for it to see who will get it." This was to fulfill what the Scripture says, "They divided my clothes among themselves, and for my clothing they cast lots." And that is what the soldiers did.

Listen as we hear a contemporary reflection by Fr. Elias Chacour:

Silent, still, I lay there, aware for the first time that I was capable of vicious, killing hatred. Aware that all men [sic] everywhere—despite the thin, polite veneer of society—are capable of hideous violence against other men [sic]. Not just the Nazis or the Zionist or the Palestinian commandos—but me! I had covered my hurts with Christian responses, but inside the anger had gnawed. With this sudden, startling view of myself, a familiar inner voice spoke firmly, without compromise, "If you hate your brother you are guilty of murder." Now I understood. I was aware of other words being spoken. A Man was dying a hideous death at the hands of His captors—a Man of Peace, who suffered unjustly—hung on a cross. Father, forgive them, I repeated. And forgive me, too.

(Elias Chacour, *Blood Brothers,* Grand Rapids, Michigan: Chosen, 1984, p. 169)

A Time of Reflection

(Volunteer shares personal reflections.)

A Time of Prayer

Response: "Kyrie Eleison" (#483, *United Methodist Hymnal*)

> **Leader:** Let us pray to the Lord:

> **Group 1:** That violence, oppression, and injustice may cease from our land, while justice and peace flourish; that the pain of all those who suffer in our land, the grief of those who mourn, and the memories of those who cannot forget the hurt, whether Muslim, Jew, or Christian, may be healed by God's loving touch; that across all the barriers of race and creed, we and all who dwell in our land may respect each other's dignity and seek to serve each other in love,

> **Leader:** Let us pray to the Lord:

> **All: Kyrie Eleison**

> **Group 2:** That our self-interest and self-concern which have increased our neighbor's bitterness against us may be forgiven; that the barriers of hatred, suspicion, anger, greed, and fear which divide the peoples of this land may be removed from our hearts and minds; that all who are now in conflict in our land may renounce violence and seek peace,

> **Leader:** Let us pray to the Lord:

> **All: Kyrie Eleison**

> **Group 1:** That we may put our trust in God and experience God's deliverance; that God's promise of justice and righteousness may be real for the peoples of this land; that they may live in freedom and peace; that the Holy Spirit may work through our struggle and confusion to accomplish the Creator's good purpose among us,

> **Leader:** Let us pray to the Lord:

> **All: Kyrie Eleison**

> **Group 2:** That the Holy Spirit may lead us from prejudice to truth and mercy, teach us truly to love our enemies, and deliver us from hatred and vengefulness; that we may commit ourselves to establishing true peace and reconciliation in

the unrelenting search for justice and a world order that is fair to the generations yet to be; that swords may be hammered into plowshares and spears into pruning knives, so that the wolves and sheep may live together in peace.

Leader: Let us pray to the Lord:

All: **Kyrie Eleison**

Jesus Dies on the Cross

A reading from Luke 23:44-47:

It was now about noon, and darkness came over the whole land until three in the afternoon, while the sun's light failed; and the curtain of the temple was torn into two. Then Jesus, crying with a loud voice, said, "Father into your hands I commend my spirit." Having said this, he breathed his last. When the centurion saw what had taken place, he praised God and said, "Certainly this man was innocent."

Listen as we hear a contemporary reflection by Rev. Dr. Mitri Raheb:

God forbids us to shed our enemy's blood. But God also summons us to resist our enemy, if that enemy attempts to shed the blood of our neighbor. We do not want to kill our enemy, but we will not let him kill our brother or sister either. Loving one's enemy without resisting him would be a cheap, abstract, and treasonable attitude. But to resist without loving one's enemy can be inhuman, brutal and violent. The one without the other would violate divine and human rights. But if we can endure the tension, both love and resistance offer the only way out for us Christians.

(Mitri Raheb, *I Am a Palestinian Christian,* Minneapolis: Fortress 1995, p. 103)

A Time of Silent Prayer

Fact Sheet: Palestinian Right of Return for Refugees

Who are the Palestinian refugees?

Palestinian refugees are the indigenous Arab inhabitants of historic Palestine—the area that now comprises Israel and the Occupied Palestinian Territories—who were forced to leave their homes during and after the first Arab-Israeli War in 1948. Two-thirds of Palestinians today are refugees. They make up one-third of the world's refugee population and are one of the world's oldest refugee populations. Today there are approximately 3.8 million Palestinian refugees from 1948 and their descendants registered by the United Nations. Another 1.5 million refugees from 1948 and their descendants are not registered by the UN. An additional 250,000 Palestinians are internally displaced within Israel while another 250,000 became refugees in 1967 following the second Arab-Israeli war. The total Palestinian refugee population is thus estimated at around 5.8 million.

How did they become refugees?

The Palestinian refugee crisis began when Israel was created as a state in 1948. During the ensuing Arab-Israeli war, 750,000 indigenous Palestinians whose families had lived in Palestine for hundreds of years were forcibly expelled by, or fled in terror of, the powerful militias that would soon become the army of the State of Israel. Some were physically driven out, others heard stories of massacres, such as that at the village of Deir Yassin in April 1948, in which 254 Palestinian civilians were killed by soldiers from the pre-state Zionist militias. The militias sent a message to its men: "As in Deir Yassin, so everywhere." Word of the massacre spread terror among Palestinians, thousands of whom fled to neighboring countries. Thousands fled the war itself, believing the fighting would end within a few weeks and they would return home. Many carried with them the keys to their houses, believing their return was imminent, and the key has become a symbol of Palestinian refugee rights. The one million or so Palestinians inside Israel today, who constitute just under 20 percent of the population, are those that remained and their descendants. The second exodus of an additional 250,000 Palestinians came in 1967 during the third Arab-Israeli war that led to the Israeli Occupation of the West Bank and Gaza Strip.

Where do Palestinian refugees live?

The majority of Palestinian refugees live within a 100-mile radius of their original homes and villages. Of the 3.8 million refugees registered by the UN, 33 percent live in 59 over-crowded and under-resourced camps administered by the UN throughout the West Bank, Gaza Strip, Jordan, Syria, and Lebanon. The other 67 percent are scattered through-out the Middle East and other countries around the world.

What are the basic rights of Palestinian refugees?

The right of return is part of international law, and Palestinians are specifically guaranteed that right by UN Resolution 194 of December 1948, which states that "refugees wishing to return to their homes and live at peace with their neighbors should be permitted to do so at the earliest practicable date, and that compensation should be paid for the property of those choosing not to return." In addition, other international laws and conventions including the Universal Declaration of Human Rights, the Fourth Geneva Convention, the Hague Convention, the International Covenant on Civil and Political Rights, and several regional conventions all support the right of refugees to return and compensation.

Why have Palestinian refugees not been able to return to their homes and villages?

Despite international law and specific UN resolutions, Israel has not allowed Palestinian refugees to return. This is in spite of the fact that Israel's admission to the UN in 1949 was conditioned on its willingness to abide by General

Assembly Resolution 194 calling for repatriation and compensation. Today, sixty years later, Israel maintains that allowing the Palestinian refugees to return would change its demographic balance, more than doubling Israel's current Palestinian population of 19 percent. Israel also claims that there is no space to accommodate Palestinian refugees seeking to return to their homes. However, around 80 percent of the Israelis currently live in approximately 15 percent of Israel. The remaining 85 percent of the land is mostly land that once belonged to the Palestinian refugees, and most of it is not used. In other words, 90 percent of depopulated Palestinian villages could be repopulated without displacing Israelis or affecting their livelihoods.

What has the United States done to support the Palestinian right of return for refugees?

The United States has not been an equal broker in its involvement in peace negotiations between the Israeli government and the Palestinian Authority. Despite the fact that it is bound by its constitution to support human rights and freedom, the United States has turned a blind eye to Israel's violations of international law and continues to supply Israel with massive financial and military support. We believe, however, that the United States could use the financial support it gives to the State of Israel to hold it accountable to international law. There can be no lasting peace in the region if the rights of Palestinian refugees are not recognized.

—US Campaign to End the Israeli Occupation

Questions for Assessing Media Reports on Palestine and Israel

When critiquing a news story about the Palestinian-Israeli conflict, ask yourself the following questions:

- How many times were UN reports/findings/resolutions mentioned?
- How many times were human rights reports/findings/statements mentioned?
- Were the terms "Occupation/occupied" used appropriately?
- Were maps of the offered Palestinian state shown?
- Was Barak's "95 percent" figure used to describe the Barak "offers"?
- How many times were the words "terror/terrorist" used to describe Palestinians/Palestinian actions as opposed to Israelis/Israeli actions?
- How many times was the word "violence" used to describe Palestinian actions as opposed to Israeli actions?
- Were the words "response/retaliation" used to describe Palestinian/Israeli actions?
- Were Palestinian actions described in context (e.g., "Palestinians launched a mortar attack after Israelis bulldozed a row of houses")?
- Were Israeli actions described in context (e.g., "Israelis bulldozed a row of houses after Palestinians launched a mortar attack")?

- Did the story describe official Palestinian denials or pleas of ignorance and innocence in violent acts?
- Did the story describe official Israeli denials or pleas of ignorance and innocence in violent acts?
- How much personal detail about Palestinian victims did the story explore?
- How much personal detail about Israeli victims did the story explore?
- Did the story appropriately use the word "alleged"?
- Did the story appropriately use double quotes?
- How many direct Palestinian/Israeli quotes did the story include?

When reading an *editorial*, ask yourself the following basic questions:

- Did the editorial mention the fact that the Palestinians are under Israeli Occupation?
- Did the editorial mention findings by human rights organizations?
- Did the editorial mention UN resolutions/findings?
- Did the editorial lament the suffering of Palestinians?
- Did the editorial mention the fact that Israel is a recipient of significant military and economic aid from the United States?

Some Key Palestinian and Israeli Websites

Environment/Land

Applied Research Institute, Jerusalem (ARIJ)
http://www.arij.org

Israeli Committee Against House Demolition (ICAHD)
http://www.icahd.org

Palestinian Agricultural Relief Committee (PARC)
http://www.pal-arc.org

Palestinian Environmental NGO Network (PENGON)
http://www.pengon.org

Human Rights

Badil - Resource Center for Palestinian Residency and
Refugee Rights
http://www.badil.org

Bat Shalom - Women with a Vision for a Just Peace
http://www.batshalom.org

B'tselem - The Israeli Information Center for Human Rights
in the Occupied Territories
http://www.btselem.org

Jerusalem Center for Women
http://www.j-c-w.org

Palestinian Center for Human Rights
(PCHR) http://www.pchrgaza.org

Medical/Social Concerns

Union of Palestinian Medical Relief Committee
(UPMRC) http://www.upmrc.org

Religious/Multifaith Issues

International Center of Bethlehem
http://www.annadwa.org

Rabbis for Human Rights
http://www.rhr.israel.net

Sabeel Ecumenical Palestinian Liberation Theology Center
http://www.sabeel.org

Multiple Issues

Ha'aretz (Israeli daily newspaper in English)
http://www.haaretz.com

Palestine Report (a weekly subscription email magazine)
www.palestinereport.org

Palestinian Academic Society for the Study of International
Affairs (PASSIA)
http://www.passia.org

Palestinian Center for Rapprochement Between People
http://www.rapprochement.org

Palestinian Conflict Resolution Center (Wi'am)
http://www.planet.edu/~alaslah

Palestinian Initiative for the Promotion of Global Dialogue
and Democracy
http://www.miftah.org

Humanitarian and Relief Organizations

ReliefWeb
www.reliefweb.int

The Humanitarian Information Center
www.ochaopt.org

Jesus Is Laid in the Tomb

A reading from Mark 15:46-47:

Then Joseph bought a linen cloth, and taking down the body, wrapped it in the linen cloth, and laid it in a tomb that had been hewn out of the rock. He then rolled a stone against the door of the tomb. Mary Magdalene and Mary the mother of Jesus saw where the body was laid.

Sing "Waa Habibi, Waa Habibi."

Share the following or summarize it in your own words.

The good news is that there is another station. The story does not end with a closed tomb but a risen Christ. As we complete this study, we do so in recognition of the power and possibility available through the spirit of resurrection. The gospel story continues in Mark 16. Listen to the next three verses: "When the Sabbath was over, Mary Magdalene, Mary the mother of James, and Salome bought spices so that they might go to anoint Jesus' body. Very early on the first day of the week, just after sunrise, they were on their way to the tomb and they asked each other, 'Who will roll the stone away from the entrance of the tomb?'" Who will roll the stone away? It is a poignant question. Through these last sessions, we learned about the many complexities of life in Israel and Palestine, of all the varied peoples and identities. We have explored issues of borders, refugees, terrorism, and racism. We've examined obstacles to a sustainable, just peace. As we draw near the end of our study, we might well ask, "Who will roll the stone away?" so that conflict gives way to relationship; so that fear and hatred give way to dignity and respect; so that oppression gives way to justice; so that violence, regardless of its sources, gives way to true peace and reconciliation. Our last session together will focus on what people have been doing to roll the stone away, and we will discuss ways that we can join that work. As we give ourselves to such efforts, we participate in the power of resurrection, where hope is reborn and life erupts from death. We thus live the next Station of the Cross!

Who Will Roll the Stone Away?

Who Will Roll the Stone Away?
Breaking the Silence

Former IDF soldiers break the silence about the human costs of Occupation to both Palestinians and Israelis. Since our discharge from the army, we all feel that we have become different. We feel that service in the Occupied Territories and the incidents we faced have distorted and harmed the moral values on which we grew up.

We all agree that as long as Israeli society keeps sending its best people to military combat service in the Occupied Territories, it is extremely important that all of us Israeli citizens know the price which the generation fighting in the territories is paying, the impossible situations it is facing, the insanity it is confronting every day, and the heavy burden it bears after being discharged from the IDF—a heavy burden that hasn't left us.

That's why we decided to break the silence, because it's time to tell. Time to tell about everything that goes on there each and every day. We all served in the territories. Some served in Gaza, some in Hebron, some in Bethlehem, and the rest served in other places. We all manned check-points, participated in patrols and arrests, and took part in the war against terror.

We all realized that the daily struggle against terror and the daily interaction with the civilian population have left us helpless. Our sense of justice was distorted, and so were our morality and emotions.

The reality we experienced was made up of innocent civilians being hurt, kids not going to school because of the curfew, and parents who can't bring food home because they can't go to work. This reality has stayed with us and will not go away. After discharge from the army, we decided that we shouldn't go on. We shouldn't forget what we ourselves did and what we witnessed. We decided to break the silence.

Our first initiative was the exhibition "Breaking the Silence—Fighters Tell about Hebron," which grew out of our will to show at home what we had never shown before. For the first time, we opened a window to the world of soldiers serving in Hebron. The reaction was overwhelming. Thousands came to see the exhibition: citizens, members of parliament, and most important—soldiers and their families.

We began to investigate, interview, and document hundreds of former combat soldiers. All this was done under guarantee of full confidentiality to all those who contact us in order to testify. The amount of testimonies we have gathered proves time and again that it is not a matter of "exceptional cases" or "stray weeds." It is a dangerous phenomenon growing from day to day. Things that were once exceptional have become the norm. Israeli society must know the price it is paying for every soldier serving in the Occupied Territories. Israeli society must realize the trap we are caught in, because while the army is trying to deal with the threat posed by terror, it is creating a disaster.

We are discharged soldiers who have decided not to keep silent. To stop keeping to ourselves everything we've been through in the past three years. So far, hundreds of discharged combat soldiers have decided to break the silence, and every day more people follow.

During our combat service we've handled many different missions. We have one mission left: to talk, tell, and not keep anything hidden. "Breaking the Silence" ("Shovrim Shtika" in Hebrew) should serve as a warning sign to Israeli society. We are alerting [people] about irreversible corruption.

(From the website http://www.shovrimshtika.org/index_e.asp, October 2006)

Who Will Roll the Stone Away?
Wi'am—Palestinian Conflict Resolution Center

The hallmark of a truly democratic and just society—one whose ideals are resilient even in challenging situations—is by having diverse groups of citizens. These citizens feel empowered when they can create peaceful change in their society by holding their leaders accountable, and by possessing a fundamental faith in the rule of law and a nonviolent means of resolving conflicts.

Wi'am believes that societies will be transformed into cultures of peace when they are in continual dialogue with each other. Then they will be capable of managing conflicts in ways that bring about positive change and a potential for learning and development.

For the construction of peace to be successful, policies from "above" are not sufficient. It is necessary to gain knowledge, motivation, and participation from "below." For this to happen, the people must feel empowered to present the learning, skills, information, and actions for their community. This will promote the integral development of the community and reinforce a sense of social responsibility among community members that a peaceful society needs to survive.

Sulha is a traditional form of reaction to violent conflicts. It is a tradition that has been developed by our ancestors as a set of skills and techniques for resolving conflicts by favoring an "arms of dialogue" versus a "dialogue of arms."

Women community leaders, grassroots peace-builders, and activists can no longer be excluded from community development and sharing in decision-making equally with men. A paradigm shift must take place from marginalizing the role of women in constructive societal development toward gender equality that respects diversity and personal choice. We are proud of our marches and sit-ins that call for social reform or women's equal rights, and for an end to the unjust Occupation and its harsh measures on the ground. We continually protest against the "Separation Wall" and identify with the people who are directly devastated by the Wall. We write petitions, articles to advocate nonviolence, and call for an end to an unjust political reality. By the same token, we are

periodically orienting international groups about the current political situation and call upon the international community to advocate peace and justice for all.

Our societies will be transformed into cultures of peace when they are in continual dialogue. This also happens when they are capable of managing conflicts in ways that bring out the positive potential for learning and development that conflicts can bring!

(From the website http://www.planet.edu/~alaslah/Newsletter2005/ Newsletter205.htm, October 2006)

Who Will Roll the Stone Away?
B'Tselem: The Israeli Information Center
for Human Rights

B'Tselem was established in 1989 by a group of prominent academics, attorneys, journalists, and Knesset members. It endeavors to document and educate the Israeli public and policymakers about human rights violations in the Occupied Territories, combat the phenomenon of denial prevalent among the Israeli public, and help create a human rights culture in Israel.

In Hebrew, B'Tselem literally means "in the image of," and is also used as a synonym for human dignity. The word is taken from Genesis 1:27: "And God created humans in his image. In the image of God did He create him." It is in this spirit that the first article of the Universal Declaration of Human Rights states that "All human beings are born equal in dignity and rights."

As an Israeli human rights organization, B'Tselem acts primarily to change Israeli policy in the Occupied Territories and to ensure that its government, which rules the Occupied Territories, protects the human rights of residents there and complies with its obligations under international law.

B'Tselem has attained a prominent place among human rights organizations. In December 1989 it received the Carter-Menil Award for Human Rights. Its reports have gained B'Tselem a reputation for accuracy, and the Israeli authorities relate to them seriously. B'Tselem ensures the reliability of information it publishes by conducting its own fieldwork and research, whose results are thoroughly cross-checked with relevant documents, official government sources, and information from other sources, among them Israeli, Palestinian, and other human rights organizations.

(From the website www.btselem.org)

Who Will Roll the Stone Away?
Dar Annadwa Addawliyya—
The International Center of Bethlehem

In contexts of conflicts, people are concentrating mainly on those who "kill the body," but often they forget about those who "kill the soul," i.e., the dignity, creativity, and vision of a people. Without a vision, nations "cast off restraints." Culture is the art for the soul not only to survive but to thrive. Culture is the art to refuse being just on the receiving end, to resist being perceived only as a mere victim. Culture is the art of becoming an actor rather than a spectator. It is the art of celebrating life in a context still dominated by forces of death and domination, an art of resisting creatively and nonviolently.

However, culture is a necessity not only in times of conflict. Culture is crucial not mainly in resisting Occupation but essential in a positive way of expressing oneself the way one is and communicating one's story the way one wants. Culture has thus to do with self-determination. Culture is the place where we determine who we are as we define ourselves and not as defined by others. Culture is the medium through which we communicate what we really want in a language that is different [from] political semantics and religious formulas. The role culture will play in our future state is what will determine for many [whether] Palestine is not only [our] homeland by birth but

by choice, too. What happens in the cultural zone will indicate the direction Palestine is heading towards: a democratic state where there is not only freedom from Occupation but also a state that guarantees legally freedom of expression and allocates resources to ensure that the cradle of the three monotheistic religions will become a major cultural hub for humanity.

Last but not least, culture is an important bridge between Palestine and the rest of the world. Although culture has to do with expressing oneself as one is, this is done always in relation to others. Encountering the other is always important in understanding oneself. It is in the light of meeting a different context that one realizes one's own unique context. Culture becomes thus the space where people can meet others and themselves, where they can discover a language that is local and yet universal, and where they realize that in order to breathe, one has to keep windows wide open to new winds and fresh air brought across the seas and oceans. Simultaneously, what Palestine needs are ambassadors of its culture who can express the unique spirit of the land and its people. Culture is the means that empowers us to give face to our people, write melodies to our narrative, and develop an identity that is deeply rooted in the Palestinian soil like an olive tree, whose branches reach out into the open skies.

It is for these reasons that we, at the International Center of Bethlehem, have decided in 2007 to focus and invest most of our resources on culture. We opened in 1999 the "Cave" Arts and Crafts Center with workshops, a gallery, and a gift shop; and we dedicated in 2003 the Addar Cultural and Conference Center with a state-of-the-art multipurpose auditorium. Out of this same conviction, we opened in September 2006 the Dar al-Kalima College as the first of its kind that is offering vital, accredited, and comprehensive higher education in arts, multimedia, and communication. This is our contribution to strengthen the civil society, cultivate talent, and communicate hope so that a fresh spirit will continue to blow within, throughout, and across Palestine, and we all can breathe.

(From a message by Rev. Dr. Mitri Raheb, Pastor of Christmas Lutheran Church and General Director of the International Center of Bethlehem, www.mitriraheb.org, www.annadwa.org)

Who Will Roll the Stone Away?
The Coalition of Women for Peace

The Coalition of Women for Peace has become one of the leading voices in Israel advocating for a just and viable peace between Israel and Palestine ever since its founding in November 2000, just six weeks after the current Intifada began. The Coalition brings together independent women and nine women's peace organizations, some newly formed, and others promoting coexistence since the founding of the State of Israel. We are a mix of Jewish and Palestinian women (all citizens of Israel), and we take action to amplify the voices of women calling for peace and justice for all inhabitants of the region.

Our Principles

The Coalition of Women for Peace seeks to mobilize women in support of human rights and a just peace between Israel and its Arab neighbors, as we work to strengthen democracy within Israel. Our principles:

- An end to the Occupation.
- The full involvement of women in negotiations for peace.
- Establishment of the State of Palestine side-by-side with the State of Israel based on the 1967 borders.
- Recognition of Jerusalem as the shared capital of two states.
- Israel must recognize its share of responsibility for the results of the 1948 war and cooperate in finding a just solution for the Palestinian refugees.
- Opposition to the militarism that permeates the entirety of Israeli society.

- Equality, inclusion, and justice for Palestinians in Israel.
- Equal rights for women and all residents of Israel.
- Social and economic justice for Israel's citizens and integration in the region.

What We Do

The Coalition has provided emergency supplies to women and children in refugee camps, and school supplies to thousands of Palestinian children. Together with Palestinian women, we recently completed the International Human Rights March of Women, marching for three weeks in Israel and Palestine and calling for an end to the Occupation and creation of a just peace between our peoples. With the escalation of violence over recent years, it has become harder and harder for peace movements in Israel to rally public support. Nevertheless, the Coalition has persisted, both independently and in collaboration with others, and believes that peace is possible, and that women have a key role in making it happen.

(From the website http://coalitionofwomen.org/home/english/about)

Who Will Roll the Stone Away?
Sabeel Ecumenical Liberation Theology Center

Sabeel is an ecumenical grassroots liberation theology movement among Palestinian Christians. Inspired by the life and teaching of Jesus Christ, this liberation theology seeks to deepen the faith of Palestinian Christians, to promote unity among them toward social action. Sabeel strives to develop a spirituality based on love, justice, peace, nonviolence, liberation, and reconciliation for the different national and faith communities. The word "Sabeel" is Arabic for "the way" and also a "channel" or "spring" of life-giving water.

By learning from Jesus—his life under Occupation and his response to injustice—this theology hopes to connect the true meaning of Christian faith with the daily lives of all those who suffer under Occupation, violence, discrimination, and human rights violations. Additionally, this blossoming theological effort promotes a more accurate international awareness of the current political situation and encourages Christians from around the world to work for justice and to stand in solidarity with the Palestinian people.

Sabeel affirms its commitment to make the gospel relevant ecumenically and spiritually in the lives of the local indigenous church. Our faith teaches that following in the footsteps of Christ means standing for the oppressed, working for justice, and seeking peace-building opportunities, and it challenges us to empower local Christians. Since a strong civil society and a healthy community are the best supports for a vulnerable population, Sabeel strives to empower the Palestinian community as a whole and to develop the internal strengths needed for participation in building a better world for all. Only by working for a just and durable peace can we provide a sense of security and create ample opportunities for growth and prosperity in an atmosphere void of violence and strife.

(From the website www.sabeel.org)

Who Will Roll the Stone Away?
Parents Circle – Families Forum

The Parents Circle – Families Forum consists of more than 500 Israeli and Palestinian families, all of whom have lost an immediate family member due to the ongoing conflict. We call on all parties to promote reconciliation as the only way to reach true coexistence and peace. To achieve this goal we work consistently to imbue both sides with a sense of tolerance and reconciliation instead of hatred and revenge, sharing with others personal and painful stories. Each day, through our activities and outreach, the Families Forum reaffirms the sanctity of life and the need to safeguard human dignity and freedom. Though our members have all paid the highest price, we fervently seek to bring reconciliation to this war-ridden region.

The most basic goal of all the Families Forum's actions is to end further bereavement and the loss of life. The long-term goals of the Families Forum are to promote reconciliation between the Israeli and Palestinian societies.

By allowing both Israelis and Palestinians to come to terms with the consequences of the escalating violence, both sides will begin to change their beliefs, which are at the root of the conflict. Currently the parties are too immersed in their own pain to be willing to acknowledge the other's suffering. By acknowledging the personal narratives of victims of both sides, a new chapter in the relations between the sides may, at last, begin. Past activities of the Families Forum have generated empathy for bereaved families of the opposing side, by gradually exposing both societies to each other's loss.

Palestinians and Israelis have so far avoided recognizing the pain of the other side. A reconciliation process initiated by the Families Forum can put victims, who refuse to revenge their loss and [instead] choose to reconcile, at the forefront of public awareness. In doing so, it will humanize both sides and will act as an example to the Israeli and Palestinian people.

(From the website http://www.theparentscircle.com/default.asp)

Solidarity: Creating a Circle of Concern and Response

Through over ten years of living and working in Palestine and Israel, I've encouraged people to develop their desire for solidarity in five areas as a way to build and express their commitment to those struggling for a just peace in that broken land. The areas are listed below. They are not listed in terms of priority, as they overlap and intersect each other in different ways. In fact, as they are held in tension with each other, they both hold us accountable not to demonize those who do not agree with us and push us to go beyond our comfort zones as we continually listen for the silenced and muted voices yearning for peace. I hope you find these helpful and that we will strive together to create ever larger circles of concern.

1. **Pray without ceasing.** This seems obvious, yet intentionality in our prayers is very important for our work of solidarity. This is more than the prayer, "Let there be peace and justice in the Middle East" during Sunday morning worship. That's a good place to begin but doesn't go nearly far enough. Prayer makes people part of our family, part of our network of concern. As we continue to pray for the people, the leaders, and projects, our circle of concern and caring grows. Specificity in prayer helps us to connect to the human dimension and moves it from "that conflict over there." For example, the General Board of Global Ministries and the Women's Division have many projects in the region that we help support through our giving. Discover them, find out their needs and what struggles they are facing. Find out what joys are helping keep hope alive. Get to know the projects and people and keep them close in your life of meditation and prayer. Another way is to go to www.rememberthechildren.org and get the list of all the children killed since September 28, 2000. This includes both Palestinian and Israeli children. Tragically there are over a thousand families who have lost their children to the violence of the conflict in

these last years. We can name them specifically in our prayers, offering our own comfort as these families grieve and heal. As we seek to work for change, prayer is one of the foundations for nonviolent response. Jim Wallis, the founding editor of Sojourners magazine, expressed it well in a short reflection.

Prayer: Antidote to Violence
by Jim Wallis

Prayer is a necessity. Without it we see only our point of view and ignore the perspective of our enemies. Prayer breaks down those distinctions. To do violence to others, you must make them enemies. Prayer, on the other hand, makes enemies into friends.

*When we bring our enemies into our hearts through prayer, it becomes most difficult to maintain the hostility necessary for violence. In bringing them close to us, prayer serves to protect our enemies. **Thus prayer undermines the propaganda and policies of governments designed to make us hate and fear our enemies** [editor's emphasis]. By softening our hearts toward our adversaries, prayer can become treasonous. Fervent prayer for our enemies is a great obstacle to war and the feelings that lead to it.*

Jesus says love our neighbors, including our enemies, "as yourself." Here lies the key to peacemaking. If we seek our security and peace at the expense of someone else's, it can only fuel the cycle of retribution. Caring for the well-being of our enemies—loving our enemies— is the only thing that can break the cycle of violence and ultimately protect our own well-being.

(From "Living with Christ," NOVALIS, July 2004)

2. **Give to support ministries of healing and hope.**
Through The United Methodist Church, there are many opportunities to participate in enabling a variety of remarkable ministries. Whether you have special concerns for children, youth, women, training, health care, or human rights, you can support vital ministries in each of these areas through your monetary gifts. This is

particularly important today, as the Christian community in the Holy Land cannot carry their projects/ministries out on their own. Over 60 percent of Palestinians are currently unemployed, and financial resources are extremely limited. Yet the work of the church communities, whose members make up only about 2 percent of the population, is remarkable. Christians are providing some of the most important gifts of hope that exist there now. The October *Response* magazine each year lists the projects for United Methodist Women.

3. **Study to develop effective tools for solidarity.** Gain knowledge about the realities that goes beyond the sound bites of mainstream media. Many Americans know little to nothing of the realities of the Occupation and its impact on the daily lives of the people there. Too few know about the amount of US foreign aid or the impact it has on the ongoing conflict. As Christians committed to the reign of God on earth, we need to be persistent in searching for justice and peace for all peoples of the world. Informed study is critical to our mission.

One of the best ways to study is to participate in an educational exposure trip. If you cannot travel, there are many resources available to help congregations gain more information about this region. It is important for people to know what their churches have said and positions they have taken. You have already begun by using this study. Current UM resolutions can be found in *The Book of Resolutions*. The Mennonite Central Committee has developed a program called Building Bridges not Walls. Excellent educational resources are available there (http://www.mcc.org/us/washington/index.html).

Global Ministries is a member of the US Campaign to End the Occupation, which has created a number of short bulletins on key issues (www.endtheoccupation.org).

In conflicts that engender such strong emotions, one of the only avenues we have available to us to ensure justice for the various parties is the guidance of international law and UN conventions and resolutions. Understanding those that apply to the Israel-Palestine conflict is important. For a list of recommended readings and resources or a selection of websites with reliable information, you can contact Mission Contexts and Relationships at the General Board of Global Ministries or Global Ministries mission personnel serving in the region. Their contact information can be found on the Global Ministries website (www.gbgm-umc.org).

4. **Engage in interfaith dialogue** and work on this issue. For too long the question of the Israel-Palestine conflict has often been left out of interfaith interactions. It has been seen as too divisive. Many are afraid of rupturing long-time relationships with Jewish neighbors and colleagues. Yet if we do not face the differences we may have on the issues, it is going to be a great stumbling block among those of us of different faith traditions. We also miss the opportunity to find communities that would be willing to work with us in education and advocacy. We must listen respectively to differing views but also be able to be clear about our church's stances toward Israeli government policies and Palestinian actions. It is important for the Christian community not to be cowed into thinking that a position against certain Israeli government policies is anti-Semitic. But we must also be willing to listen carefully in order to distinguish when statements and actions *are* anti-Semitic.

5. **Advocate for action on the issues.** Advocacy is at least a two-pronged process. One critical avenue is to consistently and systematically inform our elected officials about our positions on the conflict and to let them know that at the root of much of the struggle in the Middle

East are ongoing US positions vis-à-vis Israel-Palestine. People outside the United States see our government's policies as lopsided because they are. There are a number of direct advocacy groups that can help you attend to legislative issues in this region.

- You can get on the Action Alert mailing for Churches for Middle East Peace. This is an ecumenical advocacy group representing numerous Christian churches www.cmep.org. Visit to register to receive information.

- The General Board of Global Ministries – UMC is also a member of the US Campaign to End the Occupation, one of the largest interfaith and secular coalitions working on education and advocacy. They have great resources on the website and offer an Action Alert every Wednesday. Visit www.endtheoccupation.org to find out how to join this campaign.

- Organizing interdenominational and interfaith groups to speak to your congressperson or senator is a very effective way to share your concerns for justice in this region.

- Another avenue of advocacy is within the media. Begin to watch how the stories are told. Whose perspectives dominate? What words are used to describe the various parties in the conflict? Palestine Media Watch (www.pmwatch.org) is a helpful site to visit in order to help build an effective media advocacy team.

There is no shortage of creative activities that can be done through advocacy. It is also a critical piece towards building solidarity with those searching for a just peace.

Churches for Middle East Peace (CMEP)

110 Maryland Ave. NE, #311

Washington, DC 20002

www.cmep.org

Phone: 202-543-1222

Fax: 202-543-5025

Email inquiries: info@cmep.org

Churches for Middle East Peace is a coalition of twenty-one public policy offices of national churches and agencies—Orthodox, Catholic, and Protestant. CMEP began its work in 1984 out of the conviction that the policy perspectives and long Middle East experience of our member bodies should be more widely known in the public policy arena. We therefore seek to maintain an ongoing dialogue with Congress, the Administration, and the diplomatic community to advance such concerns, assessments, and advocacy positions.

The work of CMEP focuses on Washington in the knowledge that sound United States policy is crucial to achieving and maintaining just and stable relationships throughout the Middle East. In addition, CMEP seeks to help the members of our organizations advocate in a knowledgeable, timely, and effective way their concerns about justice and peace for all people and countries in the region.

Among our principal advocacy concerns are the avoidance and resolution of armed conflicts, human rights, arms control, foreign aid, and the unique nature of Jerusalem—sacred to Christians, Jews, and Muslims.

Fellowship of Reconciliation (FOR)

521 N. Broadway

Nyack, NY 10960

www.forusa.org

Phone: 845-358-4601

Since 1915, the Fellowship of Reconciliation has carried on programs and educational projects concerned with domestic and international peace and justice, nonviolent alternatives to conflict, and the rights of conscience. We envision a world of justice, peace, and freedom. It is a revolutionary vision of a beloved community where differences are respected, conflicts are addressed nonviolently, oppressive structures are dismantled, and people live in harmony with the earth, nurtured by diverse spiritual traditions that foster compassion, solidarity, and reconciliation.

FOR seeks to replace violence, war, racism, and economic injustice with nonviolence, peace, and justice. We are an interfaith organization committed to active nonviolence as a transforming way of life and as a means of zradical change. We educate, train, build coalitions, and engage in nonviolent and compassionate actions locally, nationally, and globally.

Interfaith Peace-Builders sends delegations to Israel and Palestine so that US citizens can see the conflict with their own eyes. Participants have the opportunity to learn directly from Israeli and Palestinian nonviolent peace/human-rights activists, to spend time in Palestinian and Israeli homes, and to experience the situation of Palestinians living under military Occupation. The delegations focus on seeing, listening to, and recording the experiences and perspectives of a wide range of Palestinian and Israeli voices.

Interfaith Peace-Builders places a strong emphasis on continuing work on the conflict when participants return to their homes. The program asks for a commitment from participants to educate people in their communities and organizations about the conflict, to write and speak about their experiences, to join with FOR and other local and national organizations working to end the conflict, and to work to change US policy in the region.

MENUM: Middle East Network of United Methodists
212 East Capitol Street, NE
Washington, DC 20003
www.mfsaweb.org
Phone: 202-546-8806
Fax: 202-546-6811
Email: mfsa@mfsaweb.org

MENUM is a subgroup of the Methodist Federation for Social Action (MFSA). MFSA works primarily through the ministries of The United Methodist Church, supporting and augmenting peace and justice ministries at the local, conference, and national levels. As an independent organization, we call our church to expand its understanding of the radical call of the gospel to be the inclusive, justice-seeking, risk-taking Body of Christ. MFSA lives out our belief that to be faithful witnesses to the gospel of Jesus Christ is to be involved in the transformation of the social order.

TIKKUN Communities
2342 Shattuck Avenue, #1200
Berkeley, CA 94704
Phone: 510-644-1200
Fax: 510-644-1255
Email: magazine@tikkun.org
community@tikkun.org
info@spiritualprogressives.org

We are an international community of many faiths calling for social justice and political freedom in the context of new structures of work, caring communities, and democratic social and economic arrangements. We seek to influence public discourse to inspire compassion, generosity, nonviolence, and recognition of the spiritual dimensions of life.

There are many ways to be involved in the TIKKUN Community. We are creating groups of like-minded people at our annual meetings of professional associations, at national conventions of unions and political parties, or at the national gatherings of our religious communities.

Some of us are engaged in solidarity work with the Israeli peace movement or in developing local initiatives to challenge the Occupation. Some of us are developing teach-ins about Israeli-Palestinian peace, and in other ways challenging the mainstream interpretation of that struggle. Some of us are bringing these ideas into the anti-globalization, ecological, and social-justice movements or affinity groups of which we are part. Some of us are trying to do that in the Democratic Party, the Natural Law Party, the Green Party, and other political parties.

Some of us are challenging local and national media, insisting that they recognize the distorted and cynical nature of their presentations, and educating the public to alternative ways to think about reality. Some of us are retirees who are making phone calls and writing letters to the media or to neighbors about these ideas.

The TIKKUN community is a place to talk about these ideas and give each other mutual support for being unequivocally utopian and committed to large-scale TIKKUN *olam* (transformation of the world). We get this nurturance through *TIKKUN* magazine, the TIKKUN website and email group, and annual TIKKUN Community national gatherings.

US Campaign to End the Israeli Occupation
P.O. Box 21539
Washington, DC 20009
www.endtheoccupation.org
Phone: 202-332-0994
(For general information on or to become involved with the US Campaign, email us at: us_campaign@endtheoccupation.org.)

The US Campaign is a diverse coalition of groups and organizations—local, state, regional, and national—working for freedom from Occupation and equal rights for all by challenging US policy towards the Israeli-Palestinian conflict. The Campaign is based on human rights and international law, providing a non-sectarian framework for everyone who supports its Call to Action. Its strategy is to inform, educate, and mobilize the public so as to change the US role in the Israeli-Palestinian conflict to support peace, justice, human rights, and international law.

Our Principles and Purpose
- We stand for freedom from Occupation and equal rights for all. International law guarantees these human rights, including the right to exist in peace and security.
- We aim to change those US policies that sustain Israel's forty-year Occupation of the Palestinian West Bank, Gaza, and East Jerusalem and that deny equal rights for all.

Our Goals
- We will inform, educate, and mobilize the public regarding the US Government's current as well as potential role in the Israeli-Palestinian conflict.
- We seek to change such policies as the billions of US military and economic aid dollars provided despite Israel's violations of US and international law.
- We call for the US to work within the UN to implement a just and lasting peace.

Our Campaign
- Our campaign will build on existing opposition to settlements, land confiscation, house demolitions, and other violations of international law, by providing a common platform to challenge US policies supporting the Israeli Occupation of Palestine.

- We include civil and human rights activists, faith-based organizations, peace activists, Arab-American organizations, Jewish groups opposing the Occupation, students, and others who promote peace and justice in Israel and Palestine. We invite all who support this call to contribute to the fulfillment of its purpose.

World Council of Churches Ecumenical Accompaniment Program
EAPPI
International Affairs, Peace and Human Security
World Council of Churches
Box 2100
1211 Geneva 2
Switzerland
Fax: +4122 791 6406
(For US application, go to: http://www.pepm.org/accompaniment.html. For information, email: info@pepm.org)

The EAPPI is an initiative of the World Council of Churches under the *Ecumenical Campaign to End the Illegal Occupation of Palestine: Support a Just Peace in the Middle East*. Its mission is to accompany Palestinians and Israelis in their nonviolent actions and concerted advocacy efforts to end the Occupation. Participants of the program are monitoring and reporting violations of human rights and international humanitarian law, supporting acts of nonviolent resistance alongside local Christian and Muslim Palestinians and Israeli peace activists, offering protection through nonviolent presence, engaging in public policy advocacy, and in general standing in solidarity with the churches and all those struggling against the Occupation.

Ecumenical accompaniers, who serve a minimum of three months, work in various capacities with local churches, Palestinian and Israeli NGOs, as well as Palestinian communities, to try to reduce the brutality of the Israeli Occupation and improve the daily lives of both peoples.

Since the program was launched in August 2002, accompaniers have participated from more than 30 churches and ecumenical partners in fourteen countries: Canada, Denmark, Finland, France, Germany, Iceland, Ireland, New Zealand, Norway, South Africa, Sweden, Switzerland, the UK, and the US.

Objectives

While the program's mission is to accompany Palestinians and Israelis in nonviolent actions and concerted advocacy efforts to end the Occupation, its detailed objectives are to:

- Expose the violence of the Occupation
- End the brutality, humiliation, and violence against civilians
- Construct a stronger global advocacy network
- Ensure the respect of Human Rights and International Humanitarian Law
- Influence public opinion in the home country and affect foreign policy on the Middle East in order to end the Occupation and create a viable Palestinian State
- Express solidarity with Palestinian and Israeli peace activists and empower local Palestinian communities/churches

Be an active witness that an alternative, nonviolent struggle for justice and peace is possible to end the illegal Occupation of Palestine.

Endnotes

Introduction

1. Lisa Alcalay Klug, "In Israel, Where Art Imitates Messy Life," *The New York Times,* December 31, 2005, p. B-9.
2. David Budbill, *While We've Still Got Feet: New Poems,* Port Townsend, Washington: Copper Canyon Press, 2005, p. 41.
3. Adapted from *Wikipedia,* the Free Encyclopedia, http://en.wikipedia.org.
4. Grace Halsell, *Journey to Jerusalem: A Journalist's Account of Christian, Jewish, and Muslim Families in the Strife-Torn Holy Land,* New York: Macmillan Publishing Co., Inc., 1981, pp. 113-114. I had the opportunity some years ago to be with Grace Halsell in Jerusalem before her death. She was a remarkable journalist and advocate for justice. I have used this passage as an introduction to my presentations. Her book serves as a wonderful introduction to Palestine-Israel. Limited copies are still available through Americans for Middle East Understanding (AMEU).

Chapter 1

5. Adapted from *Wikipedia,* the Free Encyclopedia, http://en.wikipedia.org.
6. David J. Goldberg, *To The Promised Land: A History of Zionist Thought,* London: Penguin Books, 1996, p. 25.
7. *Encarta Encyclopedia* © 1993-2003 Microsoft Corporation. All rights reserved.
8. "Jewish Massacre Denounced," *The New York Times,* April 28, 1903, p. 6. As cited in *Wikipedia,* the Free Encyclopedia, http://en.wikipedia.org.
9. Ghassam Andoni is a Palestinian native of Beit Sahour in the Bethlehem area. He is a professor of physics at Bir Zeit University.
10. ISM is a pro-Palestinian organization whose stated mission is to resist the Israeli Occupation using nonviolent tactics.
11. Quoted from the website: http://www.theisraelforum.org.
12. Tony Judt, "A Lobby, Not A Conspiracy," *The New York Times,* April 19, 2006.
13. See Stephen Goldstein, "Then and Now: Israel 1980 – Palestine 1992," *New World Outlook,* July-August 1992, pp. 18-21.
14. Israeli Ministry of Foreign Affairs: http://www.mfa.gov.il/MFA.
15. *Encarta Encyclopedia* © 1993-2003 Microsoft Corporation. All rights reserved.
16. Riah Abu El-Assal was enthroned as the Anglican Diocesan Bishop in Jerusalem at St. George's Cathedral in August 1987. He retired in 2006.
17. Riah Abu El-Assal, *Caught in Between: The Extraordinary Story of an Arab Palestinian Christian Israeli,* London: SPCK, 1999, pp. 3-5.
18. Ibid., p. x.

19. There are 4,283,892 registered refugees living in the West Bank and Gaza, Jordan, Syria, and Lebanon, of which 1,265,987 are living in 59 refugee camps. There are 1,400,000 Palestinians living in Israel. *Diary 2006,* PASSIA (Palestinian Academic Society for the Study of International Affairs), Jerusalem-Al-Quds, p. 293.
20. Goldstein, op. cit., p. 19.
21. Abu El-Assal, op. cit., p. xv.

Chapter 2

22. Alex Awad, *Through the Eyes of the Victims: The Story of the Arab-Israeli Conflict,* Bethlehem: Bethlehem Bible College, October 2001, p. 13.
23. Israel Finkelstein and Neil Asher Silberman, *The Bible Unearthed: Archaeology's New Vision of Ancient Israel and the Origin of Its Sacred Texts,* New York: Simon and Schuster, 2002, p. 40 ff.
24. William W. Hallo, "Babylon," *Oxford Companion to the Bible,* 1993, edited by Bruce M. Metzger and Michael D. Coogan (electronic version).
25. Robert North, "Diaspora," and Philip Stern, "Exile," *Oxford Companion to the Bible,* 1993, edited by Bruce M. Metzger and Michael D. Coogan (electronic version).
26. John Rose, *The Myths of Zionism,* London and Ann Arbor, Michigan: Pluto Press, 2004, p. 29. "When Rome took control of the disintegrating Ptolemaic Greek Empire, and certainly by the first century of the common era, *the majority of Jews were living outside Judaea* (Barclay 1996: 4n.1)."
27. Material in this section is adapted from information at http://www.palestinehistory.com/history/brief/brief.htm and "Early History: Islam in Palestine" at http://palestinefacts.org/pf_early_palestine_when_islam.php.
28. *Encarta Encyclopedia* © 1993-2003 Microsoft Corporation. All rights reserved.
29. Ibid.
30. H. I. Bach, *The German Jew: A Synthesis of Judaism and Western Civilization 1730-1930,* London and New York: Oxford University Press, 1984, p. 150.
31. *Encarta Encyclopedia* © 1993-2003 Microsoft Corporation. All rights reserved.
32. Bach, op. cit., pp. 150-151.
33. Charles P. Cozic, ed., *Israel: Opposing Viewpoints,* San Diego, California: Greenhaven Press, Inc. 1994, p. 18.
34. Goldberg, *To the Promised Land,* op. cit., pp. 18-19.
35. Ibid., n. 1, p. 20.
36. Ibid., p. 25.
37. The Jewish Agency for Israel. Entry taken from *Junior Judaica: Encyclopedia Judaica for Youth,* CD-ROM, by C.D.I. Systems 1992, Ltd., Keter, and Goldberg, p. 28.
38. Bach, op. cit., p.153.

39. Ibid., pp. 156-157.
40. Ibid., p. 158.
41. Ibid.
42. Quoted by Avi Shlaim in *The Iron Wall: Israel in the Arab World,* New York: W. W. Norton & Company, 2000, p. 3.
43. Colin Chapman, *Whose Promised Land? The Continuing Crisis over Israel and Palestine,* Grand Rapids, Michigan: Baker Books, 2002, p. 27.
44. Michel Warschawski, *On the Border,* translated by Levi Laub, Cambridge, Massachusetts: South End Press, 2005, p. 35.
45. Ibid.
46. *Diary 2006,* PASSIA (Palestinian Academic Society for the Study of International Affairs), Jerusalem-Al-Quds, p. 278.
47. Norman G. Finkelstein, *Image and Reality of the Israel-Palestine Conflict,* London and New York: Verso, 1995, p. 10.
48. Fareed Taamallah, *The International Herald Tribune* (electronic edition), May 24, 2006.
49. Michael Neumann, *The Case Against Israel,* Scotland and Petrolia, California: CounterPunch and AK Press, 2005, p. 18.
50. Resolution adopted by the General Assembly on the Report of the Third Committee (A/10320), 3379 (XXX). "Elimination of all forms of racial discrimination," November 10, 1975.
51. Amos Elon, *The Israelis: Founders and Sons,* New York: Penguin, 1981, p. 149.
52. When I met with Jeff Halper in January 2006, he told me that he was going to be nominated for the 2006 Nobel Peace Prize. He was nominated, along with the Palestinian peace activist Ghassan Andoni. ("Muhammad Yunus was awarded the 2006 Nobel Peace Prize, along with Grameen Bank...." *Wikipedia,* the Free Encyclopedia, http://en.wikipedia.org.)
53. Tom Segev, *One Palestine Complete: Jews and Arabs under the British Mandate,* translated by Haim Watzman, New York: Metropolitan Books, Henry Holt and Company, 2000, p. 42 ff.
54. Jeff Halper, ICAHD, distributed via email, May 25, 2006.
55. The Jewish Virtual Library, A Division of the American-Israeli Cooperative Enterprise, 2006.
56. Israel Defense Forces, the Israeli army.
57. Alain Gresh and Dominique Vidal, *A to Z of the Middle East,* translated by Bob Cumming, London and New Jersey: Zed Books, Ltd., 1990, pp. 20-21.
58. Segev, op. cit., p. 46.
59. Gresh and Vidal, op. cit., p. 189.
60. Quoted in Segev, op. cit., p. 45, and note 35, p. 528.
61. Quoted in Gresh and Vidal, op. cit., p. 19.
62. Quoted in Segev, op. cit., p. 50.
63. Ibid., p. 50.
64. Gresh and Vidal, op. cit., p. 219.
65. Gregory Harms with Todd M. Ferry, *The Palestine-Israel Conflict: A Basic Introduction,* London and Ann Arbor, Michigan: Pluto Press, 2005, p. 61.
66. Howard M. Sachar, *A History of Israel from the Rise of Zionism to Our Time,* Second Edition, Revised and Updated, New York: Alfred A. Knopf, 1996, p. 73.
67. Ibid.
68. Ibid.
69. Gresh and Vidal, op. cit., p. 219. A *dunum* is approximately 1/4 acre.
70. Ibid.
71. *Fallah* (pl. *fallahin*): peasant. Also transliterated as *fellah*. From the glossary in Samih K. Farsoun with Christina E. Zacharia, *Palestine and the Palestinians,* USA: Westview Press, 1997, p. 344.
72. Walter Laquer and Barry Rubin, eds., *The Israel-Arab Reader: A Documentary History of the Middle East Conflict, Revised and Updated Edition,* New York: Penguin Books, 2001, p. 31.
73. David Fromkin, *A Peace to End All Peace: The Fall of the Ottoman Empire and the Creation of the Modern Middle East,* New York: Avon Books, 1989, p. 521.
74. Ibid., p. 522 ff.
75. Ibid., p. 527.
76. Neumann, op. cit., p. 37.
77. Harms, op. cit., p. 63.
78. Quoted in Benny Morris, *Righteous Victims: A History of the Zionist-Arab Conflict 1881-1999,* New York: Knopf Publishing Group, 2001, p. 36.

Chapter 3

79. David Hirst, *The Gun and the Olive Branch: The Roots of Violence in the Middle East,* London and Sydney: MacDonald and Company, 1977, p. 46.
80. Palestine Documents, 1967 (Arabic), Beirut: Institute for Palestine Studies, 1968, pp. 264, 1,084; quoted in Hirst, op. cit., p. 47, and note 1, p. 338.
81. Sadiq Al-Azm, *Left Studies on the Palestinian Problem* (Arabic), Beirut: Dar al-Tali'ah, 1970, pp. 53, 55; quoted in Hirst, op. cit., p. 48, n. 2.
82. Harms, op. cit., p. 76.
83. Farsoun, op. cit., p. 103.
84. Ibid.
85. Philip Mattar, *The Mufti of Jerusalem: Al-Hajj Amin Al-Husayni and the Palestinian National Movement,* New York: Columbia University Press, 1988, p. 1 ff.
86. In a speech delivered to the United States Congress on January 8, 1918: President Woodrow Wilson's Fourteen Points.
87. Henry King, president of Oberlin College and Charles Crane, a Chicago businessman; in Harms, op. cit., p. 74.
88. Laqueur and Rubin, op. cit., p. 24.
89. Farsoun, op. cit., p. 100.
90. Mattar, op. cit., p. 1.
91. Hirst, op. cit., p. 73.

92. Elon, *The Israelis,* op. cit., p. 21.
93. Ibid., p. 22.
94. Shlaim, op. cit., p. 17.
95. Mark Tessler, *A History of the Israeli-Palestinian Conflict,* Bloomington and Indianapolis: Indiana University Press, 1994, p. 138.
96. Shlaim, op. cit., p. 11.
97. Elon, op. cit., p. 158.
98. Shlaim, op. cit., p. 12.
99. Tessler, op. cit., p. 137
100. Shlaim, op. cit., p. 12.
101. Ibid., p. 13.
102. Ibid.
103. Shlaim, op. cit., p. 14.
104. Ibid., p. 19.
105. Ibid., p. 15.
106. Farsoun, op. cit., p. 104.
107. Ibid., p. 105 ff.
108. Ibid., p. 107.
109. Ibid.
110. Harms, op. cit., p. 80.
111. Laqueur and Rubin, op. cit., p. 43.
112. Ibid.
113. Ibid.
114. Farsoun, op. cit., p. 108.
115. Ibid.
116. Hirst, op. cit., p. 93.
117. Farsoun, op. cit., p. 108.
118. Ibid.
119. Harms, op. cit., n. 21, p. 197.
120. Thomas W. Lippman, "The Day FDR Met Saudi Arabia's Ibn Saud," AMEU: *The Link,* Volume 38, Issue 2, April-May 2005, p. 1.
121. Ibid.
122. Ibid., p. 6.
123. Quoted from Col. William Eddy's 1954 book, *F.D.R. Meets Ibn Saud,* by John F. Mahoney, Executive Director, Americans for Middle East Understanding, in his introduction to Lippmann, AMEU: *The Link,* Volume 38, Issue 2, April-May 2005.
124. Baylis Thomas, *How Israel Was Won: A Concise History of the Arab-Israeli Conflict,* Lanham, Boulder, New York, Oxford: Lexington Books, 1999, p. 38.
125. Ibid., p. 39.
126. Ron David, *Arabs and Israel for Beginners,* New York: Writers and Readers Publishing, Inc., 1993, p. 112.
127. Thomas, op. cit., p. 39.
128. Ibid., p. 41.
129. Ibid.
130. Sacher (1996), op. cit., p. 271.
131. Sacher, op. cit., p. 272 and Thomas, op. cit., p. 42.
132. Thomas, op. cit., p. 41.
133. Quoted by Michael J. Cohen, *Palestine and the Great Powers,* 1945-1948, Princeton: Princeton University Press, 1982, p. 139 in Thomas, op. cit., n. 14. p. 44.
134. Thomas, op. cit., 43.
135. Ibid.
136. Sacher, op. cit., p. 278.
137. Peter Davies, "The Palestine-Israel Conflict: A War of Liberation, 2000" (unpublished).

Chapter 4

138. *Diary 2006,* PASSIA, p. 292.
139. Shlaim, op. cit., p. 34.
140. Tom Hayes, "People and the Land": Coming to a PBS Station Near You? AMEU: *The Link,* Volume 30, Issue 5, November-December 1997, p. 1.
141. Ilan Pappé, "Israeli Historians Ask: What Really Happened 50 Years Ago?" AMEU: *The Link,* Volume 31, Issue 1, January-March 1998, p. 1.
142. Ibid.
143. Ibid., pp. 3-4.
144. Michael Palumbo, "What Happened to Palestine? The Revisionists Revisited," AMEU: *The Link,* Volume 23, Issue 4, September-October 1990, p. 2.
145. Ibid., p. 5.
146. Farsoun, op. cit., p. 113.
147. Ibid.
148. Quoted in Palumbo, op. cit., p. 5.
149. Ibid., p. 1.
150. Ibid., p. 114.
151. Pappé, op. cit., p. 4.
152. Tessler, op. cit., p. 259.
153. Ilan Pappé, *The Making of the Arab-Israeli Conflict, 1947-1951,* London and New York: I. B. Tauris and Co. Ltd., 1994, p. 76.
154. Ibid.
155. Intelligence Report, December 6, 1947, CO 537/2294, quoted in Pappé, Ibid. p. 77, n. 77.
156. Harms, op. cit., p. 94.
157. Michael Palumbo, *The Palestinian Catastrophe: The 1948 Expulsion of a People from Their Homeland,* London and New York: Quartet Books, 1987, p. 48.
158. An Israeli historian—and, at the time, a Haganah soldier—interviewed by Michael Palumbo.
159. Palumbo (1987), op. cit., p. 50.
160. Ibid.
161. Jabotinsky Archives, Tel Aviv, quoted in Palumbo (1987), op. cit., p. 55, n. 12.
162. Colonial Office Papers, Public Records Office, 733/477/5, London; quoted in Palumbo (1987), op. cit., p. 55, n. 13.
163. Menachem Begin, "The Revolt," London: W. H. Allen, 1964, pp. 162-166; quoted in Daniel A. McGowan, "Deir Yassin

Remembered," AMEU: *The Link,* Volume 29, Issue 4, September-October 1996, p. 1.

164. Harms, op. cit., p. 94.

165. Ibid., p. 7.

166. Palumbo (1987), op. cit., p. xviii.

167. Laquer and Rubin, op. cit., pp. 82-83.

168. Shlaim (2000), op. cit., p. 35.

169. Shlaim (2001), "Israel and the Arab Coalition in 1948," in E. L. Rogan, et al., eds., *The War for Palestine: Rewriting the History of 1948,* Cambridge: Cambridge University Press, pp. 79-103. Quoted in Harms, op. cit.; also in "Grubb, John," *Wikipedia,* the Free Encyclopedia, http://en.wikipedia.org.

170. Farsoun, op. cit., p. 116.

171. Avi Shlaim, *War and Peace in the Middle East: A Concise History,* Revised and Updated, New York: Penguin Books, 1994, 1995, p. 22.

172. Ronald Bleier, "In the Beginning, There Was Terror," AMEU: *The Link,* Volume 36, Issue 3, July-August 2003, p. 1.

173. Ibid., p. 1.

174. Ibid., p. 2. Quoted from Baylis Thomas, op. cit., p. 93, n. 39.

175. Kati Marton, *A Death in Jerusalem: The Assassination by Jewish Extremists of the First Arab/Israeli Peacemaker,* New York: Pantheon Books, 1994, p. ix ff.

176. Charles D. Smith, *Palestine and the Arab-Israeli Conflict,* Second Edition, New York: St. Martin's Press, 1992, p. 146.

177. Thomas, op. cit., p. 95.

178. Shlaim, *The Politics of Partition: King Abdullah, the Zionists, and Palestine 1921-1951,* Oxford and New York: Oxford University Press, 1988, p. 342.

179. Ibid., p. 343.

180. *Encarta Encyclopedia* © 2004 Microsoft Corporation. All rights reserved.

181. Shlaim, *War and Peace in the Middle East,* op. cit., p. 28.

182. Ibid., pp. 24-25.

183. Rashid Khalidi, *Palestinian Identity: The Construction of a Modern National Consciousness,* New York: Columbia University Press, 1997, p. 182.

184. Steven L. Spiegel, *The Other Arab-Israeli Conflict,* Chicago: University of Chicago Press, 1985, p. 64; quoted in Thomas, *How Israel Was Won,* op. cit., p. 117.

185. Thomas, op. cit., p. 117.

186. *Encarta Encyclopedia* © 2004 Microsoft Corporation. All rights reserved.

187. Ibid.

188. Uri Avnery, quoted in Shlaim, *The Iron Wall,* op. cit., p. 102.

189. Ibid.

190. Quoted in Shlaim, *War and Peace in the Middle East,* op. cit., p. 30.

191. Ibid., p. 31.

192. Shlaim, *Iron Wall,* op. cit., p. 233.

193. Ibid.

194. Ibid.

195. Quoted in ibid.

196. Ibid.

197. Ibid., p. 219.

198. Ibid., p. 210.

199. Smith, op. cit., p. 179.

200. Khalidi, op. cit., p. 194.

201. Quoted in Shlaim, *The Iron Wall,* op. cit., pp. 229-230.

202. Khalidi, *Palestinian Identity,* op. cit., pp. 179-180.

203. Shlaim, *The Iron Wall,* op. cit., p. 230.

204. Ibid., pp. 230 ff.

205. Ibid., p. 236.

206. Shlaim, *The Iron Wall,* op. cit., p. 236 ff.

207. Ibid., pp. 237-238.

208. Ibid.

209. Ibid.

210. Yitzhak Rabin, *The Rabin Memoirs,* London: Weidenfeld & Nicolson, 1979, pp. 58-59, quoted in ibid., p. 239.

211. Ibid., p. 239 ff.

212. Smith, op. cit., p. 197.

213. Harms, op. cit., p. 110.

214. Ibid.

215. Smith, op. cit., pp. 198-199.

216. Ibid., p. 199.

217. John Borne, "Remember the Liberty," AMEU: *The Link,* Volume 30, Issue 3, July-August 1997, p. 1.

218. Ibid.

219. Shlaim, *The Iron Wall,* op. cit., pp. 241-242.

220. Farsoun, op. cit., p. 181.

221. Harms, op. cit., p. 111, citing B. Morris, *Righteous Victims,* 2001, p. 336; Farsoun breaks it down differently, noting: "Following the 1967 war, Israel's military enveloped an estimated 1.3 million Palestinians, created over 400,000 new refugees, and added at least 20,000 to the camps" (pp. 218-219).

222. Fred Bush, from an unpublished paper, June 2006.

223. Quoted in Smith, op. cit., p. 200; from Donald Neff, *Warriors for Jerusalem: The Six Days That Changed the Middle East,* New York: Linden Press, Simon & Schuster, 1984, p. 299.

224. Shlaim, *The Iron Wall,* op. cit., p. 256. The Latrum salient is a section of "greater Jerusalem north of the city almost bordering Ramallah, the major Palestinian city."

225. Quoted in Smith, op. cit., p. 208.

226. Quoted from an interview with Hussein in Shlaim, *Iron Wall,* op. cit., p. 259.

227. Ibid., p. 260.

228. Michael Palumbo, *Imperial Israel: The History of the Occupation of the West Bank and Gaza,* London: Bloomsbury, 1990, p. 53.

229. Ibid.

230. Morris, *Righteous Victims,* op. cit., p. 362.

231. Ibid., p. 363.
232. Quoted in ibid.
233. Quoted in Morris, *Righteous Victims,* op. cit., p. 389, and secondarily in Harms, op. cit., p. 123.
234. Thomas, op. cit., p. 196.
235. Ibid., pp. 196-197.
236. Ibid., p. 197.
237. Ibid.
238. Morris, op. cit., p. 402.
239. Ibid., p. 433.
240. Harms, op. cit., p. 125.
241. Ibid., p. 124.
242. Shlaim, *Iron Wall,* op. cit., p. 319.
243. Ibid., p. 323.
244. Ibid., p. 324.

Chapter 5

245. Palumbo, *Imperial Israel,* op. cit., p. 15.
246. Ibid., p. 16.
247. Ibid., p. 17.
248. Israel Shahak and Norton Mezvinsky, *Jewish Fundamentalism in Israel,* London and Stirling, Virginia: Pluto Press, 1999, p. 65.
249. Michel Warschawski, *On The Border,* op cit., p. 169. Michel Warschawski was born in the French city of Strasbourg, a town historically part of both Germany and France, where his father was the rabbi.
250. Quoted in Farsoun, op. cit., p. 182.
251. Not all feda'iyyin were associated with Fateh as yet.
252. Ibid., Farsoun.
253. Ibid., p. 183.
254. Khalidi, op. cit., p. 197.
255. Farsoun, op. cit., p. 185.
256. Khalidi, op. cit., p. 198. The complicity of two Israelis and two Syrian liaison officers in the massacre in two of the refugee camps was confirmed in the testimony heard in the inquiry in the Israeli Knesset from Ariel Sharon defending himself against charges of involvement in the massacre in the Sabra and Shatila refugee camps following Israel's invasion in 1982. (See note 42, p. 264 in Khalidi.)
257. Ibid.
258. Ibid.
259. Ibid., p. 200.
260. A shtetl was typically a small town or village with a large Jewish population in pre-Holocaust Central and Eastern Europe.
261. Amos Elon, *A Blood-Dimmed Tide,* New York: Columbia University Press, 1997, pp. 268-269.
262. Ibid.
263. Amira Hass, translated by Elana Wesley and Maxine Kaufman-Lacusta, *Drinking the Sea at Gaza,* New York: Henry Holt and Company, 1999, pp. 6-7.
264. Ibid., p. 7.
265. Marc Ellis, *Ending Auschwitz: The Future of Jewish and Christian Life,* Louisville, Kentucky: Westminster John Knox Press, 1994, p. 137.
266. Ibid., p. 141.
267. Ibid., p. 140.
268. Marc H. Ellis, *Israel and Palestine: Out of the Ashes, The Search for Jewish Identity in the Twenty-First Century,* London, Sterling Virginia: The Pluto Press, 2002, p. 7.

Chapter 6

269. Robert Fisk, "No Wonder the UN Can't Find Volunteers," *The Independent,* August 19, 2006 (electronic version).
270. "Hopes and Fantasies," Editor's Desk, August 22, 2006, *The Christian Century Magazine,* http://www.christiancentury.org/article.lasso?id=2273.
271. Thomas, op. cit., p. 203.
272. I highly recommend Robert Fisk's book on the period, *Pity the Nation,* New York: Atheneum, 1990, which is excellent background for the period from the Civil War through the Israeli invasion.
273. Farsoun, op. cit., p. 222.
274. Ibid.
275. General Assembly Resolution 3236 and 3237, November 22, 1974, http://domino.un.org/UNISPAL.NSF.
276. Farsoun, op. cit., p. 222.
277. Edward W. Said, "Intifada and Independence," p. 11, quoted in Farsoun, op. cit., p. 222, n. 25.
278. Tessler, op. cit., p. 292. Also cited in Harms, op. cit., p. 127.
279. Quoted in John and Janet Wallach, *Still Small Voices: The Untold Human Stories Behind the Violence on the West Bank and Gaza,* San Diego, New York, London: Harcourt Brace Jovanovich, Publishers, 1989, p. 29.
280. Tessler, op. cit., p. 507.
281. Thomas, op. cit., p. 212.
282. The Fourth Geneva Convention states: "Section III. Occupied Territories Art. 47. Protected persons who are in occupied territory shall not be deprived, in any case or in any manner whatsoever, of the benefits of the present Convention by any change introduced, as the result of the occupation of a territory, into the institutions or government of the said territory, nor by any agreement concluded between the authorities of the occupied territories and the Occupying Power, *nor by any annexation by the latter of the whole or part of the occupied territory."* (Emphasis added.) And SC 242 states: "...the inadmissibility of the acquisition of territory by war and the need to work for a just and lasting peace in which every State in the area can live in security...."
283. Thomas, op. cit., p. 213.
284. Ibid., p. 214.

285. Quoted in Tessler, op. cit., p. 519.
286. Ibid., pp. 520-521.
287. Jeff Halper, *Obstacles to Peace: A Critical Re-Framing of the Israeli-Palestinian Conflict,* written and presented by Jeff Halper, Coordinator, The Israeli Committee Against House Demolitions (ICAHD); maps prepared and designed by Michael Younan and PalMap of GSE, April 2005, Third Edition, pp. 8-10.
288. Ibid.
289. Edward W. Said, *The Politics of Dispossession: The Struggle for Palestinian Self-Determination, 1969-1994,* New York: Pantheon Books, 1999, p. xxvii.
290. Ibid., p. 166.
291. Tessler, op. cit., p. 697.
292. Thomas, op. cit., p. 252.
293. Quoted in Thomas, op. cit., p. 253, n. 64 p. 261.
294. Ritchie Ovendale, *The Origins of the Arab-Israeli Wars,* Second Edition, London and New York: LongmanGroup UK, Ltd., 1984, 1992, p. 258.
295. Ibid., p. 259.
296. Ibid., pp. 258-259.
297. Ibid., p. 256.
298. Ibid., p. 259.
299. Ibid., 254.
300. Quoted in Thomas, op. cit., p. 255.
301. *Encarta Encyclopedia* © 1993-2003 Microsoft Corporation. All rights reserved.
302. Shlaim, *The Iron Wall,* op. cit., p. 487.
303. Ibid.
304. Ibid., p. 488.
305. Ibid., pp. 488-489.
306. Ibid., p. 489.

307. Ibid., p. 492.
308. Ibid.
309. Ibid., p. 493.
310. Quoted in ibid., p. 496.
311. Gershom Gorenberg, *The Accidental Empire: Israel and the Birth of the Settlements, 1967-1977,* New York: Times Books, Henry Holt and Company, 2006, p. 369.
312. *Ha'aretz,* November 1, 2000, quoted in Tanya Reinhart, *Israel/Palestine: How To End the War of 1948,* Second Edition, New York: Seven Stories Press, 2002, 2005, p. 101.
313. Said, op. cit., p. xxxii.
314. Quoted in ibid., p. xxxv.
315. PASSIA, op. cit., p. 318.
316. Said, op. cit., p. xxxvi.
317. Halper, op. cit., p. 20.
318. Said, op. cit., p. xxxvi.
319. PASSIA, op. cit., p. 280.
320. *Encarta Encyclopedia* © 1993-2003 Microsoft Corporation. All rights reserved.
321. Reinhart, op. cit., p. 21.
322. Hussein Agha and Robert Malley, "Camp David: The Tragedy of Errors," *The New York Review of Books,* Volume 48, Number 13, August 9, 2001, (electronic version).
323. Ibid.
324. Ibid.
325. Reinhart, op. cit., p. 30.
326. Ibid., p. 54.
327. Ibid., p. 60.
328. Jeff Halper, "A Most Ungenerous Offer," Americans for Middle East Understanding, AMEU: *The Link,* Volume 35, Issue 4, September-October 2002, p. 1.
329. Ibid., p. 1.

About the Authors

The Reverend Stephen Goldstein is the Assistant General Secretary for the Mission Personnel Program Unit of the General Board of Global Ministries. His office is responsible for assisting with the recruitment, selection, training, assigning, and commissioning and coordination of the Mission Personnel Unit's almost five hundred missionaries.

In addition he does interpretation for the General Board of Global Ministries in local churches, districts, and conferences and at general church events throughout the five jurisdictions.

Rev. Goldstein, a clergy member of the New York Conference, has served parishes in both New York and Connecticut and also was Associate Program Director in the New York Conference.

Sandra Olewine is a clergy member of the California-Pacific Annual Conference of The United Methodist Church. She served two congregations before becoming the General Board of Global Ministries Liaison to Jerusalem. Throughout her ministry, Sandra has worked across social, racial, and economic borders, attempting to create a sense of solidarity among diverse communities. Driven by a passion for the gospel, she seeks the healing of creation through acts of compassion, justice, and mercy. Known as an inspired preacher, writer, and teacher, Sandra is now assigned to a new ministry start, The Neighborhood, in downtown Long Beach, California. She continues to witness with authority about life under Occupation and its effects on both Palestinians and Israelis.

He is married to Pamela Blair, an author and therapist with a practice in Westchester County. He has two grown sons, Jeremiah and Jacob Jones-Goldstein, and two grown stepchildren, Aimee Blair and Ian Ferris. He and Pamela reside in Hawthorne, New York.

Additional Resources

Children of the Nakba, by the Central Committee, has been selected as the primary video resource for this study. It discusses why the issue of the Palestinian refugees is an integral part of resolving the conflict. Comes with useful study guides. This 26-minute video is available in VHS and DVD formats from the Mennonite Central Committee.
To order, call 888-563-4676 or go to www.mcc.org/shop (click on MCC Store).
(VHS) $19.99, (DVD) $15.99

"The Middle East," a full-color educational wall poster by the Knowers Ark Educational Foundation, is a two-sided map that highlights historical, political, economic, and human concerns in the Middle East, with a concentration on Israel and Palestine.

(#3805) $12.95

Israel-Palestine. By Stephen Goldstein. This four-page brochure of the 2007-2008 mission study in Spanish and Korean gives a history of the relationships between Israel and Palestine.

(Korean #M5003) Free for postage and handling
(Spanish #M5004) Free for postage and handling

From Palestine to Seattle: Becoming Neighbors & Friends— Children's Storybook on Israel and Palestine. By Mary Davies. A full-color storybook for children, aged six to twelve, describing a trip by American United Methodist kids to Palestine. Children learn about the joys and dangers of life in Israel and Palestine today.

(#M3004) $6.00

From Palestine to Seattle: Becoming Neighbors & Friends— Teacher's Guide. By Faye Wilson. From recipes to songs and stories, this guide is aimed at children, aged six to twelve, offering three sessions for children and an intergenerational experience. Each session begins with worship and Bible study. Includes a wide variety of activities for different age levels.

(#M3005) $9.00

Order from the e-store:
www.missionresourcecenter.org
Please mail order with check payable to:

MISSION RESOURCE CENTER
1221 Profit Drive, Dallas, TX 75247

Call toll-free: 1-800-305-9857
Fax: 1-214-630-0079

For further assistance, you may email:
cs@missionresourcecenter.org

A publication of the Women's Division produced by the General Board of Global Ministries, The United Methodist Church

#M3006
$8.50 + shipping & handling